mental_floss

Trivia

Brisk REFRESHING FACTS
without the ice cream headache!

Sandy Wood & Kara Kovalchik

D0096531

PUZZLE WRIGHT PRESS

New York

PUZZLE WRIGHT PRESS

New York

An Imprint of Sterling Publishing
387 Park Avenue South
New York, NY 10016

ISBN 978-1-4027-8937-3

Distributed in Canada by Sterling Publishing
c/o Canadian Manda Group, 165 Dufferin Street
Toronto, Ontario, Canada M6K 3H6
Distributed in the United Kingdom by GMC Distribution Services
Castle Place, 166 High Street, Lewes, East Sussex, England BN7 1XU
Distributed in Australia by Capricorn Link (Australia) Pty. Ltd.
P.O. Box 704, Windsor, NSW 2756, Australia

For information about custom editions, special sales, and premium and corporate purchases, please contact Sterling Special Sales at 800-805-5489 or specialsales@sterlingpublishing.com.

Printed in China

2 4 6 8 10 9 7 5 3 1

www.puzzlewright.com

INTRODUCTION

Do you remember the first "anatomically correct" doll? How about the only U.S. president to be a Rhodes scholar? Or the original name of Mickey Mouse's dog Pluto? Those are just three of the 2,150 trivia tidbits you'll be tested on in this titanic tome! Each test features five multiple choice questions on themes such as Literary Animals, Controversial Covers, and Chock Full of Chocolate. To check the answers to any test, just turn the page—the correct responses appear at the end of the following test (sometimes featuring bonus factoids). Your chance to triumph at trivia begins ... now!

STRAWBERRY SHORTCUT

1. What classic Charles Ward song featured lyrics by John Palmer, which began with the words: "Casey would waltz with a strawberry blonde"?

A. "Down by the Old Mill Stream"
B. "The Band Played On"
C. "A Bicycle Built for Two"
D. "Waltzing Matilda"

2. A "strawberry roan" has reddish hair mixed with white. What type of animal is a strawberry roan?

A. a horse
B. a collie
C. an otter
D. a rabbit

3. In 1983, Darryl Strawberry was named Rookie of the Year as a member of what National League team?

A. the San Francisco Giants
B. the Philadelphia Phillies
C. the Los Angeles Dodgers
D. the New York Mets

4. What company's headquarters are located on Strawberry Lane in the town of Orrville, Ohio?

A. Birds Eye Foods
B. the J.M. Smucker Company
C. Breyer's Ice Cream
D. the Sara Lee Corporation

5. What renowned director's 1957 film *Wild Strawberries* depicted the life of an elderly professor?

A. Ingmar Bergman
B. Billy Wilder
C. Cecil B. DeMille
D. Orson Welles

88 KEYS BUT NO LOCKS

1. In 1993, who won an Academy Award for Best Supporting Actress for her role in the motion picture *The Piano*?

A. Holly Hunter
B. Anna Chulmsky
C. Anna Paquin
D. Beverly Mitchell

2. What is the highest musical note on a standard 88-key piano? (For reference, middle C is C4.)

A. A7
B. C7
C. E7
D. F7

3. What company introduced the first Japanese piano in 1887, and is still famous for pianos, organs, and keyboards to this day?

A. Farfisa
B. Suzuki
C. Mitsubishi
D. Yamaha

4. Before he felt the call to the ministry, Jimmy Swaggart spent much of his childhood singing and playing piano with what rock-and-roll legend (who happened to be his cousin)?

A. Bill Haley
B. Jerry Lee Lewis
C. Eddie Cochran
D. Buddy Holly

5. We've all seen comedy skits where someone's hand gets caught in it—that hinged cover that protects the keyboard of a piano. What is its proper name?

A. a fallboard
B. a whippen
C. a frontslip
D. a black jack

Answer 1: B—"The Band Played On."

Answer 2: A—a horse.

Answer 3: D—the New York Mets.

Answer 4: B—the J.M. Smucker Company.

Answer 5: A—Ingmar Bergman.

ABBREVIATIONS & ACRONYMS

1. A letter addressed to the state abbreviated MS should arrive where?

A. Minnesota
B. Missouri
C. Massachusetts
D. Mississippi

2. For what does the letter C in the acronym ASCAP stand?

A. Composers
B. Cinematographers
C. Conductors
D. Copywriters

3. The college degree D.D. is an abbreviation for a Doctorate of what?

A. Dentistry
B. Divinity
C. Dianetics
D. Dermatology

4. Common Internet addresses end in .COM (for commercial sites) and .EDU (for educational sites). What does .CA mean at the end of an Internet address?

A. the site is subject to a Citizens Advisory
B. the site has free Computer Access
C. the site is based in Canada
D. the site is part of the University of California

5. Mn is the chemical symbol for which element?

A. manganese
B. molybdenum
C. magnesium
D. mendelevium

Answer 1: C—Anna Paquin (Holly Hunter also won an Oscar, but hers was for Best Actress).

Answer 2: B—C7.

Answer 3: D—Yamaha.

Answer 4: B—Jerry Lee Lewis.

Answer 5: A—a fallboard.

MORNING MUNCHING

1. In the early 1970s, Quaker began national distribution of what short-lived orange-flavored cereal as a companion to Quisp and Quake?

A. Sunny Morning
B. Citrus Crunch
C. Quangaroos
D. OJs

2. In the 1990s, what cereal first added special green pine tree–shaped marshmallows for an Earth Day promotion?

A. Apple Jacks
B. Kaboom
C. Kix
D. Lucky Charms

3. There have been several varieties of Cap'n Crunch over the years, including one called Cinnamon Crunch, which featured Cap'n Crunch's pirate nemesis as its mascot. Name him.

A. Jean LaFoote
B. Cap'n Kidd
C. Short John Silver
D. Pegleg Pete

4. During the 1960s, what TV personality performed the voice for Sugar Bear on commercials for Sugar Crisp cereal?

A. Sterling Holloway
B. Carl Reiner
C. Sheldon Leonard
D. Scatman Crothers

5. Five cereals made up General Mills' original "monster" line—two of them were Count Chocula and Frankenberry. Which was NOT one of the other three?

A. Cool Ghoul
B. Fruit Brute
C. Boo Berry
D. Yummy Mummy

Answer 1: D—Mississippi.

Answer 2: A—Composers. The organization's full name is the American Society of Composers, Authors and Publishers.

Answer 3: B—Divinity.

Answer 4: C—the site is based in Canada.

Answer 5: A—manganese.

TRADEMARKED NAMES

1. This term has come to be both a noun and a verb, but it is also a trademark for a powder or paste designed to fill cracks and holes in interior walls, ceilings, and partitions. Name it.

A. grout
B. plaster of Paris
C. spackle
D. putty

2. In 1925, B.F. Goodrich attempted to trademark what name for a closing device used in a line of overshoes, only to lose out after a lawsuit?

A. shoelace
B. zipper
C. hook-and-eye
D. button snap

3. The tranquilizer diazepam is better known by what trademarked name?

A. Valium
B. Xanax
C. Halcion
D. Morphine

4. What term, used to refer to a program of a theatrical performance, is a trademarked name?

A. featurette
B. synopsis
C. marquee
D. playbill

5. This trademark is used by the Solder Seal Company to refer to its degreasing solvent, but is commonly used to describe any thick, greasy substance. Name it.

A. goop
B. gunk
C. sludge
D. muck

Answer 1: C—Quangaroos.

Answer 2: D—Lucky Charms (originally, the cereal only had four marshmallow shapes—pink hearts, yellow moons, orange stars, and green clovers).

Answer 3: A—Jean LaFoote.

Answer 4: B—Carl Reiner.

Answer 5: A—Cool Ghoul.

"FREE" AND EASY

1. What is the name of Detroit's oldest newspaper?

A. The Free Times
B. The Free Press
C. The Free Lance
D. The Free Journal

2. What was founded in 1787 by British abolitionists as a home for liberated slaves?

A. the Lake Isle of Innisfree
B. Orange Free State
C. Freeport, Brazil
D. Freetown, Sierra Leone

3. Keiko was the real name of the animal that was the focus of what popular film?

A. Breaking Free
B. Free Willy
C. Butterflies Are Free
D. Born Free

4. What short-lived political party was formed in 1848 to oppose slavery in new U.S. territories, and was absorbed into the then-new Republican Party by 1854?

A. the Free Soil Party
B. the Freedmen's Bureau
C. the Freedom Party
D. the Free State Party

5. Which song from the 1970s hit the charts twice for the same artist (in both studio and live-concert versions)?

A. "Free Ride"
B. "Philadelphia Freedom"
C. "Freebird"
D. "Free Man in Paris"

Answer 1: C—spackle.

Answer 2: B—zipper.

Answer 3: A—Valium.

Answer 4: D—playbill.

Answer 5: B—gunk.

RADICALS AND REVOLUTIONARIES

1. What was the motto of the Black Panther Party?

A. Burn, Baby, Burn
B. Free Huey
C. Black Is Beautiful
D. Power to the People

2. What revolutionary name did heiress Patricia Hearst adopt when she joined forced with the Symbionese Liberation Army?

A. Zoya
B. Squeaky
C. Tania
D. Yolanda

3. What actor portrayed the role of Hans Gruber, the leader of the terrorists that took over the Nakatome Plaza, in the original *Die Hard* motion picture?

A. Rutger Hauer
B. Alan Rickman
C. William Sadler
D. Ricardo Montalban

4. What John Lennon/Plastic Ono Band album includes songs about such radical figures as Angela Davis and John Sinclair?

A. *Life With the Lions*
B. *Shaved Fish*
C. *Some Time in New York City*
D. *Approximately Infinite Universe*

5. What 1977 Best Supporting Actress Academy Award winner punctuated her acceptance speech with praise for the Palestinian Liberation Organization?

A. Vanessa Redgrave
B. Jane Fonda
C. Ellen Burstyn
D. Meryl Streep

Answer 1: B—*The Free Press.*

Answer 2: D—Freetown, Sierra Leone.

Answer 3: B—*Free Willy.*

Answer 4: A—the Free Soil Party.

Answer 5: C—"Freebird" (by Lynyrd Skynyrd).

HERE COME THE JUDGES

1. Mike Judge is best known for creating what two popular characters?

A. Tom & Jerry
B. Beavis & Butt-head
C. Itchy & Scratchy
D. Ren & Stimpy

2. Though some scholars disagree, the Old Testament book of Judges is traditionally attributed to what judge of Israel?

A. Joshua
B. Saul
C. Benjamin
D. Samuel

3. What late actor portrayed Judge Chamberlain Haller in the hit 1992 film *My Cousin Vinny*?

A. Fred Gwynne
B. Wally Cox
C. Jason Bernard
D. William Schallert

4. Which Major League Baseball Commissioner was a former U.S. District Judge?

A. Bowie Kuhn
B. William Eckert
C. Kennesaw Mountain Landis
D. Happy Chandler

5. What character did Christopher Lloyd portray in the 1988 film *Who Framed Roger Rabbit*?

A. Judge Dredd
B. Judge Mint
C. Judge Judy
D. Judge Doom

Answer 1: D—Power to the People.

Answer 2: C—Tania.

Answer 3: B—Alan Rickman.

Answer 4: C—*Some Time in New York City*.

Answer 5: A—Vanessa Redgrave.

THE YEAR 1974

1. What television show premiered in 1974 and opened each week with an answering machine playing a different message?

A. *The Rockford Files*
B. *Mission: Impossible*
C. *Mannix*
D. *Marcus Welby, M.D.*

2. Who passed away in 1974 after authoring a few books, including one titled *We*?

A. Otto Kruger
B. Tex Ritter
C. Charles Lindbergh
D. Walter Brennan

3. On March 2, 1974, the U.S. First Class postal rate rose again (as it had three years before). What was the new rate?

A. eight cents
B. ten cents
C. twelve cents
D. thirteen cents

4. In what city did Hammerin' Hank Aaron hit his 715th home run on April 8, 1974, breaking Babe Ruth's record for most career homers?

A. Los Angeles
B. Cincinnati
C. San Francisco
D. Atlanta

5. Produced by Francis Ford Coppola, what Academy Award–winning film (for Best Picture) was released in 1974?

A. *The Godfather*
B. *The Godfather, Part II*
C. *American Graffiti*
D. *The Conversation*

Answer 1: B—Beavis & Butt-head (Mike Judge also developed the cartoon series *King of the Hill*).

Answer 2: D—Samuel.

Answer 3: A—Fred Gwynne (best known for his role as Herman on TV's *The Munsters*).

Answer 4: C—Kennesaw Mountain Landis.

Answer 5: D—Judge Doom.

KIDS' LUNCHBOXES

1. What cartoon legend became the first licensed lunch box character back in 1935?

A. Woody Woodpecker
B. Mickey Mouse
C. Krazy Kat
D. Popeye the Sailor Man

2. The late 1950s lunch box for what television show misspelled Marshal Dillon as Marshall?

A. *Gunsmoke*
B. *Rawhide*
C. *Bat Masterson*
D. *Bonanza*

3. A Howdy Doody lunch box was pulled off the shelves after the actress who portrayed Princess Summerfallwinterspring starred in an Elvis Presley film. Name this actress.

A. Dolores Hart
B. Donna Dixon
C. Ann-Margret
D. Judy Tyler

4. Which of the following companies did NOT enter the kids' lunch box market?

A. Aladdin
B. Ohio Art
C. Rubbermaid
D. Thermos

5. In 1985, a lunch box featuring what Sylvester Stallone character became the last full-metal kids' lunchbox made in the U.S.?

A. John Rambo
B. Lincoln Hawk
C. Rocky Balboa
D. Ray Tango

Answer 1: A—*The Rockford Files.*

Answer 2: C—Charles Lindbergh.

Answer 3: B—ten cents.

Answer 4: D—Atlanta (Aaron hit the pitch off L.A. Dodgers pitcher Al Downing).

Answer 5: B—*The Godfather, Part II.*

ADVERTISING QUESTIONS

Name the product/company:

1. How do you spell relief?

A. Tums
B. Mylanta
C. Rolaids
D. Pepto-Bismol

2. Who made the salad?

A. Seven Seas
B. Hidden Valley
C. Wishbone
D. Miracle Whip

3. Where do you want to go today?

A. Greyhound
B. Toyota
C. Charmin
D. Microsoft

4. What's the best tuna?

A. Starkist
B. Chicken of the Sea
C. Empress
D. Bumblebee

5. Does she or doesn't she?

A. Miss Clairol
B. L'Oreal
C. Helene Curtis
D. Maybelline

Answer 1: B—Mickey Mouse.

Answer 2: A—*Gunsmoke*.

Answer 3: D—Judy Tyler.

Answer 4: C—Rubbermaid.

Answer 5: A—John Rambo.

ALBERT EINSTEIN

1. Fill in the blank of this Albert Einstein quote: "_____ is what remains after one has forgotten everything he learned in school."

A. Nothing
B. History
C. Common sense
D. Education

2. As a child, Albert Einstein had eight years of training in what musical instrument?

A. the piano
B. the violin
C. the trombone
D. the oboe

3. Before applying for American citizenship in 1940, Albert Einstein was a citizen of what nation?

A. Switzerland
B. Austria
C. Germany
D. Italy

4. With the atomic number 99, what is the symbol for the synthetic element named for Albert Einstein, known as einsteinium?

A. Ei
B. E
C. Es
D. En

5. In 1952, Albert Einstein was offered (but refused) the presidency of what country?

A. South Africa
B. France
C. Israel
D. Holland

Answer 1: C—Rolaids.

Answer 2: A—Seven Seas.

Answer 3: D—Microsoft.

Answer 4: B—Chicken of the Sea.

Answer 5: A—Miss Clairol.

TAKE IT TO THE BANK

1. In the movie *Take the Money and Run*, Woody Allen's character Virgil Starkwell attempts to rob a bank but hits a snag when the tellers can't read his stickup note, misreading the word "gun" as:

A. gub
B. gow
C. gip
D. gak

2. "You can take that to the bank!" was a catchphrase of what hard-bitten TV cop?

A. McCloud
B. Kojak
C. Cannon
D. Baretta

3. The first American blood bank was established in 1937 at Cook County Hospital in what city?

A. New York
B. Houston
C. Chicago
D. Los Angeles

4. Which savings & loan, headed by Charles Keating, was at the center of one of the biggest financial scandals of the 1980s?

A. Madison
B. Washington
C. Hibernia
D. Lincoln

5. Composed by Paul Williams, what hit song was originally written for a Crocker National Bank TV commercial?

A. "An Old-Fashioned Love Song"
B. "We've Only Just Begun"
C. "Close to You"
D. "Save It for a Rainy Day"

Answer 1: D—Education.

Answer 2: B—the violin.

Answer 3: A—Switzerland (he renounced his German citizenship in 1896, and became a Swiss citizen five years later).

Answer 4: C—Es.

Answer 5: C—Israel.

CLOTHES-UP

1. What British designer introduced the miniskirt in 1965?

A. Jean Shrimpton
B. Roy Halston
C. Yves St. Laurent
D. Mary Quant

2. "Elephant bells" are what type of garment?

A. pants
B. shoes
C. shoulder pads
D. bloomers

3. What legendary American pioneer was said to have traveled barefoot, wearing shabby clothes and a tin pot as a hat?

A. Daniel Boone
B. Johnny Appleseed
C. Davy Crockett
D. John Armstrong

4. The Mustela vison and Mustela luterola provide which type of clothing?

A. silk shirts
B. woolen sweaters
C. mink furs
D. leather jackets

5. What was the name of the TV production company that brought us the NBC show *Late Night With David Letterman*?

A. Hams & Shirts
B. Over Underwear
C. Black Tie
D. Worldwide Pants

Answer 1: A—gub.

Answer 2: D—Baretta.

Answer 3: C—Chicago.

Answer 4: D—Lincoln Savings & Loan.

Answer 5: B—"We've Only Just Begun."

THE YEAR 1972

1. In 1972, the Soviet spacecraft Venus 8 made a soft landing on what planet?

A. Mercury
B. Venus
C. Mars
D. Jupiter

2. In April 1972, what company unveiled the SX-70 system, in which a color photograph developed outside the camera while the photographer watched?

A. Kodak
B. Minolta
C. Fuji
D. Polaroid

3. In 1972, Bobby Fischer became the first American to win the world chess title after winning a match in Reykjavik, Iceland, against what Russian grandmaster?

A. Boris Spassky
B. Paul Keres
C. Leonid Stein
D. Garry Kasparov

4. A dog named Boots was the mascot for the team on what Jack Webb TV production, which made its debut in 1972 and was on the air for five seasons?

A. *The Rookies*
B. *Adam-12*
C. *Emergency!*
D. *Dragnet*

5. What company was founded in Memphis in 1972 by Frederick W. Smith, whose father built the Greyhound bus system?

A. U.S. Air
B. Federal Express
C. Kinko's Copies
D. Smith-Corona

Answer 1: D—Mary Quant.

Answer 2: A—pants.

Answer 3: B—Johnny Appleseed.

Answer 4: C—mink furs.

Answer 5: D—Worldwide Pants.

SNAILS ON THE TRAIL

1. What's the most obvious physical difference between snails and slugs?

A. the tentacles
B. the overall size
C. the shell
D. the eyes

2. How many feet do snails have?

A. one
B. six
C. eight
D. around 600

3. The line "I pity snails and all that carry their homes on their backs" was spoken by Samwise Gamgee in which famous novel?

A. *Oliver Twist*
B. *Charlotte's Web*
C. *Animal Farm*
D. *The Fellowship of the Ring*

4. Snails are members of the class Gastropoda, which literally means:

A. shell carrier
B. stomach foot
C. fuel warmth
D. slime trail

5. A snail can be seen three times in the background of each episode of what children's television show?

A. *Sesame Street*
B. *Blue's Clues*
C. *Rugrats*
D. *The Bear in the Big Blue House*

Answer 1: B—Venus.

Answer 2: D—Polaroid.

Answer 3: A—Boris Spassky.

Answer 4: C—*Emergency!*

Answer 5: B—Federal Express.

I'M HENRY VIII, I AM

1. How many of Henry VIII's wives did he order to be executed?

A. one
B. two
C. three
D. five

2. Henry VIII was a member of what dynastic house of the English monarchy?

A. York
B. Stuart
C. Hanover
D. Tudor

3. Long before he appeared in the film *Cleopatra*, what British actor portrayed Henry VIII in the original 1948 Broadway production of *Anne of the Thousand Days*?

A. John Gielgud
B. Rex Harrison
C. Laurence Olivier
D. Michael Caine

4. Which of Henry VIII's wives was the only one to bear him a legitimate, surviving son?

A. Jane Seymour
B. Catherine of Aragon
C. Anne Boleyn
D. Catherine Howard

5. What was the original title of William Shakespeare's play, *Henry VIII*?

A. *The Unfortunate Six*
B. *Glutton for Punishment*
C. *All Is True*
D. *You Do Me Honour*

Answer 1: C—the shell.

Answer 2: A—one.

Answer 3: D—*The Fellowship of the Ring.*

Answer 4: B—stomach foot.

Answer 5: B—*Blue's Clues.*

LITERARY ANIMALS

1. In the book *Animal Farm*, what prize boar originally encouraged the other animals to rebel against Farmer Jones?

A. Old Major
B. Snowball
C. Napoleon
D. Boxer

2. In what book did Rudyard Kipling introduce us to a mongoose named Rikki Tikki Tavi?

A. *Wee Willie Winkie*
B. *Just So Stories*
C. *Kim*
D. *The Jungle Book*

3. How many puppies did Missis Pongo give birth to in the Dodi Smith classic *The Hundred and One Dalmatians*?

A. 10
B. 15
C. 18
D. 99

4. *Treasure Island* pirate Long John Silver had a parrot named Captain Flint, whose favorite phrase was:

A. "Pieces of eight!"
B. "Yo ho ho!"
C. "Walk the plank!"
D. "Flint wants a cracker!"

5. In the popular book by Anna Sewell, what was the name of Black Beauty's mother?

A. Princess
B. Ginger
C. Merrylegs
D. Duchess

Answer 1: B—two (they were #2, Anne Boleyn, and #5, Catherine Howard).

Answer 2: D—Tudor.

Answer 3: B—Rex Harrison.

Answer 4: A—Jane Seymour (the child was Edward VI).

Answer 5: C—*All Is True.*

ANDY WARHOL

1. Andy Warhol was born with the name Andrew Warhola in what country?

A. Poland
B. Germany
C. Russia
D. USA

2. The March 19, 1984 cover of *Time* magazine featured a Warhol rendering of what music legend?

A. Michael Jackson
B. John Lennon
C. Bruce Springsteen
D. Elton John

3. Which of these was NOT the title of a film directed by Warhol?

A. *Dracula*
B. *Soup*
C. *Bad*
D. *Frankenstein*

4. What magazine was founded by Warhol back in 1969?

A. *The Face*
B. *Ω Magazine*
C. *Interview*
D. *Fangoria*

5. One of Andy's most famous album covers was *Sticky Fingers* by the Rolling Stones, originally packaged with a working zipper. Which of these other Stones albums also featured Warhol's work on the cover?

A. *Goat's Head Soup*
B. *Love You Live*
C. *Some Girls*
D. *Tattoo You*

Answer 1: A—Old Major (Napoleon was a younger pig that led the rebellion after Old Major died).

Answer 2: D—*The Jungle Book.*

Answer 3: B—15.

Answer 4: A—"Pieces of eight!"

Answer 5: D—Duchess.

PICK THE ODD ONE OUT

1. Which of the following is NOT a city in Canada?

A. Medicine Hat
B. Head Smashed In
C. Yellow Knife
D. Beaver Tooth

2. Which of the following is NOT a bone in the human ear?

A. horseshoe
B. anvil
C. stirrup
D. hammer

3. Which of the following is NOT an officially recognized type of poodle?

A. Standard
B. Toy
C. French
D. Miniature

4. Which of the following football players was NOT one of the legendary "Four Horsemen" of Notre Dame?

A. Jim Crowley
B. Daniel Ruettiger
C. Elmer Layden
D. Don Miller

5. Which of the following was NOT one of the Bobbsey Twins from the book series of the same name?

A. Sally
B. Freddie
C. Nan
D. Bert

Answer 1: D—USA (he was born in Pittsburgh).

Answer 2: A—Michael Jackson.

Answer 3: B—*Soup*.

Answer 4: C—*Interview*.

Answer 5: B—*Love You Live*.

OSCAR THE GROUCH

1. During the first season of *Sesame Street*, Oscar wasn't the dirty green color he is now. What color was he then?

A. blue
B. orange
C. yellow
D. brown

2. Caroll Spinney, the voice behind Oscar, is perhaps even better known for his role as what other *Sesame Street* character?

A. Ernie
B. Grover
C. Gordon
D. Big Bird

3. What kind of animal is Oscar's pet, Slimey?

A. a worm
B. a snake
C. a snail
D. an octopus

4. The late Jeffrey Moss (co-creator of Oscar) wrote the Grouch's signature tune in 1970. Name this song.

A. "Junkyard Blues"
B. "I Love Trash"
C. "Oscar's Can-Can"
D. "Dance This Mess Around"

5. What 1999 feature film was set in Oscar's world, where the population bathes with stinky cheese instead of soap?

A. *Dirt*
B. *Nothing but Garbage*
C. *Elmo in Grouchland*
D. *Limburger Hill*

Answer 1: D—Beaver Tooth.

Answer 2: A—horseshoe.

Answer 3: C—French.

Answer 4: B—Daniel Ruettiger (better known as Rudy).

Answer 5: A—Sally.

THE U.S. FLAG

1. When the American flag is displayed vertically on a wall, in which corner should the field of stars appear?

A. lower left
B. lower right
C. upper left
D. upper right

2. How many red stripes appear on the American flag?

A. six
B. seven
C. eight
D. thirteen

3. What is the only U.S. building on which another flag properly flies above the American flag?

A. The U.S. Capitol Building
B. Independence Hall
C. United Nations Headquarters
D. The Canadian Embassy

4. What must be done before the American flag is flown at half-staff in a symbol of mourning?

A. It must be hoisted to the top of the pole
B. "The Star-Spangled Banner" must be played
C. A death certificate must be presented
D. The sun must rise in the sky

5. In what year did the U.S. Congress first adopt a resolution containing the uniform code of etiquette for the American flag?

A. 1777
B. 1865
C. 1923
D. 1942

Answer 1: B—orange.

Answer 2: D—Big Bird.

Answer 3: A—a worm (Oscar also has an elephant named Fluffy).

Answer 4: B—"I Love Trash."

Answer 5: C—*Elmo in Grouchland.*

LAND O' LAKES

1. What ship famously sank in Lake Superior on November 10, 1975?

A. the *Achille Lauro*
B. the *Daniel J. Morrell*
C. the *Edmund Fitzgerald*
D. the *Arthur M. Anderson*

2. In which U.S. state would you find the Finger Lakes?

A. New York
B. Wisconsin
C. Maine
D. Minnesota

3. Before joining the trio of Emerson, Lake & Palmer, bassist Greg Lake was a founding member of which progressive rock band?

A. Yes
B. The League of Gentlemen
C. King Crimson
D. Traffic

4. In what bucolic village are Garrison Keillor's *Prairie Home Companion* stories set?

A. Lake Placid
B. Lake Gitchegumee
C. Lake Havasu
D. Lake Wobegon

5. Actor Arthur Lake is best known for his movie portrayals of which comic strip character?

A. Dagwood Bumstead
B. Leroy Lockhorn
C. Snuffy Smith
D. Hägar the Horrible

Answer 1: C—upper left.

Answer 2: B—seven (there are six white stripes).

Answer 3: C—United Nations Headquarters (the U.N. flag flies above all countries; the American flag flies secondary, in tandem with the flags of all other member nations).

Answer 4: A—It must be hoisted to the top of the pole (when a half-staff flag is lowered, it again should be raised to the peak before being taken down).

Answer 5: D—1942.

STREETWISE

1. London's Fleet Street has long been associated with:

A. the stock market
B. the press
C. the police
D. the government

2. The first mile of paved concrete street in the world was Woodward Avenue, located in what city?

A. Paris
B. New York City
C. Munich
D. Detroit

3. What Academy Award–winning actor co-starred with Karl Malden on TV's *The Streets of San Francisco*?

A. Michael Douglas
B. Gene Hackman
C. Richard Dreyfuss
D. Jack Nicholson

4. What literary character lived at 221B Baker Street?

A. Miss Marple
B. Sam Spade
C. Sherlock Holmes
D. Charlie Chan

5. What is the subtitle of "The 59th Street Bridge Song," recorded by both Simon & Garfunkel and Harpers Bizarre?

A. "Don't Look Back"
B. "C'mon, Get Happy"
C. "Walk on By"
D. "Feelin' Groovy"

Answer 1: C—the Edmund Fitzgerald.

Answer 2: A—New York.

Answer 3: C—King Crimson.

Answer 4: D—Lake Wobegon.

Answer 5: A—Dagwood Bumstead.

NAMING NAMES

1. Big Ben is the nickname for what specific part of the structure atop London's Houses of Parliament?

A. the tower
B. the clock's second hand
C. the largest bell
D. the clock's face

2. Which ingredient is NOT part of the Caesar salad, as originally created by the renowned chef Cesare Cardini?

A. anchovies
B. croutons
C. garlic
D. eggs

3. Which ailment is often referred to as Lou Gehrig's disease?

A. scleroderma
B. lupus
C. multiple sclerosis
D. amyotrophic lateral sclerosis

4. Sadie Hawkins' Day, the one day of the year when women are expected to make advances to unattached men, originated in which classic comic strip?

A. "Smokey Stover"
B. "Li'l Abner"
C. "Barney Google"
D. "Gasoline Alley"

5. "Tinkers to Evers to Chance" is still a common phrase for precision teamwork. For what baseball team did this legendary trio play?

A. the Chicago Cubs
B. the Pittsburgh Pirates
C. the Cincinnati Reds
D. the Brooklyn Dodgers

Answer 1: B—the press (it is home to the city's major newspapers).

Answer 2: D—Detroit.

Answer 3: A—Michael Douglas.

Answer 4: C—Sherlock Holmes.

Answer 5: D—"Feelin' Groovy."

MINT CONDITION

1. What image appeared on the back of the George Washington 25-cent piece before the State Quarter Series began in 1999?

A. Mount Vernon
B. the Moon landing
C. a bald eagle
D. the Washington Monument

2. Prior to the mid-1980s, American coins that did not depict either an "S" or a "D" mint mark were minted in which U.S. city?

A. Washington, D.C.
B. Philadelphia
C. Boston
D. New York City

3. In 1943, in order to save necessary metals for World War II production, pennies were made from zinc-coated:

A. copper
B. silver
C. iron
D. steel

4. The obverse (front) of which American coin has remained virtually unchanged since 1909?

A. the penny
B. the nickel
C. the dime
D. the quarter

5. Which female appeared on the 1999 U.S. dollar coin?

A. Susan B. Anthony
B. Martha Washington
C. Sacagawea
D. Betsy Ross

Answer 1: C—the largest bell (weighing 13 tons).

Answer 2: A—anchovies.

Answer 3: D—amyotrophic lateral sclerosis (which gives the disease its abbreviation of ALS).

Answer 4: B—"Li'l Abner."

Answer 5: A—the Chicago Cubs.

MAGAZINE RACK

1. On a 1972 hit single, Dr. Hook & the Medicine Show lamented their inability to make the cover of which magazine?

A. *Spin*
B. *Creem*
C. *Rolling Stone*
D. *Vibe*

2. What was the first nonhuman to appear on the cover of *Time* magazine's "Man of the Year" issue?

A. the atomic bomb
B. the personal computer
C. the television
D. the planet Earth

3. Which sitcom was set in the offices of the fictional fashion magazine *Blush*?

A. *Good Morning, Miami*
B. *Suddenly Susan*
C. *Ed*
D. *Just Shoot Me*

4. Although it's since been revealed as a work of fiction, an article in *New York* magazine entitled "Tribal Rites of the New Saturday Night" inspired which of these films?

A. *Boogie Nights*
B. *Harlem Nights*
C. *Saturday Night Fever*
D. *Uptown Saturday Night*

5. What magazine is the official publication of the Boy Scouts of America?

A. *Boys' Life*
B. *Discover*
C. *Guideposts*
D. *Outdoor Life*

Answer 1: C—a bald eagle.

Answer 2: B—Philadelphia.

Answer 3: D—steel.

Answer 4: A—the penny.

Answer 5: A—Susan B. Anthony (these coins were minted in 1979–81 and again in 1999).

PAST PRESENT

1. On October 18, 1954, what comic strip (created by Mort Walker and Dik Browne) made its newspaper debut?

A. "Mutt and Jeff"
B. "Hi and Lois"
C. "Frank and Ernest"
D. "Mother Goose and Grimm"

2. After 34 years in print, the final issue of what *Life* magazine competitor hit newsstands on October 18, 1971?

A. *Love*
B. *Lines*
C. *Like*
D. *Look*

3. Boxer Thomas Hearns was born on October 18, 1958, winning championships in several weight divisions. What was Hearns's nickname?

A. the Hit Man
B. the Total Package
C. the Big Hurt
D. the Tomahawk

4. On October 18, 1767, two surveyors agreed on the boundary line that was named for them—the Mason-Dixon Line. Between what two states does this line lie?

A. Virginia and West Virginia
B. Ohio and Kentucky
C. Maryland and Pennsylvania
D. North Carolina and South Carolina

5. What artificial sweetener was banned by the U.S. Food and Drug Administration on October 18, 1969?

A. saccharin
B. cyclamate
C. galactose
D. aspartame

Answer 1: C—*Rolling Stone.*

Answer 2: B—the personal computer.

Answer 3: D—*Just Shoot Me.*

Answer 4: C—*Saturday Night Fever.*

Answer 5: A—*Boys' Life.*

FOR THE BIRDS

1. What feature on a pinball machine was originally called the stool pigeon?

A. flipper
B. plunger
C. tilt
D. bumper

2. What type of bird was Fred, the feathered companion of TV detective Baretta?

A. budgie
B. cockatoo
C. African grey
D. cockatiel

3. Who wrote the classic 1960 tale of growing up in the American south titled *I Know Why the Caged Bird Sings*?

A. Maya Angelou
B. Alice Walker
C. Toni Morrison
D. Zora Neale Hurston

4. What bird did Benjamin Franklin favor for America's national emblem?

A. the fishing hawk
B. the eagle
C. the peregrine falcon
D. the turkey

5. The character of Rooster Cogburn was first seen on the silver screen in what 1969 motion picture?

A. *True Grit*
B. *Rio Bravo*
C. *The Cowboys*
D. *The War Wagon*

Answer 1: B—"Hi and Lois."

Answer 2: D—*Look.*

Answer 3: A—the Hit Man.

Answer 4: C—Maryland and Pennsylvania.

Answer 5: B—cyclamate.

UNINTENTIONALLY EDUCATIONAL TELEVISION

1. An award-winning "Got Milk?" commercial made millions aware of the name of the gentleman who fatally shot Alexander Hamilton in a duel. Name this former vice president.

A. John Calhoun
B. Charles Lee
C. Elbridge Gerry
D. Aaron Burr

2. An episode of what 1960s sitcom showcased not only music from the Georges Bizet opera *Carmen*, but also lyrics from Shakespeare's *Hamlet*?

A. *Gilligan's Island*
B. *The Dick Van Dyke Show*
C. *Bewitched*
D. *The Mothers-in-Law*

3. On a popular episode of *The Honeymooners*, Ralph Kramden learned that it wasn't his pal and neighbor Ed Norton who wrote "Swanee River." Who did pen this classic tune?

A. Scott Joplin
B. Cole Porter
C. Stephen Foster
D. Ira Gershwin

4. In an episode of *The Little Rascals*, it took a magnifying glass to set off the firecrackers in Alfalfa's pocket, but the explosions hilariously punctuated his recital of what poem by Alfred, Lord Tennyson?

A. "Break, Break, Break"
B. "The Charge of the Light Brigade"
C. "Morte d'Arthur"
D. "Mariana"

5. The "Password" episode of what popular sitcom taught viewers not only that Abraham Lincoln liked mayonnaise, but that Aristophanes wrote a play called *The Birds*?

A. *Maude*
B. *Green Acres*
C. *Family Ties*
D. *The Odd Couple*

Answer 1: C—tilt.

Answer 2: B—cockatoo.

Answer 3: A—Maya Angelou.

Answer 4: D—the turkey.

Answer 5: A—*True Grit*.

THE MILKY WAY

1. In 1947, both the live and animated Borden cow Elsie gave birth to a son. What was his name?

A. Elmer
B. Beauregard
C. Walter
D. Bocephus

2. Since 1995, which state has led the U.S. in milk production?

A. California
B. Texas
C. Nebraska
D. Wisconsin

3. What Western star rode a horse named Buttermilk?

A. Calamity Jane
B. Annie Oakley
C. Belle Star
D. Dale Evans

4. Which late rock legend released a posthumous album entitled *Milk & Honey*?

A. John Lennon
B. Jimi Hendrix
C. "Mama" Cass Elliott
D. Jim Morrison

5. On what sitcom was a combination of milk and Pepsi the preferred refreshment for one of the lead characters?

A. *Happy Days*
B. *Mork and Mindy*
C. *The Facts of Life*
D. *Laverne and Shirley*

Answer 1: D—Aaron Burr.

Answer 2: A—*Gilligan's Island*.

Answer 3: C—Stephen Foster.

Answer 4: B—"The Charge of the Light Brigade."

Answer 5: D—*The Odd Couple*.

SOUTH AMERICA

1. In land area, what is the largest country in South America?

A. Colombia
B. Peru
C. Brazil
D. Argentina

2. What makes Bolivia and Paraguay unique in comparison to the rest of the countries in the South American continent?

A. they have no coastline
B. they are ruled by the same government
C. they both lie on the Equator
D. they use the same form of currency

3. What South American country is home to Atacama Desert, one of the most arid regions in the world?

A. Venezuela
B. Brazil
C. Uruguay
D. Chile

4. What is the capital of Guyana?

A. Georgetown
B. Jamestown
C. Capetown
D. Freetown

5. What is the name of the island promontory that is the southernmost point of South America?

A. Cape of Good Hope
B. Cape Verde
C. Cape Horn
D. Cape San Lucas

Answer 1: B—Beauregard (Elmer was Elsie's husband).

Answer 2: A—California.

Answer 3: D—Dale Evans.

Answer 4: A—John Lennon.

Answer 5: D—*Laverne and Shirley* (played by Penny Marshall, Laverne DeFazio was a fan of the odd liquid mixture).

HAIR APPARENT

1. When a person "wears a hair shirt," he or she is:

A. repenting
B. toweling off
C. exercising
D. showing off

2. What author penned the classic Jazz Age short story titled *Bernice Bobs Her Hair*?

A. D.H. Lawrence
B. Jack London
C. F. Scott Fitzgerald
D. Ernest Hemingway

3. Which celebrity popularized the "wedge" haircut?

A. Twiggy
B. Dorothy Hamill
C. Cathy Rigby
D. Jennifer Aniston

4. Which of these songs was NOT featured in the Broadway musical *Hair*?

A. "Almost Cut My Hair"
B. "Let the Sun Shine In"
C. "Easy to Be Hard"
D. "Good Morning, Starshine"

5. The story of Samson, who lost his strength after Delilah had someone cut his hair, appears in which book of the Old Testament?

A. Leviticus
B. Numbers
C. Esther
D. Judges

Answer 1: C—Brazil (which takes up nearly half of the continent).

Answer 2: A—they have no coastline (are landlocked).

Answer 3: D—Chile.

Answer 4: A—Georgetown.

Answer 5: C—Cape Horn.

"WAR" AND "PEACE"

1. Who was awarded a Special Congressional Medal for his World War I–era anthem, "Over There"?

A. John Philip Sousa
B. Glenn Miller
C. George M. Cohan
D. Irving Berlin

2. The John Knowles novel *A Separate Peace* is narrated by which character?

A. Brinker
B. Gene
C. Edwin
D. Phineas

3. Which controversial story was set in the town of Grover's Mill?

A. *War and Peace*
B. *The War of the Roses*
C. *The Winds of War*
D. *The War of the Worlds*

4. What festival was billed as "Three Days of Peace and Music"?

A. The Monterey Pop Festival
B. Live Aid
C. Woodstock
D. The Isle of Wight Festival

5. "Remember the Maine!" was the rallying cry for what war?

A. the Spanish-American War
B. the American Civil War
C. the French and Indian War
D. the Seven Years' War

Answer 1: A—repenting.

Answer 2: C—F. Scott Fitzgerald.

Answer 3: B—Dorothy Hamill.

Answer 4: A—"Almost Cut My Hair."

Answer 5: D—Judges.

BEN FRANKLIN

1. Ben Franklin's mug adorned what U.S. coin from 1948 to 1963?

A. the nickel
B. the half-dollar
C. the quarter
D. the dime

2. Where was Ben Franklin born on January 17, 1706?

A. Manchester, England
B. Philadelphia, Pennsylvania
C. Wilmington, Delaware
D. Boston, Massachusetts

3. While visiting Paris in 1783, Ben Franklin's hotel room window allowed him a pleasant view of the Montgolfier brothers' initial public demonstration of:

A. the steam locomotive
B. the hot air balloon
C. the microscope
D. the glider

4. Which of these items did Ben Franklin NOT invent?

A. the Franklin stove
B. bifocal eyeglasses
C. the fountain pen
D. the lightning rod

5. After 40 years on Broadway, Howard Da Silva's last theater role was that of Benjamin Franklin in what 1969–72 musical (and the film version as well)?

A. *Independence*
B. *The American Adventure*
C. *Lafayette*
D. *1776*

Answer 1: C—George M. Cohan.

Answer 2: B—Gene.

Answer 3: D—*The War of the Worlds.*

Answer 4: C—Woodstock.

Answer 5: A—the Spanish-American War.

COSMOPOLITAN CANINES

1. In some areas of the world, this dog is called an Alsatian; in the U.S., it's called:

A. a German shepherd
B. a Staffordshire terrier
C. an English bulldog
D. an Irish terrier

2. A Newfoundland named Nana was a nurse in what children's story?

A. *Charlotte's Web*
B. *Peter Pan*
C. *Stuart Little*
D. *Mary Poppins*

3. What type of dog was the title character in Jim Kjelgaard's classic novel *Big Red*?

A. a Brussels griffon
B. a Siberian Husky
C. a Welsh corgi
D. an Irish setter

4. The title of what song from the Beatles' "White Album" contained the name of Paul McCartney's Old English Sheepdog?

A. "Sexy Sadie"
B. "Martha, My Dear"
C. "Julia"
D. "Dear Prudence"

5. The Borzoi is sometimes called:

A. the Russian wolfhound
B. the Chesapeake Bay retriever
C. the German wirehaired pointer
D. The West Highland white terrier

Answer 1: B—the half-dollar.

Answer 2: D—Boston, Massachusetts.

Answer 3: B—the hot air balloon.

Answer 4: C—the fountain pen.

Answer 5: D—*1776.*

COMPACT CARS

1. In 1969, Ford introduced what compact car (a cheaper companion to the Mustang) in hopes of competing with Volkswagen and other foreign makes?

A. the Escort
B. the Fiesta
C. the Pinto
D. the Maverick

2. Which foreign car company, whose vehicles included the Fuego, saved AMC from bankruptcy back in 1979 by purchasing a controlling interest?

A. Renault
B. Audi
C. Peugeot
D. Fiat

3. Chevrolet marketed a souped-up version of what compact car as the Z24?

A. the Chevette
B. the Cavalier
C. the Corsica
D. the Citation

4. What Dodge/Plymouth compact car's initial sales pitch was a simple "Hi!" to take advantage of the vehicle's cute, bug-like front end?

A. the Laser
B. the Neon
C. the Colt
D. the Shadow

5. In 1982, this automobile manufacturer made Ohio the site of the first U.S. assembly plant for Japanese cars. Name the company.

A. Nissan
B. Toyota
C. Honda
D. Mitsubishi

Answer 1: A—a German shepherd.

Answer 2: B—*Peter Pan*.

Answer 3: D—an Irish setter.

Answer 4: B—"Martha, My Dear."

Answer 5: A—a Russian wolfhound.

THE GOOD, THE BAD, AND THE UGLY

1. To what religious order did Mother Teresa belong?

A. Sisters of Our Lady Immaculate
B. Sisters of Divine Compassion
C. Sisters of Charity
D. Little Sisters of the Poor

2. "Reverence for life, and a compassion for all living things" was the personal philosophy of what Nobel Peace Prize winner?

A. Albert Schweitzer
B. Dr. Martin Luther King Jr.
C. Nelson Mandela
D. The 14th Dalai Lama

3. In what classic film did tough guy James Cagney smash half a grapefruit into Mae Clark's face?

A. *White Heat*
B. *Little Caesar*
C. *The Public Enemy*
D. *Scarface*

4. Depression-era bank robber Pretty Boy Floyd's first name was:

A. Charles
B. Fred
C. George
D. Lester

5. What breed of dog was *The Ugly Dachshund* in the 1966 Disney film?

A. a basset hound
B. a greyhound
C. a bloodhound
D. a Great Dane

Answer 1: D—the Maverick.

Answer 2: A—Renault.

Answer 3: B—the Cavalier.

Answer 4: B—the Neon.

Answer 5: C—Honda.

TRIPLE YOUR PLEASURE

1. Which of these is NOT a legitimate Roman numeral?

A. CCC
B. LLL
C. XXX
D. MMM

2. The musical abbreviation fff stands for fortississimo, meaning the music should be played in the _____ manner.

A. loudest
B. quickest
C. softest
D. slowest

3. Who was president of the U.S. when the SSS (Selective Service System) first went into effect?

A. Lyndon Johnson
B. Jimmy Carter
C. Harry Truman
D. Franklin D. Roosevelt

4. The Better Business Bureau—known as the BBB—was founded in 1920 in what city?

A. Minneapolis
B. Miami
C. Memphis
D. Montpelier

5. Tim Berners-Lee is best known for:

A. devising the first EEE-sized shoe
B. developing the WWW (World Wide Web)
C. founding the AAA (American Automobile Association)
D. starring in XXX-rated films

Answer 1: D—Little Sisters of the Poor.

Answer 2: A—Albert Schweitzer.

Answer 3: C—*The Public Enemy.*

Answer 4: A—Charles.

Answer 5: D—a Great Dane.

PUMPKINS

1. What rock and roll composer founded the Barking Pumpkin record label?

A. Marilyn Manson
B. David Byrne
C. Alice Cooper
D. Frank Zappa

2. What nursery rhyme character kept his wife "in a pumpkin shell"?

A. Simple Simon
B. Peter
C. Old King Cole
D. Jack Sprat

3. Genetically, pumpkins are most directly related to which of these vegetables?

A. squash
B. green peppers
C. tomatoes
D. carrots

4. In what film did a young character named Pumpkin (portrayed by Tim Roth) rob a restaurant while Vincent Vega (John Travolta) was dining nearby?

A. *Broken Arrow*
B. *Phenomenon*
C. *Pulp Fiction*
D. *Blow Out*

5. Which character from the Peanuts comic strip waits up every Halloween night for a visit from the Great Pumpkin?

A. Schroeder
B. Charlie Brown
C. Linus
D. Peppermint Patty

Answer 1: B—LLL (since L equals 50, the number 150 would be CL instead of LLL).

Answer 2: A—loudest.

Answer 3: D—Franklin D. Roosevelt.

Answer 4: A—Minneapolis.

Answer 5: B—developing the WWW (World Wide Web).

PAPERWORK

1. What term is used to describe the art of folding paper sculptures?

A. origami
B. calligraphy
C. papier-mâché
D. decoupage

2. What singer had a #1 country hit at the tender age of 14 with her rendition of "Paper Roses"?

A. Jessica Andrews
B. Tanya Tucker
C. LeAnn Rimes
D. Marie Osmond

3. What writer played quarterback at an NFL summer camp in Detroit and recounted his experience in the book *Paper Lion*?

A. Norman Mailer
B. Gore Vidal
C. George Plimpton
D. Truman Capote

4. In the famous photograph, Harry Truman was holding aloft what newspaper containing the headline "Dewey Defeats Truman"?

A. *The Chicago Tribune*
B. *The St. Louis Post-Dispatch*
C. *The Cleveland Plain Dealer*
D. *The Washington Post*

5. The TV series *The Paper Chase* focused on the lives of a group of students attending:

A. business school
B. law school
C. a school of the performing arts
D. medical school

Answer 1: D—Frank Zappa.

Answer 2: B—Peter (a.k.a. Peter Peter, pumpkin eater).

Answer 3: A—squash.

Answer 4: C—*Pulp Fiction*.

Answer 5: C—Linus.

MMM, MEATY

1. In his book *The Four Million*, what author was the first to use the term "filet mignon"?

A. Ernest Hemingway
B. F. Scott Fitzgerald
C. O. Henry
D. Sherwood Anderson

2. From what bird do we get the meat known as squab?

A. pigeon
B. dove
C. pheasant
D. starling

3. What poultry magnate's slogan was "It takes a tough man to make a tender chicken"?

A. Hamilton Church
B. Frank Perdue
C. John Tyson
D. Harland Sanders

4. Ham is taken from what part of a pig?

A. the shoulder
B. the underbelly
C. the back
D. the hind leg

5. What cut of steak got its name from the New York City coach stop where it was first served?

A. London broil
B. New York strip
C. Porterhouse
D. Club steak

Answer 1: A—origami.

Answer 2: D—Marie Osmond.

Answer 3: C—George Plimpton.

Answer 4: A—*The Chicago Tribune.*

Answer 5: B—law school.

HAVING A BALL

1. In the 1950s, the NFL experimented with a new football that was what color?

A. orange
B. white
C. red
D. yellow

2. Which of these sport/game balls has the smallest diameter?

A. baseball
B. croquet ball
C. softball
D. tennis ball

3. The official Spalding NBA basketball (as used in all league games) is divided by black lines into how many segments?

A. four
B. six
C. eight
D. ten

4. In order to help raise slumping batting averages, baseballs used in professional games in 1910 were produced using what material as the core center?

A. cork
B. balsa wood
C. plastic
D. rubber

5. Which factor makes Wilson's official NCAA football different than the company's official NFL football?

A. the size
B. the number of lacings
C. the weight
D. the stripes

Answer 1: C—O. Henry.

Answer 2: A—pigeon.

Answer 3: B—Frank Perdue.

Answer 4: D—the hind leg.

Answer 5: C—Porterhouse.

BALLOT SLIPPERS

1. In 1800, the Electoral College vote was split evenly between Thomas Jefferson and what Republican opponent?

A. John Adams
B. George Clinton
C. Aaron Burr
D. James Madison

2. What successful presidential candidate used the Western expansion slogan "54-40 or Fight" in his campaign?

A. James Polk
B. Millard Fillmore
C. James Buchanan
D. Martin Van Buren

3. Theodore Roosevelt, Robert LaFollette, and Henry Wallace all left their original party affiliations to run for president as members of what 'third' party?

A. People's Party
B. State's Right Party
C. American Independent Party
D. Progressive Party

4. What president signed the Voting Rights Act, considered by many to be the end of the civil rights movement?

A. Jimmy Carter
B. George Bush
C. Lyndon Johnson
D. Richard Nixon

5. Of the list below, which was the last group given the right to vote in U.S. presidential elections?

A. District of Columbia residents
B. African-Americans
C. women
D. Native Americans

Answer 1: B—white (since regular footballs were difficult to see on black-and-white TV broadcasts).

Answer 2: D—tennis ball.

Answer 3: C—eight.

Answer 4: A—cork.

Answer 5: D—the stripes (the NCAA football is identical in proportion to the NFL ball, but has white stripes near each end).

PICK A PAIR

1. 1950s era nuclear attack advice:

A. tuck & roll
B. sit & spin
C. duck & cover
D. slip & slide

2. Susan St. James and Jane Curtin:

A. *Cagney & Lacey*
B. *Kate & Allie*
C. *Laverne & Shirley*
D. *Thelma & Louise*

3. Crossed the continental divide in 1805:

A. Lewis & Clark
B. Bliss & Laughlin
C. Sperry & Hutchinson
D. Bell & Howe

4. Bud Fisher comic strip characters used to describe opposites:

A. Eek & Meek
B. Frank & Ernest
C. Hi & Lois
D. Mutt & Jeff

5. Mythological brothers who joined Jason and his Argonauts and later became the constellation Gemini:

A. Damon & Pythias
B. Castor & Pollux
C. Romulus & Remus
D. Poseidon & Hades

Answer 1: C—Aaron Burr.

Answer 2: A—James Polk.

Answer 3: D—Progressive Party.

Answer 4: C—Lyndon Johnson.

Answer 5: A—District of Columbia residents (in 1961, with the passing of the Twenty-third Amendment).

COFFEE

1. What sitting president visited the Maxwell House Hotel in Nashville and was the first person to declare their coffee to be "good to the last drop"?

A. Dwight Eisenhower
B. James Buchanan
C. John Quincy Adams
D. Theodore Roosevelt

2. Coffee heiress Abigail Folger was one of the unlucky victims of which celebrated criminal?

A. Charles Manson
B. Ted Bundy
C. Richard Speck
D. Albert DeSalvo

3. In what 1980 movie did a group of secretaries mistakenly believe they'd killed their boss with poisoned coffee?

A. *Take This Job and Shove It*
B. *Working Girl*
C. *Office Space*
D. *Nine to Five*

4. A nervous character named Tweek, whose parents own a coffee shop, appeared in which of these animated TV shows?

A. *King of the Hill*
B. *South Park*
C. *Daria*
D. *The Simpsons*

5. Which of these is NOT one of the cup sizes offered by Starbucks Coffee?

A. medium
B. venti
C. tall
D. grande

Answer 1: C—duck & cover.

Answer 2: B—*Kate & Allie.*

Answer 3: A—Lewis & Clark.

Answer 4: D—Mutt & Jeff.

Answer 5: B—Castor & Pollux.

HAVE A HEART

1. Though it's recently been reduced to tiny text, what state's license plates long featured the slogan "Heart of Dixie"?

A. Louisiana
B. Mississippi
C. Alabama
D. Georgia

2. What comic strip character usually wears clothing that has a tiny heart decoration near the neckline?

A. Cathy
B. Juliet Jones
C. Mary Worth
D. Nancy

3. Who was the first person to receive an artificial heart implant?

A. Christiaan Barnard
B. Robert Jarvik
C. Louis Washkansky
D. Barney Clark

4. What politico died of a heart attack during a rendezvous with his mistress, Megan Marshak?

A. Spiro Agnew
B. Lyndon Johnson
C. Hubert Humphrey
D. Nelson Rockefeller

5. Which confectioner invented the heart-shaped Valentine's Day candy box?

A. Henri Nestle
B. Fanny Farmer
C. Milton Hershey
D. Richard Cadbury

Answer 1: D—Theodore Roosevelt.

Answer 2: A—Charles Manson.

Answer 3: D—*Nine to Five.*

Answer 4: B—*South Park.*

Answer 5: A—medium.

ATOMIC DOGS

1. Three Mile Island, a nuclear reactor that suffered a core meltdown in 1979, is located in which U.S. state?

A. New York
B. Maryland
C. Connecticut
D. Pennsylvania

2. In what year did the Chernobyl nuclear plant suffer an explosion that released moderate amounts of radiation into the atmosphere?

A. 1979
B. 1986
C. 1991
D. 1995

3. What David Bowie song told a fictional story of the possible aftermath after a 1966 near meltdown of the Enrico Fermi nuclear power plant?

A. "Ashes to Ashes"
B. "Diamond Dogs"
C. "Panic in Detroit"
D. "Space Oddity"

4. What 1956 John Wayne film was shot near nuclear testing grounds in the Utah desert, leading many to believe it led to the cancer deaths of many of its stars, including Susan Heyward and Agnes Moorehead?

A. *The Conqueror*
B. *Hondo*
C. *The Longest Day*
D. *Rio Bravo*

5. What activist was killed in a suspicious 1974 auto accident on the way to deliver documents that would have exposed unsafe occurrences at his/her former employer, the Kerr-McGee plutonium processing plant?

A. Linus Palding
B. Daniel Ellsberg
C. Karen Silkwood
D. Allen Ginsberg

Answer 1: C—Alabama (since 2002, it has appeared inside a small heart).

Answer 2: A—Cathy.

Answer 3: D—Barney Clark.

Answer 4: D—Nelson Rockefeller.

Answer 5: D—Richard Cadbury.

THE GOLDEN AGE OF SCIENCE FICTION

1. What late Russian-born sci-fi legend, despite his many books on space travel, preferred land-based transportation since he was afraid of heights and flying?

A. Aldous Huxley
B. Ivan Efremov
C. Isaac Asimov
D. Alexander Tyurin

2. What writer's work of science (and social) fiction, *The Martian Chronicles*, was published in Great Britain under the title *The Silver Locusts*?

A. Frank Herbert
B. Carl Sagan
C. C.S. Lewis
D. Ray Bradbury

3. In the genre's golden age, *Astounding Science Fiction* was the most popular sci-fi magazine. Today, it's also the oldest continuously running sci-fi magazine. Under what title is it now published?

A. *Analog*
B. *Artemis*
C. *Starlog*
D. *Fantasy & Sci-Fi*

4. Writer and editor John W. Campbell wrote a novella titled *Who Goes There?*, which was made into films in 1951, 1982, and again in 2011, all three under what different title?

A. *Zapped!*
B. *The Thing*
C. *Blade Runner*
D. *Alien*

5. This late writer and former naval officer received four Hugo awards and wrote 31 novels, including *Starship Troopers*. Name him.

A. Philip K. Dick
B. Robert A. Heinlein
C. Fritz Lieber
D. Harlan Ellison

Answer 1: D—Pennsylvania.

Answer 2: B—1986.

Answer 3: C—"Panic in Detroit."

Answer 4: A—*The Conqueror*.

Answer 5: C—Karen Silkwood.

U.S. NAVY RANKS, INSIGNIAS & UNIFORMS

1. The sleeve insignia of a First Class Petty Officer in the U.S. Navy is a spread eagle over how many chevrons?

A. zero
B. one
C. two
D. three

2. The gold embroidery on the bill of a U.S. Naval officer's cap is known to enlisted men by what colloquial name?

A. scrambled eggs
B. lace
C. needlepoint
D. mustard

3. Which U.S. Navy uniforms are worn exclusively in the wintertime?

A. dress whites
B. dungarees
C. khakis
D. dress blues

4. What part of a sailor's uniform can be used in an emergency as a flotation device?

A. hat
B. collar
C. shoes
D. belt

5. Which of these U.S. Navy rank titles is no longer used?

A. Commander
B. Ensign
C. Commodore
D. Vice Admiral

Answer 1: C—Isaac Asimov.

Answer 2: D—Ray Bradbury.

Answer 3: A—*Analog*.

Answer 4: B—*The Thing*.

Answer 5: B—Robert A. Heinlein.

THE SPICE OF LIFE

1. Christopher Columbus thought he'd found pepper in the Caribbean, but when he returned to Spain, it was determined that he'd actually discovered:

A. cloves
B. allspice
C. sage
D. turmeric

2. Of the five original Spice Girls' nicknames, what was the only actual spice among them?

A. Vanilla
B. Saffron
C. Ginger
D. Cinnamon

3. Which mint was the first to be used as a gum flavoring by the Wrigley Company?

A. spearmint
B. wintergreen
C. peppermint
D. basil

4. Which U.S. state is nicknamed the Nutmeg State?

A. Delaware
B. Vermont
C. Rhode Island
D. Connecticut

5. On the children's TV show *Blue's Clues*, what is the name of the little daughter of Mr. Salt and Mrs. Pepper?

A. Cilantro
B. Paprika
C. Anise
D. Rosemary

Answer 1: D—three.

Answer 2: A—scrambled eggs (the thick yellowish-gold embroidery against the dark background looks like scrambled eggs).

Answer 3: D—dress blues.

Answer 4: A—hat (a sailor's cover is waterproof and can be folded down to trap air inside).

Answer 5: C—Commodore (this rank is now known as Rear Admiral Lower Half).

NAME THE COLLEGE MASCOT

Each set of colleges/universities has the same college mascot.

1. Mississippi State, Drake, Fresno State:

A. Tigers
B. Bulldogs
C. Demons
D. Rebels

2. Clark, Houston, Brigham Young:

A. Cougars
B. Redmen
C. Trojans
D. Rockets

3. Rice, Oregon Tech, Temple:

A. Falcons
B. Ducks
C. Hawks
D. Owls

4. New Hampshire, Kansas State, Baker:

A. Spartans
B. Wildcats
C. Bears
D. Jayhawks

5. Holy Cross, Southeastern, Valparaiso:

A. Crusaders
B. Lions
C. Patriots
D. Titans

Answer 1: B—allspice.

Answer 2: C—Ginger (a.k.a. Geri Halliwell, she was the first to leave the girl group).

Answer 3: A—spearmint.

Answer 4: D—Connecticut.

Answer 5: B—Paprika.

GRIN AND BEAR IT

1. What motel chain's mascot is Sleepy Bear?

A. Super 8
B. Travelodge
C. Best Western
D. Motel 6

2. What former star of the NFL's Chicago Bears has his own restaurant at the Tremont Hotel on Chestnut Street in Chicago?

A. Mike Ditka
B. Jim McMahon
C. Walter Payton
D. William Perry

3. Which literary bear got its name from a London railway station?

A. Teddy Ruxpin
B. Paddington Bear
C. Winnie the Pooh
D. Rupert Bear

4. What type of bear made its commercial debut in a Coca-Cola ad in 1993?

A. polar bear
B. teddy bear
C. koala bear
D. panda bear

5. What TV cop show featured a streetwise informant called "Huggy Bear"?

A. *Simon & Simon*
B. *Baretta*
C. *Kojak*
D. *Starsky & Hutch*

Answer 1: B—Bulldogs.

Answer 2: A—Cougars.

Answer 3: D—Owls.

Answer 4: B—Wildcats.

Answer 5: A—Crusaders.

ART FOR ART'S SAKE

1. In the Grant Wood painting *American Gothic* (depicting a woman and a farmer holding a pitchfork), what relationship is the woman to the man?

A. daughter
B. sister
C. wife
D. mother

2. Who painted the cover art for the 1993 Billy Joel album *River of Dreams*?

A. Salvador Dalí
B. Christie Brinkley
C. Ryan White
D. Billy Joel

3. What color hair does the *Mona Lisa* have?

A. blonde
B. red
C. brown
D. black

4. By display area, what is the largest art museum in the United States?

A. Metropolitan Museum of Art (NYC)
B. National Gallery of Art (Washington, DC)
C. Philadelphia Museum of Art
D. High Museum of Art (Atlanta)

5. What artist also directed many films, including his own warped versions of horror classics like *Dracula* and *Frankenstein*?

A. Salvador Dalí
B. Andy Warhol
C. LeRoy Neiman
D. Peter Max

Answer 1: B—Travelodge.

Answer 2: A—Mike Ditka.

Answer 3: B—Paddington Bear.

Answer 4: A—polar bear.

Answer 5: D—*Starsky & Hutch*.

HANDLE WITH CARE

1. What CB channel is reserved for police and emergency use only?

A. channel 3
B. channel 9
C. channel 13
D. channel 19

2. This 1977 film was full of beer, car chases, and CB talk, and was even nominated for an Oscar. Okay, it was only for editing, but still.... Name it.

A. *Smokey & the Bandit*
B. *Duel*
C. *Convoy*
D. *Cannonball Run*

3. Many 10-codes became popular lingo, such as "10-4" (message received) and "10-10" (standing by). What does the code "10-20" represent?

A. busy
B. out of service
C. a location
D. repeat message

4. How many channels did CB radios originally offer when they first became a national fad in the mid-'70s?

A. 9
B. 19
C. 23
D. 33

5. Claude Akins and Frank Converse starred in what mid-'70s TV show about truckers, a hit in the midst of the CB craze?

A. *CHiPs*
B. *Keep On Truckin'*
C. *B.J. and the Bear*
D. *Movin' On*

Answer 1: A—daughter (many people mistakenly believe the woman is his wife).

Answer 2: B—Christie Brinkley (his wife at the time).

Answer 3: D—black.

Answer 4: A—Metropolitan Museum of Art (NYC).

Answer 5: B—Andy Warhol.

THE YEAR 1981

1. The Iran hostages were released in January 1981 after 444 days of captivity; what was their first stop on the way home?

A. Karachi
B. Addis Ababa
C. Istanbul
D. Algiers

2. MTV made its debut in August 1981; which of the following was NOT one of the original VJs?

A. Mark Goodman
B. Rosie O'Donnell
C. Alan Hunter
D. Nina Blackwood

3. Mehmat Ali Agca was accused of shooting whom in 1981?

A. Pope John Paul II
B. Francois Mitterand
C. Ronald Reagan
D. Anwar Sadat

4. On July 29, 1981, a nervous Lady Diana Spencer mistakenly mangled the order of Prince Charles's names and ended up taking whom as her lawful husband?

A. Arthur
B. George
C. Philip
D. William

5. What single, the biggest hit of 1981 (and the decade), was #1 throughout the holiday season, from Thanksgiving until after the next New Year's Day?

A. "The Tide Is High"
B. "Bette Davis Eyes"
C. "Endless Love"
D. "Physical"

Answer 1: B—channel 9.

Answer 2: A—*Smokey & the Bandit*.

Answer 3: C—a location.

Answer 4: C—23 (when the airwaves became too crowded, the FCC expanded the CB range to 40 stations).

Answer 5: D—*Movin' On*.

FELINE GROOVY

1. What breed of cat is tailless?

A. Scottish fold
B. Manx
C. Cornish rex
D. Maine coon

2. What was the name of the jungle cat that growled on cue in those classic Mercury Cougar commercials?

A. Chauncey
B. Morris
C. Christopher
D. Charlie

3. Legendary ballpark Tiger Stadium was located on a Detroit street named for what American League star?

A. Denny McLain
B. Ty Cobb
C. Mickey Lolich
D. Al Kaline

4. Which continent is NOT home to at least one extant species of cat?

A. South America
B. Antarctica
C. Africa
D. Australia

5. What sultry actress portrayed the title character in the 1965 big-screen Western *Cat Ballou*?

A. Nancy Sinatra
B. Mia Farrow
C. Jane Fonda
D. Marlo Thomas

Answer 1: D—Algiers.

Answer 2: B—Rosie O'Donnell (she was an original VJ for MTV's sister station, VH-1).

Answer 3: A—Pope John Paul II.

Answer 4: C—Philip.

Answer 5: D—"Physical."

THE UN-QUIZ

1. Murray Langston was better known to the public as:

A. the Unicorn Killer
B. the Unknown Comic
C. the Unabomber
D. the Unknown Soldier

2. What Undersecretary of the United Nations became the first African-American to win the Nobel Peace Prize?

A. Andrew Young
B. Dr. Martin Luther King Jr.
C. Thurgood Marshall
D. Ralph Bunche

3. Which of the following films starred Bruce Willis?

A. *Unforgiven*
B. *The Untouchables*
C. *Unbreakable*
D. *Unfaithfully Yours*

4. The UPC is the bar code appearing on most consumer products. For what do the letters UPC stand?

A. Unscanned Purchase Code
B. Union Packaging Code
C. Universal Product Code
D. Unsold Premium Code

5. What Czech author penned the 1984 novel *The Unbearable Lightness of Being*?

A. Milan Kundera
B. Josef Hora
C. Vaclav Havel
D. Jan Neruda

Answer 1: B—Manx.

Answer 2: A—Chauncey.

Answer 3: D—Al Kaline (technically, the field's address was at the corner of Michigan Avenue and Trumbull Street, but the length of Trumbull near the stadium was renamed Al Kaline Drive).

Answer 4: B—Antarctica.

Answer 5: C—Jane Fonda.

PLANET, SCHMANET

1. Neptune, the Roman god of water, was known by what name in Greek mythology?

A. Poseidon
B. Artemis
C. Ulysses
D. Jason

2. What U.S. state is the home of General Motors' original Saturn automobile plant?

A. Kentucky
B. Michigan
C. Tennessee
D. Delaware

3. The Jupiter II spacecraft was featured in what TV series?

A. *Star Trek: Enterprise*
B. *Lost in Space*
C. *Battlestar Galactica*
D. *Space: 1999*

4. Mickey Mouse's faithful dog Pluto was originally known by what name?

A. Fido
B. Buster
C. Spot
D. Rover

5. What British rock-and-roll legend recorded a 1975 album titled *Venus and Mars*?

A. Elton John
B. Paul McCartney
C. David Bowie
D. Eric Clapton

Answer 1: B—the Unknown Comic.

Answer 2: D—Ralph Bunche.

Answer 3: C—*Unbreakable*.

Answer 4: C—Universal Product Code.

Answer 5: A—Milan Kundera.

THE OTHER WHITE MEAT

1. Ham was one of the sons of what Biblical patriarch?

A. Moses
B. Adam
C. Noah
D. Job

2. The cover of what colorful band's 1977 album *Animals* depicts a large, inflatable pig flying over London's Battersea Power Station?

A. Pink Floyd
B. Deep Purple
C. Black Sabbath
D. The Moody Blues

3. Francis Bacon was knighted in 1603 for his proposals related to the unification of England and which other nation?

A. Ireland
B. Holland
C. Scotland
D. France

4. Because it was the center of the salt pork industry in 19th-century America, what Midwestern city garnered the nickname Porkopolis?

A. Cincinnati
B. Des Moines
C. Rockford
D. Kansas City

5. In what television show did a gentleman with the last name Hogg own an establishment called the Boar's Nest?

A. *The Beverly Hillbillies*
B. *Green Acres*
C. *The Dukes of Hazzard*
D. *The Andy Griffith Show*

Answer 1: A—Poseidon.

Answer 2: C—Tennessee.

Answer 3: B—*Lost in Space.*

Answer 4: D—Rover.

Answer 5: B—Paul McCartney (with his band, Wings).

KING ME

1. What American beer has long been promoted as the "King of Beers"?

A. Pabst
B. Coors
C. Budweiser
D. Miller

2. The animated Fox sitcom *King of the Hill* was set in the fictitious town of Arlen, located in what state?

A. Texas
B. Florida
C. Arkansas
D. Kentucky

3. Disc jockey Howard Stern is occasionally referred to as "The King of All ..." what?

A. Microphones
B. Media
C. Morons
D. Markets

4. As the largest member of its breed, what type of dog is known as the "King of the Terriers"?

A. Skye terrier
B. Wire fox terrler
C. Airedale
D. Scottish terrier

5. Which singer/songwriter had a 1964 hit with "King of the Road"?

A. Roy Orbison
B. Ferlin Husky
C. B.J. Thomas
D. Roger Miller

Answer 1: C—Noah.

Answer 2: A—Pink Floyd.

Answer 3: C—Scotland.

Answer 4: A—Cincinnati.

Answer 5: C—*The Dukes of Hazzard.*

QUIZ, BOND QUIZ

1. Who sings the theme song for the 007 film *Die Another Day* (and also has a brief cameo appearance in the film)?

A. Moby
B. Cher
C. Brandy
D. Madonna

2. In what year were there two "official" James Bond films released, *Octopussy* and *Never Say Never Again*?

A. 1977
B. 1980
C. 1983
D. 1986

3. Which actor appeared in his last James Bond movie at the age of 56, making him older than any other on-screen 007?

A. Pierce Brosnan
B. Sean Connery
C. Roger Moore
D. Timothy Dalton

4. What was the title of the very first James Bond film adaptation, released back in 1962?

A. *Dr. No*
B. *On Her Majesty's Secret Service*
C. *You Only Live Twice*
D. *The Man With the Golden Gun*

5. The theme song from which of these 007 films was NOT sung by Shirley Bassey?

A. *Goldfinger*
B. *Diamonds Are Forever*
C. *From Russia With Love*
D. *Moonraker*

Answer 1: C—Budweiser.

Answer 2: A—Texas.

Answer 3: B—Media.

Answer 4: C—Airedale.

Answer 5: D—Roger Miller.

I DON'T LIKE MONDAYS

1. In what year did the Black Monday event occur, in which the Dow Jones Average dropped 500 points (over 22%)?

A. 1929
B. 1972
C. 1987
D. 1992

2. Which of the following was NOT part of the original broadcast team when *Monday Night Football* made its debut in 1970?

A. Howard Cosell
B. Fran Tarkenton
C. Don Meredith
D. Keith Jackson

3. Which of these "Monday" songs peaked at #1 on the *Billboard* pop chart?

A. "Monday, Monday"
B. "Blue Monday"
C. "New Moon on Monday"
D. "Manic Monday"

4. Rick Monday was a National League All-Star selection in 1978 from which Western Division team?

A. the San Francisco Giants
B. the California Angels
C. the Los Angeles Dodgers
D. the San Diego Padres

5. Which of these was not included in the 1971 Uniform Monday Law, in which Congress moved certain holiday occurrences to Monday (to give American workers more three-day weekends)?

A. Columbus Day
B. Independence Day
C. Presidents' Day
D. Memorial Day

Answer 1: D—Madonna.

Answer 2: C—1983.

Answer 3: C—Roger Moore (who was 56 when he starred in 1985's *A View to a Kill*).

Answer 4: A—*Dr. No.*

Answer 5: C—*From Russia With Love.*

IS IT TUESDAY YET?

1. Which French term literally means "Fat Tuesday"?

A. tour de force
B. bête noire
C. Mardi Gras
D. joie de vivre

2. What cartoon character often promised that he would "gladly pay you Tuesday for a hamburger today"?

A. Shaggy
B. Wimpy
C. Jughead
D. Beavis

3. Which of these "Tuesday" songs peaked at #1 on the *Billboard* pop chart?

A. "Tuesday's Gone"
B. "Ruby Tuesday"
C. "Everything's Tuesday"
D. "Tuesday Afternoon"

4. *The Tuesday Club Murders* was a novel written by what mystery writer?

A. Agatha Christie
B. Mary Higgins Clark
C. Lois Duncan
D. Janet Evanovich

5. Born with the first name Susan, Tuesday Weld was nominated for a Best Supporting Actress Oscar for her role in what 1978 motion picture?

A. *Pretty Poison*
B. *Who'll Stop the Rain*
C. *Thief*
D. *Looking for Mr. Goodbar*

Answer 1: C—1987.

Answer 2: B—Fran Tarkenton.

Answer 3: A—"Monday, Monday."

Answer 4: C—the Los Angeles Dodgers.

Answer 5: B—Independence Day.

WHEN'S WEDNESDAY?

1. What duo's debut album was titled *Wednesday Morning, 3 A.M.?*

A. Hall & Oates
B. Simon & Garfunkel
C. Ashford & Simpson
D. Sonny & Cher

2. What is Sheffield Wednesday?

A. a British football (soccer) team
B. a particular breed of sheep
C. a New England holiday
D. a comic strip character

3. According to the nursery rhyme, "Wednesday's child is ..." what?

A. full of grace
B. loving and giving
C. full of woe
D. fair of face

4. Wednesday, September 2, 1752, was the last "old style" date used by Great Britain and her colonies before a switch to what calendar?

A. Gregorian
B. Lunar
C. Julian
D. Roman

5. What poet penned "Ash Wednesday" back in 1930?

A. Ezra Pound
B. Ogden Nash
C. Edna St. Vincent Millay
D. T.S. Eliot

Answer 1: C—Mardi Gras.

Answer 2: B—Wimpy.

Answer 3: B—"Ruby Tuesday."

Answer 4: A—Agatha Christie.

Answer 5: D—*Looking for Mr. Goodbar.*

ANOTHER THURSDAY

1. Thursday Island is located in the Torres Strait off the coast of what country?

A. Chile
B. Portugal
C. Australia
D. Somalia

2. With the exception of a break during World War II, which pro football team has participated in a Thursday game every Thanksgiving Day since 1934?

A. the Detroit Lions
B. the Philadelphia Eagles
C. the New York Giants
D. the Dallas Cowboys

3. What actress from TV's *My Sister Sam*, killed by a deranged fan at age 21, was a spokesperson for a teen assistance charity known as Thursday's Child?

A. Dominique Dunne
B. Amy Boyer
C. Dorothy Stratten
D. Rebecca Schaeffer

4. Whose novel *Sweet Thursday* formed the basis for the 1955 Rodgers & Hammerstein musical *Pipe Dream*?

A. John Steinbeck
B. William Faulkner
C. F. Scott Fitzgerald
D. Ernest Hemingway

5. What John Ford film featured John Wayne and Shirley Temple, and starred Henry Fonda in the role of Lt. Colonel Owen Thursday?

A. *How the West Was Won*
B. *Fort Apache*
C. *Rio Grande*
D. *The Longest Day*

Answer 1: B—Simon & Garfunkel.

Answer 2: A—a British football (soccer) team.

Answer 3: C—full of woe.

Answer 4: A—Gregorian.

Answer 5: D—T.S. Eliot.

EVERY FRIDAY IS A GOOD FRIDAY

1. In what decade did the Vatican withdraw their requirement that Catholics refrain from eating meat on Friday?

A. the 1920s
B. the 1940s
C. the 1960s
D. the 1980s

2. In what city was the very first T.G.I. Friday's (sporting the same red-and-white canopies that distinguish the restaurants' locations to this day) opened back in 1965?

A. New York City
B. Sacramento
C. Dallas
D. Vancouver

3. What railroad financier led the United States into an 1869 panic known as Black Friday before going on to own the *New York World* and the Western Union Telegraph Company?

A. Cornelius Vanderbilt
B. John Jacob Astor
C. Jay Gould
D. J.P. Morgan

4. What religious sleuth's debut came in the Edgar Award–winning 1964 Harry Kemelman novel *Friday the Rabbi Slept Late*?

A. Mother Lavinia Gray
B. Father Frank Dowling
C. Rabbi David Small
D. Sister Mary Helen

5. Which of these TV characters had the middle name "Friday"?

A. Queen Sara Saturday (*Mister Rogers' Neighborhood*)
B. Joe Friday (*Dragnet*)
C. Wednesday Addams (*The Addams Family*)
D. June Tuesday (*That '80s Show*)

Answer 1: C—Australia.

Answer 2: A—the Detroit Lions.

Answer 3: D—Rebecca Schaeffer.

Answer 4: A—John Steinbeck.

Answer 5: B—*Fort Apache*.

S, A, T-U-R, D-A-Y, RIGHT!

1. Which of these sporting events is always held on a Saturday?

A. the Kentucky Derby
B. the Major League Baseball All-Star Game
C. the Super Bowl
D. the Indianapolis 500

2. Notwithstanding a two-year hiatus from 1969 to 1971, which of the following magazines has been published since way back in 1821?

A. *Every Saturday*
B. *The Saturday Review*
C. *Saturday Magazine*
D. *The Saturday Evening Post*

3. Members of which of these religious denominations celebrate their sabbath day on Saturday?

A. Buddhists
B. Seventh-day Adventists
C. Roman Catholics
D. Muslims

4. The *Saturday Night Fever* soundtrack is #2 on the RIAA's list of best-selling soundtrack albums of all time. What soundtrack album holds the #1 spot?

A. *Cocktail*
B. *The Bodyguard*
C. *O Brother, Where Art Thou?*
D. *The Sound of Music*

5. Which of these actors was NEVER a regular cast member on TV's *Saturday Night Live*?

A. Billy Crystal
B. Steve Martin
C. Ben Stiller
D. Randy Quaid

Answer 1: C—the 1960s.

Answer 2: A—New York City.

Answer 3: C—Jay Gould.

Answer 4: C—Rabbi David Small.

Answer 5: C—Wednesday Addams.

SUNNY SUNDAY

1. According to legend, what laws were so named because of the color of the paper used when the ordinances were first printed in 1781 in New Haven, Connecticut?

A. red laws
B. blue laws
C. white laws
D. peach laws

2. Who starred alongside Cuba Gooding Jr. as Master Chief Billy Sunday in the 2000 motion picture *Men of Honor*?

A. Karl Malden
B. Bill Paxton
C. Gene Hackman
D. Robert De Niro

3. What began on the early morning of Sunday, September 2, 1666, near London Bridge?

A. the Hundred Years' War
B. the Great Fire of London
C. the founding of Freemasonry
D. the first services of the Church of England

4. The Stephen Sondheim Broadway musical *Sunday in the Park With George* was based on a painting by ... whom?

A. Georges Braque
B. George Bellows
C. Georg Baselitz
D. Georges Seurat

5. Daylight saving time has changed dates in recent years, but still occurs at the same specific time on a Sunday. Name this hour.

A. midnight
B. 1 A.M.
C. 2 A.M.
D. 3 A.M.

Answer 1: A—the Kentucky Derby.

Answer 2: D—*The Saturday Evening Post.*

Answer 3: B—Seventh-day Adventists.

Answer 4: B—*The Bodyguard.*

Answer 5: B—Steve Martin (he's been a frequent guest, but never a regular cast member on the show).

I CAN SEE FOR MILES

1. Roger Bannister, the first athlete in history to run one mile in less than four minutes, was a native of which nation?

A. the United States
B. New Zealand
C. Great Britain
D. Canada

2. How many furlongs are in one regular (statute) mile?

A. five
B. eight
C. twelve
D. twenty

3. Which of these movies was NOT set in prison?

A. *The Last Mile*
B. *The Jericho Mile*
C. *8 Mile*
D. *The Green Mile*

4. What color are the standard mile marker signs used on the Interstate Highway System in the United States?

A. yellow
B. orange
C. green
D. blue

5. Mile High Stadium in Denver was built in 1948 and was then known by what name?

A. Rocky Mountain Grounds
B. Gates Stadium
C. Comanche Field
D. Bears Stadium

Answer 1: B—blue laws.

Answer 2: D—Robert De Niro.

Answer 3: B—the Great Fire of London.

Answer 4: D—Georges Seurat.

Answer 5: C—2 A.M.

DON'T CROSS ME

1. Which of these four-sided geometric shapes can have just two parallel sides?

A. a trapezoid
B. a rectangle
C. a parallelogram
D. a rhombus

2. What type of musical instrument is often crafted with two parallel pipes, one known as a chanter and the other known as a drone?

A. the theremin
B. the pipe organ
C. the bagpipe
D. the trombone

3. Before the popularity of the USB port, which of these computer peripherals were most commonly attached to PCs by a cable connected to a parallel port?

A. a keyboard
B. a printer
C. a monitor
D. a diskette drive

4. What new wave band recorded the 1978 album titled *Parallel Lines*?

A. The Pretenders
B. Blondie
C. XTC
D. Talking Heads

5. Which of these U.S. states borders the 49th parallel, an area disputed with Great Britain until the Oregon Treaty in 1846?

A. Wyoming
B. Colorado
C. Washington
D. Nebraska

Answer 1: C—Great Britain.

Answer 2: B—eight (a furlong equals 660 feet).

Answer 3: C—*8 Mile*.

Answer 4: C—green.

Answer 5: D—Bears Stadium (after the Denver Bears, the city's minor league baseball team at the time).

DIDACTIC VS.

1. The November 17, 1968, New York Jets vs. Oakland Raiders game has earned a place in football history, and is often referred to by what colloquial name?

A. the Ice Bowl
B. the Heidi Game
C. the Greatest Game Ever Played
D. Miracle in the Meadowlands

2. What rock band's 1993 album *Vs.* was unique for the time in that no related singles or videos were released in the U.S.?

A. Pearl Jam
B. Stone Temple Pilots
C. Alice in Chains
D. Soundgarden

3. The Supreme Court decision that legalized abortion in America was referred to by what case name?

A. *Gideon vs. Wainwright*
B. *Plessy vs. Ferguson*
C. *Miranda vs. Arizona*
D. *Roe vs. Wade*

4. Which of these films earned the most money at U.S. box offices?

A. *Joe vs. the Volcano*
B. *Godzilla vs. Mechagodzilla*
C. *Kramer vs. Kramer*
D. *The People vs. Larry Flynt*

5. In 1978, DC Comics issued a collector's edition series of comic books pitting Superman against some unlikely opponents. Which of these was NOT part of the series?

A. *Superman vs. Muhammad Ali*
B. *Superman vs. the Flash*
C. *Superman vs. Bigfoot*
D. *Superman vs. Wonder Woman*

Answer 1: A—a trapezoid (in all the other shapes, each of the four sides is parallel to its opposite side).

Answer 2: C—the bagpipe.

Answer 3: B—a printer.

Answer 4: B—Blondie.

Answer 5: C—Washington.

DUCKS GET DOWN

1. The duck-billed platypus is one of only three mammals in the world that:

A. can breathe underwater
B. has webbed feet
C. lays eggs
D. has a five-chambered heart

2. Which of the following NEVER served a "lame duck" period while president of the United States?

A. Ronald Reagan
B. John F. Kennedy
C. Gerald R. Ford
D. Jimmy Carter

3. What humorist often reminisces about his high school rock band, the Federal Duck?

A. Michael Moore
B. P.J. O'Rourke
C. Tom Bodett
D. Dave Barry

4. Which character starred in the animated short *Duck Dodgers in the 24½th Century*?

A. Daffy Duck
B. Yakky Doodle
C. Howard the Duck
D. Donald Duck

5. A male duck is properly known as a:

A. mallard
B. drake
C. gander
D. cob

Answer 1: B—the Heidi Game.

Answer 2: A—Pearl Jam.

Answer 3: D—*Roe vs. Wade*.

Answer 4: C—*Kramer vs. Kramer* (grossing over $100 million).

Answer 5: C—*Superman vs. Bigfoot* (and just so you know, Ali beat the tar out of a superpower-less Superman in the boxing ring).

WHAT A DOLL!

1. "Shrimp on the barbie" is a seafood dish with origins in what country?

A. Brazil
B. Australia
C. Morocco
D. Liberia

2. You may not have been aware that your Barbie doll (or your sister's Barbie doll) has a last name. What is it?

A. Handler
B. Bouvier
C. Roberts
D. Sanders

3. Just one year before she found great success on a hit TV series, what actress landed the role of Barbie Keeley in the 1996 comedy film *The Birdcage*?

A. Debra Messing
B. Calista Flockhart
C. Kristin Davis
D. Jennifer Aniston

4. In 1987, Klaus Barbie, an SS officer during World War II, was put on trial for the war crimes he committed while in charge of a Gestapo in what European country?

A. France
B. Austria
C. Italy
D. Czechoslovakia

5. Mattel sued MCA Records for trademark violations in 1998 over what band's hit song, titled "Barbie Girl"?

A. ABBA
B. Allure
C. Aqua
D. Asia

Answer 1: C—lays eggs.

Answer 2: B—John F. Kennedy (he was assassinated, and thus never spent a period when he was in sitting in office while waiting for his replacement to take over).

Answer 3: D—Dave Barry.

Answer 4: A—Daffy Duck.

Answer 5: B—drake.

THE SPACE SHUTTLE

1. What was the name of the very first Space Shuttle, initially launched into space on April 12, 1981?

A. Columbia
B. Endeavour
C. Atlantis
D. Discovery

2. What foreign country started its own space shuttle program in 1988, but had to stop work on it in 1993 (and has never completed the project)?

A. China
B. Japan
C. Russia
D. France

3. How many unfortunate crew members perished when the space shuttle Challenger exploded during takeoff on January 28, 1986?

A. three
B. four
C. five
D. seven

4. All of these films focused on the actions of an American space shuttle. Which appeared in theatres before the first space shuttle mission in 1981?

A. *Armageddon*
B. *Space Cowboys*
C. *Moonraker*
D. *Airplane II: The Sequel*

5. Which American president signed the bill that authorized the $5.5 billion needed to develop the Space Shuttle?

A. Jimmy Carter
B. Lyndon Johnson
C. Richard Nixon
D. Ronald Reagan

Answer 1: B—Australia.

Answer 2: C—Roberts (her full name is Barbara Millicent Roberts).

Answer 3: B—Calista Flockhart.

Answer 4: A—France.

Answer 5: C—Aqua.

LIKE SANDS THROUGH THE ...

1. What poisonous spider can be identified by a small rod hourglass-shaped marking on the underside of its abdomen?

A. brown recluse
B. tarantula
C. black widow
D. katipo

2. In 1978, what Kimberly-Clark product was advertised as having a snug "elastic fit" and an "hourglass shape"?

A. Cross-Your-Heart bras
B. Huggies diapers
C. Living girdles
D. Curad disposable bandages

3. What musical brothers went to L.A. in the 1960s and recorded two albums with friends on the Liberty Records label under the name the Hourglass?

A. Eddie & Alex Van Halen
B. John & Chuck Panozzo
C. Gregg & Duane Allman
D. Phil & Don Everly

4. What game comes packaged with a small plastic hourglass and sixteen different letter cubes?

A. Boggle
B. Perquackey
C. UpWords
D. Pictionary

5. When Dorothy is held captive in the 1939 film *The Wizard of Oz*, the Wicked Witch of the West threatens her with death after an hourglass runs out of time. What color was the sand in this hourglass?

A. blue
B. green
C. red
D. black

Answer 1: A—Columbia.

Answer 2: C—Russia.

Answer 3: D—seven.

Answer 4: C—*Moonraker*.

Answer 5: C—Richard Nixon (in 1972).

I'M YOUR CAPTAIN

1. "I am the master of my fate, I am the captain of my soul ..." is from which famous poem?

A. "Avalon"
B. "Beowulf"
C. "To Hope"
D. "Invictus"

2. Captain James Cook discovered what country in 1769 and claimed it for Great Britain?

A. New Zealand
B. Tahiti
C. Australia
D. Canada

3. Who was the sadistic commander of the HMS *Bounty*?

A. Captain Blood
B. Captain Queeg
C. Captain Bligh
D. Captain Morgan

4. For what does the "T" stand in the name of *Star Trek* captain James T. Kirk?

A. Thor
B. Tyrone
C. Thomas
D. Tiberius

5. Which Captain & Tennille hit was written by Neil Sedaka?

A. "Shop Around"
B. "Love Will Keep Us Together"
C. "Do That to Me One More Time"
D. "Muskrat Love"

Answer 1: C—black widow.

Answer 2: B—Huggies diapers.

Answer 3: C—Gregg & Duane Allman.

Answer 4: A—Boggle.

Answer 5: C—red.

STATE OF MIND

1. Which of the following had a pop hit with the single "Indiana Wants Me"?

A. James Taylor
B. Mick Taylor
C. Livingston Taylor
D. R. Dean Taylor

2. A Michigan loader is:

A. a Great Lakes barge
B. a scam artist
C. a piece of earth-moving equipment
D. a freight elevator

3. What U.S. president endorsed the Louisiana Purchase, which was approved by the Senate in 1803?

A. James Madison
B. Thomas Jefferson
C. James Monroe
D. John Adams

4. Through 2012, which of these stars of the motion picture *Raising Arizona* has NOT won an Academy Award?

A. Nicolas Cage
B. Holly Hunter
C. John Goodman
D. Frances McDormand

5. A New York strip steak is, by definition, most similar to which of these other cuts of beef?

A. filet mignon
B. rib eye
C. chateaubriand
D. porterhouse

Answer 1: D—"Invictus."

Answer 2: A—New Zealand.

Answer 3: C—Captain Bligh.

Answer 4: D—Tiberius.

Answer 5: B—"Love Will Keep Us Together."

WEAR YOUR PJS

1. P.J. O'Rourke served as editor-in-chief of which of these humor periodicals?

A. *Mad*
B. *The Onion*
C. *National Lampoon*
D. *Spy*

2. P.J. Clapp is better known by what name?

A. Andy Rooney
B. Eric Clapton
C. Danielle Steel
D. Johnny Knoxville

3. What African-American comedian voiced the lead character (and was co–executive producer) of the Fox animated TV series *The PJs*?

A. Eddie Murphy
B. Nipsey Russell
C. Chris Rock
D. Keenen Ivory Wayans

4. P.J. Proby, P.J. Kelly, and P.J. Harvey are all best known for their contributions to what field?

A. literature
B. medicine
C. music
D. politics

5. Which of these is NOT one of P.J.'s siblings in the Bil Keane comic "The Family Circus"?

A. Billy
B. Tammy
C. Jeffy
D. Dolly

Answer 1: D—R. Dean Taylor

Answer 2: C—a piece of earth-moving equipment.

Answer 3: B—Thomas Jefferson.

Answer 4: C—John Goodman (He's won an Emmy and a Golden Globe, but has never been nominated for an Academy Award).

Answer 5: D—porterhouse.

GOLDEN YEARS

1. What was the first name of American artist Grandma Moses, who began her painting career at the age of 75?

A. Daisy
B. Anna
C. Marjorie
D. Beth

2. Which advocacy group was founded by Maggie Kuhn?

A. American Association of Retired Persons
B. 60 Plus Association
C. National Council of Senior Citizens
D. Gray Panthers

3. Who was the oldest U.S. president to take office?

A. Ronald Reagan
B. William Henry Harrison
C. Dwight Eisenhower
D. George Washington

4. Elizabeth Bowes-Lyon, who was still appearing at public engagements at the age of 100, was better known as:

A. Moms Mabley
B. the Queen Mother
C. Mother Theresa
D. Mama Celeste

5. Which of these was the oldest to ever win a Best Actor Oscar?

A. Art Carney
B. George Burns
C. Sir John Gielgud
D. Henry Fonda

Answer 1: C—*National Lampoon*.

Answer 2: D—Johnny Knoxville.

Answer 3: A—Eddie Murphy.

Answer 4: C—music.

Answer 5: B—Tammy.

SHORT SUBJECT

1. In the board game Monopoly, Short Line is a railroad. In real life, it wasn't a railroad at all. What was the Short Line?

A. a bus route
B. a trolley
C. a ferry boat
D. a subway system

2. What singer had a controversial hit with a 1977 novelty song known as "Short People"?

A. Rick Dees
B. Jim Stafford
C. Randy Newman
D. Ray Stevens

3. Sir Isaac Pitman and John Robert Gregg were two important names in the popularization of:

A. shortwave radio
B. short sleeve shirts
C. shorthand writing
D. film shorts

4. Every baseball position has a number, from the pitcher (1) to the right fielder (9). What number references the shortstop?

A. four
B. five
C. six
D. seven

5. What was the first name of Martin Short's character on his TV series *Primetime Glick*?

A. Jerome
B. Joshua
C. Jiminy
D. Jerrold

Answer 1: B—Anna.

Answer 2: D—Gray Panthers.

Answer 3: A—Ronald Reagan.

Answer 4: B—the Queen Mother.

Answer 5: D—Henry Fonda.

IN AN INSTANT

1. In 1952, M&R Dietetic Laboratories introduced Pream, which was the first brand of instant:

A. creamer
B. pudding
C. oatmeal
D. coffee

2. In 1998, what company acquired the rights to ICQ, the first widespread instant messaging service?

A. IBM
B. Intel
C. AOL
D. Corel

3. Beginning with the 2002 season, what professional sports organization announced that it would begin the use of instant replay cameras to assist officials?

A. the WTA (tennis)
B. the NHL (hockey)
C. the NBA (basketball)
D. NASCAR (stock car racing)

4. What parenthetical subtitle appeared at the end of the title on the John Lennon single "Instant Karma"?

A. "(When You're Down and Out)"
B. "(War Is Over)"
C. "(Darling Boy)"
D. "(We All Shine On)"

5. Name the 18th-century American whose "Rights of Man" revealed: "The instant formal government is abolished, society begins to act. A general association takes place, and common interest produces common security."

A. Benjamin Franklin
B. William Hill Brown
C. Thomas Paine
D. Alexander Hamilton

Answer 1: A—a bus route.

Answer 2: C—Randy Newman.

Answer 3: C—shorthand writing.

Answer 4: C—six.

Answer 5: C—Jiminy.

THE "AA" QUIZ

1. "Aardvark" is an Afrikaans word meaning ... what?

A. ant eater
B. earth pig
C. fierce claws
D. long nose

2. In Great Britain, it's known as the AA. What is it in America?

A. the AAA
B. the AARP
C. the FAA
D. the NCAA

3. What American writer published the poem "Al Aaraaf" in 1829?

A. Ralph Waldo Emerson
B. Walt Whitman
C. Edgar Allan Poe
D. Herman Melville

4. What Aaron Copland composition has been used as the theme music for several television shows around the world, including *CBS Sports Spectacular*?

A. *Appalachian Spring*
B. *Billy the Kid*
C. *Fanfare for the Common Man*
D. *Rodeo*

5. Aalen and Aachen are cities in what European country?

A. Germany
B. Netherlands
C. Denmark
D. Poland

Answer 1: A—creamer.

Answer 2: C—AOL.

Answer 3: C—the NBA (basketball).

Answer 4: D—"(We All Shine On)."

Answer 5: C—Thomas Paine.

"SPIRITED" MOVIE PERFORMANCES

1. Matt Damon provided the voice of the title character in the 2002 animated motion picture *Spirit*. What type of animal was Spirit?

A. a leopard
B. an eagle
C. a horse
D. a kangaroo

2. The animated 1991 short *The Spirit of Christmas* is the first work featuring characters that would go on to form the basis of what animated series?

A. *Beavis & Butt-head*
B. *The Brothers Grunt*
C. *South Park*
D. *Ren & Stimpy*

3. The motion picture *Blithe Spirit* was based on a play by what British luminary, who also penned *Private Lives* and *Sail Away* and was knighted in 1970?

A. Noel Coward
B. John Osborne
C. David Garrick
D. Peter Shaffer

4. Name the 1971 film (written by, directed by, and starring Tom Laughlin) in which this line of dialogue appears: "I try, I really try. But when I see this girl of such a beautiful spirit suffer this indignity … I just go BERSERK!"

A. *Shaft*
B. *The Last Picture Show*
C. *Billy Jack*
D. *The French Connection*

5. What actor starred as Charles Lindbergh in the 1957 Billy Wilder film *The Spirit of St. Louis*?

A. Charlton Heston
B. Jimmy Stewart
C. Kirk Douglas
D. Henry Fonda

Answer 1: B—earth pig.

Answer 2: A—the AAA (in the U.S. it's the American Automobile Association—in the U.K. it's simply the Automobile Association).

Answer 3: C—Edgar Allan Poe.

Answer 4: C—*Fanfare for the Common Man.*

Answer 5: A—Germany.

LIQUID REFRESHMENT

1. The water moccasin, the most poisonous snake in North America, is also known as the:

A. copperhead
B. sidewinder
C. cottonmouth
D. massasauga

2. In what work does this sentiment appear: "If I can't drink my bowl of coffee three times daily, then in my torment, I will shrivel up like a piece of roast goat"?

A. William Shakespeare's *The Merry Wives of Windsor*
B. Jim Jarmusch's *Coffee and Cigarettes*
C. Benjamin Franklin's *Poor Richard's Almanack*
D. Johann Sebastian Bach's "Coffee Cantata"

3. Alongside his friend Paul Revere, which of these American patriots was instrumental in organizing the Boston Tea Party?

A. John Jay
B. Samuel Adams
C. Nathan Hale
D. John Hancock

4. Since 1962, a character named Opie has appeared in television and print advertisements for what brand of fruit drink?

A. Hawaiian Punch
B. Juicy Juice
C. Hi-C
D. Five Alive

5. What young adult author created the characters Ponyboy and Sodapop?

A. Norma Fox Mazer
B. Judy Blume
C. Paul Zindel
D. S.E. Hinton

Answer 1: C—a horse.

Answer 2: C—*South Park.*

Answer 3: A—Noel Coward.

Answer 4: C—*Billy Jack.*

Answer 5: B—Jimmy Stewart.

SOCK IT TO ME

1. What presidential daughter brought Socks the cat to the White House?

A. Susan Ford
B. Chelsea Clinton
C. Amy Carter
D. Caroline Kennedy

2. What clothier was the first American retailer to manufacture argyle hose?

A. Brooks Brothers
B. Sears & Roebuck
C. Eddie Bauer
D. J. Crew

3. What Chicago White Sox outfielder, named A.L. Rookie of the Year in 1983, holds the record for the most rooftop home runs at old Comiskey Park?

A. Sammy Sosa
B. Carlos Lee
C. Ron Kittle
D. Chris Singleton

4. What famous hoofer made his final big-screen musical appearance in the MGM film *Silk Stockings*?

A. Fred Astaire
B. Ray Bolger
C. Donald O'Connor
D. Gene Kelly

5. Wallace Carothers invented nylon while working as a scientist for what company?

A. Union Carbide
B. Bosch
C. Burlington
D. DuPont

Answer 1: C—cottonmouth.

Answer 2: D—Johann Sebastian Bach's "Coffee Cantata."

Answer 3: B—Samuel Adams.

Answer 4: A—Hawaiian Punch (the straw hat–wearing wise guy who always ends up punching Opie is appropriately named Punchy).

Answer 5: D—S.E. Hinton (the characters first appeared in her book *The Outsiders*).

THE WHITE STUFF

1. Written in the fifth century by Greek historian Herodotus, the well-known (but unofficial) U.S. Postal Service motto begins with what four words?

A. Neither rain nor snow
B. Neither snow nor sleet
C. Neither rain nor sleet
D. Neither snow nor rain

2. Which of these singers was born in Nova Scotia, Canada?

A. Hank Snow
B. Valaida Snow
C. Kilby Snow
D. Phoebe Snow

3. Alpin, Blizzak, and SP Arctic are all brands of:

A. snow skis
B. snowmobiles
C. snow tires
D. snowblowers

4. What TV show featured a character by the name of Christmas Snow?

A. *Northern Exposure*
B. *Dick Tracy*
C. *Three's Company*
D. *The Muppet Show*

5. What David Guterson novel was made into a 1999 motion picture starring Ethan Hawke, Youki Kudoh, and Max von Sydow?

A. *Snow Day*
B. *Leopard in the Snow*
C. *Smilla's Sense of Snow*
D. *Snow Falling on Cedars*

Answer 1: B—Chelsea Clinton.

Answer 2: A—Brooks Brothers.

Answer 3: C—Ron Kittle.

Answer 4: A—Fred Astaire.

Answer 5: D—DuPont.

SUNNY DAY

Each question contains the name of a *Sesame Street* character.

1. Elmo Lincoln was the first actor to portray what character on the silver screen?

A. Superman
B. Tarzan
C. Batman
D. Sherlock Holmes

2. What classic play is set in the fictitious city of Grover's Corners?

A. *Our Town*
B. *Inherit the Wind*
C. *Twelfth Night*
D. *Arsenic and Old Lace*

3. 1997's *Titanic* took home 11 Oscars; what is the only other film to garner as many Academy Awards?

A. *Gone With the Wind*
B. *The Color Purple*
C. *Ben-Hur*
D. *All About Eve*

4. Pulitzer Prize–winning war correspondent Ernie Pyle was killed by a sniper's bullet during what war?

A. World War I
B. World War II
C. Korean War
D. Vietnam War

5. His family called him Bertie, but when his elder brother Edward abdicated, this British monarch became known as:

A. Edward VII
B. George VI
C. Henry VIII
D. William the Conqueror

Answer 1: D—Neither snow nor rain.

Answer 2: A—Hank Snow.

Answer 3: C—snow tires.

Answer 4: C—*Three's Company* (Christmas Snow was the full name of Chrissy, portrayed by Suzanne Somers).

Answer 5: D—*Snow Falling on Cedars.*

ALL ABOUT "EVE"

1. Which of these actresses had a regular role in the TV series *The Brady Bunch*?

A. Eve Brent
B. Eve Arden
C. Eve Plumb
D. Eve Gordon

2. What poet penned some of his best work in 1819, including "To Autumn," "Ode on a Grecian Urn," and "The Eve of St. Agnes"?

A. John Keats
B. Alfred, Lord Tennyson
C. Rudyard Kipling
D. William Wordsworth

3. In Great Britain, January 20 marks a day known as St. Agnes' Eve, during which young women who sleep at night are said to dream of:

A. their past lives
B. the manner of their deaths
C. their guardian angel
D. their future husbands

4. What band's albums have included *The Turn of a Friendly Card*, *Vulture Culture*, and *Eve*?

A. the Jimi Hendrix Experience
B. the Dwight Twilley Band
C. the Alan Parsons Project
D. the Michael Schenker Group

5. According to the Bible, Adam and Eve had how many sons?

A. one
B. two
C. three
D. four

Answer 1: B—Tarzan.

Answer 2: A—*Our Town*.

Answer 3: C—*Ben-Hur*.

Answer 4: B—World War II.

Answer 5: B—George VI.

BOX IT UP

1. In medical terminology, the "voice box" is known as the:

A. pharynx
B. epiglottis
C. trachea
D. larynx

2. What would you find in a bento box?

A. toys
B. food
C. cosmetics
D. stationery

3. Who was the first female to be featured on the front of a Wheaties box?

A. Mary Lou Retton
B. Babe Didrickson
C. Sonja Henie
D. Billie Jean King

4. Taking into consideration that it's summer in December down under, what sporting competition is a Boxing Day tradition in Australia?

A. water skiing
B. tennis
C. cricket
D. rowing

5. According to Greek mythology, what was the only spirit that remained in Pandora's Box?

A. Wealth
B. Hope
C. Charity
D. Faith

Answer 1: C—Eve Plumb (who played middle sister Jan Brady).

Answer 2: A—John Keats.

Answer 3: D—their future husbands.

Answer 4: C—the Alan Parsons Project.

Answer 5: C—three (Cain, Abel, and Seth).

HEAVY METAL

1. Bronze is an alloy of what two metals?

A. tin & copper
B. lead & tin
C. copper & zinc
D. iron & carbon

2. A version of Andrew Gold's 1978 hit "Thank You for Being a Friend" became the theme song for what television series?

A. *Suddenly Susan*
B. *Designing Women*
C. *Bosom Buddies*
D. *The Golden Girls*

3. Shirley Babashoff holds the record for the most Olympic silver medals (six) won by a female. What sport is her specialty?

A. swimming
B. running
C. archery
D. speed skating

4. In what country would you find the scenic Sierra Tarahumara, or Copper Canyon?

A. Ecuador
B. Mexico
C. Honduras
D. Venezuela

5. What album was the first to be certified platinum by the RIAA?

A. *Rumours* (Fleetwood Mac)
B. *Songs in the Key of Life* (Stevie Wonder)
C. *Their Greatest Hits 1971–1975* (The Eagles)
D. *Goodbye, Yellow Brick Road* (Elton John)

Answer 1: D—larynx.

Answer 2: B—food (a bento box is a prepackaged Japanese meal).

Answer 3: A—Mary Lou Retton (in 1984, after winning the all-around gymnastics gold medal at the Summer Olympic Games).

Answer 4: C—cricket.

Answer 5: B—Hope.

ON, COMET!

1. In 1994, the Comet Shoemaker-Levy 9 collided with which planet?

A. Jupiter
B. Mercury
C. Saturn
D. Neptune

2. What legendary rock-and-roller led a band known as the Comets?

A. Jerry Lee Lewis
B. Buddy Holly
C. Eddie Cochran
D. Bill Haley

3. A child born in 1986, when Halley's Comet last visited our solar system, will be how old when it makes its next visit?

A. 35
B. 54
C. 76
D. 98

4. What conglomerate introduced Comet cleanser back in 1956?

A. Bristol-Myers
B. Procter & Gamble
C. Colgate-Palmolive
D. Kimberly-Clark

5. The de Havilland Comet IV was:

A. a motorcycle
B. a jet plane
C. an outboard boat motor
D. an automobile

Answer 1: A—tin and copper.

Answer 2: D—*The Golden Girls*.

Answer 3: A—swimming.

Answer 4: B—Mexico.

Answer 5: C—*Their Greatest Hits 1971–1975* (by the Eagles, which is also the biggest-selling album in U.S. music history).

HATS OFF

1. The fez, the most recognizable symbol of the Shriners, originated in what country?

A. Morocco
B. Tunisia
C. Austria
D. Turkey

2. As depicted on an episode of the sitcom *I Love Lucy*, what Hollywood gossip columnist was known for her outrageous hats?

A. Liz Smith
B. Cindy Adams
C. Hedda Hopper
D. Louella Parsons

3. What president broke with tradition by wearing a homburg instead of the traditional top hat to his inauguration?

A. Harry Truman
B. Dwight Eisenhower
C. Lyndon Johnson
D. John Kennedy

4. What type of salad was invented by the owner of the famous Hollywood eatery the Brown Derby?

A. Waldorf salad
B. Caesar salad
C. Maurice salad
D. Cobb salad

5. "Toque blanche" is the technical name of what type of headgear?

A. a chef's hat
B. a fedora
C. a Cossack cap
D. a ten-gallon hat

Answer 1: A—Jupiter.

Answer 2: D—Bill Haley.

Answer 3: C—76.

Answer 4: B—Procter & Gamble.

Answer 5: B—a jet plane.

GRAPPLE OF DISCORD

1. In which of these forms of wrestling is it illegal to use the legs for offensive purposes?

A. Freestyle
B. Sumo
C. Greco-Roman
D. Jujitsu

2. Which of these football legends got his name from a wrestling match in which he was once involved?

A. Jack "The Assassin" Tatum
B. Paul "Bear" Bryant
C. Craig "Ironhead" Heyward
D. Elroy "Crazylegs" Hirsch

3. What actor starred alongside the late Richard Harris in a critically acclaimed 1993 motion picture titled *Wrestling Ernest Hemingway*?

A. Robert Duvall
B. Anthony Hopkins
C. Jack Nicholson
D. Sean Connery

4. The professional wrestling organization formerly known as the WWF is now known by what set of initials?

A. the WWE
B. the WCW
C. the WWWF
D. the NWA

5. According to the book of Genesis, what Old Testament character wrestled with God?

A. Esau
B. Seth
C. Jacob
D. Moses

Answer 1: A—Morocco.

Answer 2: C—Hedda Hopper.

Answer 3: B—Dwight Eisenhower.

Answer 4: D—Cobb salad.

Answer 5: A—a chef's hat.

CHAUNTICLEER-LY
All about *The Canterbury Tales.*

1. *The Canterbury Tales* were stories told by a band of pilgrims on their way to the Canterbury Cathedral to visit the shrine of:

A. Thomas à Becket
B. Roger Bacon
C. Oliver Cromwell
D. King Arthur

2. In what motion picture did Paul Bettany portray the role of *The Canterbury Tales* author Geoffrey Chaucer?

A. *Braveheart*
B. *A Knight's Tale*
C. *The Lion in Winter*
D. *Ladyhawke*

3. During the story, what prize is offered by the Innkeeper (Host) for the pilgrim who tells the best story of the bunch?

A. a meal
B. a shilling
C. a pair of shoes
D. a chalice

4. What classic rock song contains a lyrical reference to *The Canterbury Tales* with the line: "And so it was that later, as the miller told his tale"?

A. "Killer Queen"
B. "Sympathy for the Devil"
C. "A Whiter Shade of Pale"
D. "American Pie"

5. What was the name of the man believed to be the first English printer, who crafted the first book edition of *The Canterbury Tales* among his near-100 publications?

A. Richard Hoe
B. Horace Walpole
C. Stephen Day
D. William Caxton

Answer 1: C—Greco-Roman.

Answer 2: B—Paul "Bear" Bryant (who got his nickname after wrestling a bear in a theater in his younger days).

Answer 3: A—Robert Duvall.

Answer 4: A—the WWE (World Wrestling Entertainment).

Answer 5: C—Jacob.

THE "OX" QUIZ

All answers end in "ox."

1. Which of the following is a type of algae?

A. phlox
B. cowpox
C. volvox
D. lox

2. Which of these names applies to the division of Hallmark known for the humorous artwork and text in its greeting cards?

A. Mailbox
B. Shoebox
C. Tinderbox
D. Lunchbox

3. Which one of these events occurred in 1865?

A. U.S. purchase of Seward's Icebox
B. invention of vaccine for smallpox
C. Lee's surrender at Appomattox
D. the construction of Fort Knox

4. Which one of these brand names was the first to appear, back in 1913?

A. Xerox
B. Maalox
C. Magnavox
D. Clorox

5. Which one of these items is mentioned in the lyrics of the song "Roll Over Beethoven," a hit for Chuck Berry, the Beatles, and the Electric Light Orchestra?

A. jukebox
B. fusebox
C. icebox
D. toolbox

Answer 1: A—Thomas à Becket.

Answer 2: B—*A Knight's Tale*.

Answer 3: A—a meal (paid for by the other members of the party).

Answer 4: C—"A Whiter Shade of Pale."

Answer 5: D—William Caxton.

THE "STANDARD" QUIZ

1. First published in 1827, the *Evening Standard* is the only nighttime newspaper in what world capital?

A. London
B. Moscow
C. Ottawa
D. Tokyo

2. The "Standard Model" theory applies to which branch of science?

A. biology
B. chemistry
C. physics
D. mechanics

3. Which of these tycoons was once head of Standard Oil?

A. Andrew Carnegie
B. John D. Rockefeller
C. Aristotle Onassis
D. Jay Gould

4. If it is 8 P.M. Eastern Standard Time in New York City, what time is it locally in Detroit, Michigan?

A. 6 P.M.
B. 7 P.M.
C. 8 P.M.
D. 9 P.M.

5. In what year did the United States abandon the gold standard for the last time?

A. 1873
B. 1903
C. 1933
D. 1963

Answer 1: C—volvox.

Answer 2: B—Shoebox.

Answer 3: C—Lee's surrender at Appomattox.

Answer 4: D—Clorox.

Answer 5: A—jukebox.

UP AND ATOM!

1. An "atomizer" is a device most often used to distribute:

A. penicillin
B. X-rays
C. perfume
D. cellular telephone signals

2. In what they said was in contrast to the busy, colorful album covers of the era, a plain photo of a cow was depicted on the cover of what British band's 1970 album *Atom Heart Mother*?

A. Pink Floyd
B. Hawkwind
C. Jethro Tull
D. The Moody Blues

3. Which of these cartoon characters did NOT appear in segments on *The Atom Ant / Secret Squirrel Show*?

A. The Hillbilly Bears
B. Squiddly Diddly
C. Mr. Magoo
D. Winsome Witch

4. After the United States and the Soviet Union, what country became the third in the world to test an atom bomb (in 1952)?

A. Great Britain
B. China
C. France
D. Japan

5. Which of these particles orbits around the nucleus of an atom?

A. proton
B. neutron
C. photon
D. electron

Answer 1: A—London.

Answer 2: C—physics.

Answer 3: B—John D. Rockefeller.

Answer 4: C—8 P.M. (both cities are in the Eastern time zone).

Answer 5: C—1933.

NOTHING AT ALL

1. Introduced in 1920 by Frank A. Martoccio, the white fudge-covered Zero candy bar is now a product of what conglomerate?

A. Hershey
B. Nestle
C. M&M/Mars
D. Cadbury

2. What Japanese company developed the A6M fighter plane known during World War II as the Zero?

A. Fuji
B. Sanyo
C. Mitsubishi
D. Kawasaki

3. Which of these comic strips included a character named (or nicknamed) Zero?

A. "Doonesbury"
B. "Ziggy"
C. "Hägar the Horrible"
D. "Beetle Bailey"

4. The temperature known as absolute zero is equal to zero degrees on which scale?

A. Celsius
B. Kelvin
C. Fahrenheit
D. none of the above

5. A zero-insertion-force socket (also known as a ZIF socket) is most likely to be found in what type of device?

A. a jet plane
B. a compact disc player
C. an alarm clock
D. a computer

Answer 1: C—perfume.

Answer 2: A—Pink Floyd.

Answer 3: D—Winsome Witch.

Answer 4: A—Great Britain.

Answer 5: D—electron.

FANTASTIC PLASTIC

1. Which of these is considered a charge card, but not a credit card?

A. Visa
B. American Express
C. Discovery
D. MasterCard

2. After they passed what was known as Amendment 60 back in 1982, what state has had a reputation for consistently offering the lowest credit card interest rates in the country?

A. Arkansas
B. Washington
C. New Jersey
D. Hawaii

3. Back in 1950, which of the following was introduced as the world's first charge card?

A. Master Charge
B. Carte Blanche
C. Sears
D. Diner's Club

4. What letter is placed at the end of the "http" on Web addresses to indicate that the site is considered safe for entering card numbers and other financial information?

A. S
B. P
C. X
D. T

5. Before changing its name to Visa in 1975, the company's credit cards were known in the United States by what other name?

A. Citibank Card
B. Consumer Passport
C. Bank Americard
D. Union Charge

Answer 1: A—Hershey.

Answer 2: C—Mitsubishi.

Answer 3: D—"Beetle Bailey."

Answer 4: B—Kelvin.

Answer 5: D—a computer.

DANCE, DANCE, DANCE

1. "Put your right foot forward, put your left foot out" are part of the instructions for what "animal" dance?

A. the Bunny Hop
B. the Turkey Trot
C. the Lame Duck
D. the Camel Walk

2. St. Vitus's Dance is:

A. atmospheric electricity
B. an English horse race
C. a type of brain disorder
D. a yellow-flowered plant

3. Cosmo "Gus" Allegretti portrayed Dancing Bear on what kiddie TV show?

A. *Howdy Doody*
B. *The New Zoo Revue*
C. *Mister Rogers' Neighborhood*
D. *Captain Kangaroo*

4. What disco dance tune was the first single to be certified as platinum by the RIAA?

A. "Dancing Queen" (ABBA)
B. "YMCA" (The Village People)
C. "Disco Lady" (Johnnie Taylor)
D. "The Hustle" (Van McCoy)

5. What comic strip was set in the Okeefenokee Swamp?

A. "Snuffy Smith"
B. "Li'l Abner"
C. "Pogo"
D. "Broom-Hilda"

Answer 1: B—American Express (certain special Amex cards do offer "credit" services, but the standard card does not).

Answer 2: A—Arkansas.

Answer 3: D—Diner's Club.

Answer 4: A—S.

Answer 5: C—Bank Americard.

WELL, SHOOT

Each question contains the name of a gun manufacturer.

1. Introduced in 1898, the Remington #2 revolutionized the industry. What was it?

A. a razor
B. a revolver
C. a typewriter
D. a vacuum cleaner

2. Elizabeth Barrett Browning's classic poem "How Do I Love Thee" originally appeared in what collection?

A. *A Drama of Exile*
B. *Sonnets From the Portuguese*
C. *Poems Before Congress*
D. *Aurora Leigh*

3. The character of Major Charles Emerson Winchester III was a mid-series replacement on what television show?

A. *China Beach*
B. *M*A*S*H*
C. *F Troop*
D. *Combat!*

4. What chestnut colt appeared simultaneously on the covers of *Time*, *Newsweek*, and *Sports Illustrated* in 1973?

A. Seattle Slew
B. Man o' War
C. Affirmed
D. Secretariat

5. Guitarist Rick Derringer was only 16 years of age when he cowrote and played on what #1 single?

A. "Hang On Sloopy"
B. "Lightnin' Strikes"
C. "Love Is Blue"
D. "96 Tears"

Answer 1: A—the Bunny Hop.

Answer 2: C—a type of brain disorder.

Answer 3: D—*Captain Kangaroo*.

Answer 4: C—"Disco Lady" (Johnnie Taylor).

Answer 5: C—"Pogo."

THE CUTTING EDGE

1. Those poor "Three Blind Mice" of nursery rhyme fame had their tails cut off by the farmer's wife using what sharp instrument?

A. a butcher knife
B. a paring knife
C. a carving knife
D. a pocket knife

2. Yellowknife is the capital city of what part of Canada?

A. Northwest Territories
B. Prince Edward Island
C. Yukon Territory
D. Newfoundland

3. Name the Arkansas craftsman who forged the first Bowie knife, named after Alamo hero James Bowie.

A. John Snowden
B. William Travis
C. Alexander Crain
D. James Black

4. "Mack the Knife" was a Grammy-winning record and the only #1 hit single for what singer?

A. Bobby Darin
B. Ella Fitzgerald
C. Louie Armstrong
D. Billy Vaughn

5. In what motion picture did a character wield a machete at some street thugs, telling them, "That's not a knife … THAT'S a knife"?

A. *Robocop*
B. *Blade Runner*
C. *"Crocodile" Dundee*
D. *Die Hard*

Answer 1: C—a typewriter.

Answer 2: B—*Sonnets From the Portuguese.*

Answer 3: B—*M*A*S*H.*

Answer 4: D—Secretariat.

Answer 5: A—"Hang On Sloopy."

CAPITAL CANINES

1. A sculpture of the Airedale known as "Laddie Boy" was crafted from nearly 20,000 pennies raised by the Newsboys' Association. Who was his presidential master?

A. Harry Truman
B. Dwight Eisenhower
C. Warren Harding
D. Herbert Hoover

2. What was the rather appropriate name of Jimmy Carter's pooch during his stint in the White House?

A. Grits
B. Smiley
C. Peanuts
D. Georgia

3. In September, 1952, then–vice president Richard Nixon made what became known as "the Checkers speech." What breed of dog was Checkers?

A. Basset hound
B. Poodle
C. Dalmatian
D. Cocker spaniel

4. Lyndon Johnson drew the ire of pet lovers nationwide when he was photographed lifting which of his unusually named beagles by its ears?

A. She
B. Him
C. He
D. Her

5. Millie, a Springer Spaniel who "dictated" a best-selling book to Barbara Bush, had a son that lived in the second Bush White House. What was his name?

A. Rover
B. Fido
C. Spot
D. Barky

Answer 1: C—a carving knife.

Answer 2: A—Northwest Territories.

Answer 3: D—James Black.

Answer 4: A—Bobby Darin.

Answer 5: C—*Crocodile* Dundee.

SMALL SCREEN FIRSTS

1. The first interracial kiss (between a Caucasian and an African-American) on U.S. television occurred on which prime-time show?

A. *All in the Family*
B. *Julia*
C. *The Jeffersons*
D. *Star Trek*

2. Baby Maggie of TV's *The Simpsons* spoke her first word (voiced by Elizabeth Taylor) on December 3, 1992. What did she say?

A. "¡Ay, caramba!"
B. "Daddy!"
C. "Bart!"
D. "D'oh!"

3. What TV character's first spoken words were: "Goodbye, kids"?

A. Clarabell the Clown
B. Big Bird
C. Crusader Rabbit
D. Mr. Green Jeans

4. In September, 1947, the New York Yankees played against what National League team in the first televised World Series?

A. the Brooklyn Dodgers
B. the Pittsburgh Pirates
C. the Cincinnati Reds
D. the St. Louis Cardinals

5. Zenith introduced the first TV remote control in December of 1950. What was it called?

A. Couch Potato
B. Back-Seat Driver
C. Slugabed
D. Lazy Bones

Answer 1: C—Warren Harding.

Answer 2: A—Grits.

Answer 3: D—Cocker Spaniel (accused of accepting bribes, Nixon said Checkers was the only gift he had received).

Answer 4: B—Him (the beagles were named Him and Her).

Answer 5: C—Spot.

MY "BUDDY"

1. What are "buddy stores"?

A. aircraft fuel tanks
B. interlocking steel cabinets
C. retail establishments sharing a parking lot
D. military commissaries

2. What was the unusual nickname that Buddy Sorrell used to refer to his wife on the TV sitcom *The Dick Van Dyke Show*?

A. Butterfly
B. Tootsie
C. Pickles
D. Woo-Woo

3. Who danced alongside Shirley Temple in the motion picture *Captain January*?

A. Buddy Ebsen
B. Buddy DeFranco
C. Buddy Rogers
D. Buddy DeSylva

4. What is a Nutty Buddy?

A. a nut-filled candy bar
B. a flavored specialty coffee
C. an ice cream treat
D. a peanut-shaped cookie

5. Along with his band (Gene Alden, Dave Burgess, and Danny Flores), who was awarded the very first Grammy award for best R&B performance back in 1958?

A. Buddy Rich
B. Buddy Bruce
C. Buddy Holly
D. Buddy Guy

Answer 1: D—*Star Trek* (the kiss took place between stars William Shatner and Nichelle Nichols).

Answer 2: B—Daddy.

Answer 3: A—Clarabell the Clown (the normally silent clown, played by Bob "Captain Kangaroo" Keeshan, said the phrase on the last episode of *The Howdy Doody Show*).

Answer 4: A—the Brooklyn Dodgers.

Answer 5: D—Lazy Bones.

SOUNDS FISHY ...

1. Former Secretary of State Edmund Muskie was elected the governor of what state in 1954?

A. Michigan
B. Missouri
C. Montana
D. Maine

2. The lyrics to what patriotic song were inspired by the view from the top of Pikes Peak?

A. "America the Beautiful"
B. "This Land Is Your Land"
C. "Proud To Be an American"
D. "God Bless America"

3. Plymouth's answer to the Mustang was the Barracuda, which was based on which of their existing models?

A. Reliant
B. Fury
C. Valiant
D. Duster

4. A traditional "black and tan" is an alcoholic mixture of Bass Ale and:

A. Dr Pepper
B. Guinness Stout
C. Worcestershire sauce
D. hard apple cider

5. Which character in the 1978 film *Animal House* was given the Delta Tau Chi name Flounder?

A. Larry Kroger
B. Greg Marmalard
C. Kent Dorfman
D. Robert Hoover

Answer 1: A—aircraft fuel tanks (designed to transfer fuel from one plane to another while in the air).

Answer 2: C—Pickles.

Answer 3: A—Buddy Ebsen.

Answer 4: C—an ice cream treat (also known in some areas as a drumstick).

Answer 5: B—Buddy Bruce (of the Champs—their biggest hit being "Tequila").

ROYAL FLUSH

1. What was the real first name of jazz great Duke Ellington?

A. Edward
B. Charles
C. James
D. Reginald

2. When discussing dress silhouettes, a "princess waist" is most similar to:

A. mermaid
B. empire
C. A line
D. sheath

3. Dr. Martin Luther King Jr. received his Ph.D. from which school?

A. Baylor University
B. Harvard University
C. Columbia University
D. Boston University

4. According to a national advertising campaign that began 50 years ago, what day of the week is Prince Spaghetti Day?

A. Wednesday
B. Friday
C. Tuesday
D. Saturday

5. Where in Canada would you find Mount Queen Elizabeth?

A. Glacier National Park
B. Jasper National Park
C. Banff National Park
D. Point Pelee National Park

Answer 1: D—Maine.

Answer 2: A—"America the Beautiful."

Answer 3: C—Valiant.

Answer 4: B—Guinness Stout.

Answer 5: C—Kent Dorfman.

WHERE THE BUFFALO ROAM

1. From 1916 to 1938, what U.S. coin featured a buffalo (or, more accurately, a North American bison) on its reverse?

A. penny
B. nickel
C. dime
D. quarter

2. What author penned the 1990 novel *Buffalo Girls*?

A. Larry McMurtry
B. John Irving
C. Scott Turow
D. Tom Wolfe

3. The famous Anchor Bar is best known as:

A. where the rock band Buffalo Springfield formed
B. where buffalo wings were invented
C. the birthplace of "Buffalo" Bill Cody
D. the setting of the film *Buffalo Soldiers*

4. Buffalo Grove is a northwest suburb of what major U.S. city?

A. New York
B. Los Angeles
C. Houston
D. Chicago

5. The Buffalo Bills have played in four Super Bowls and lost all four of them. What other pro football team also sports an 0–4 record in the big game (through 2012)?

A. the Miami Dolphins
B. the Denver Broncos
C. the Minnesota Vikings
D. the Kansas City Chiefs

Answer 1: A—Edward (full name Edward Kennedy Ellington).

Answer 2: C—A line.

Answer 3: D—Boston University.

Answer 4: A—Wednesday.

Answer 5: C—Banff National Park.

YOU'RE DOING ADMIRABLY

1. What nickname for liquor came from Admiral Edward Vernon of the British Navy, known for watering down the rum given to his sailors?

A. rotgut
B. grog
C. firewater
D. hooch

2. What is the parent company of Admiral Appliances?

A. Whirlpool
B. Amana
C. General Electric
D. Maytag

3. In 1937, the thoroughbred War Admiral won the Triple Crown. The next year, he lost in a one-on-one match race at Pimlico against what other famous horse?

A. Man o' War
B. Citation
C. Seabiscuit
D. Whirlaway

4. Admiral John Franklin was an English explorer best known for his inadvertent discovery of what northern locale in the 1840s?

A. the Northwest Passage
B. Alaska
C. the North Pole
D. the Arctic Circle

5. What 1960s sitcom character took a ride on a U.S. Navy warship when he wore an officer's uniform on board and was mistaken by the crew for an admiral?

A. Gomer Pyle
B. Jed Clampett
C. Rob Petrie
D. Gomez Addams

Answer 1: B—nickel (commonly known as the "buffalo nickel").

Answer 2: A—Larry McMurtry.

Answer 3: B—where buffalo wings were invented.

Answer 4: D—Chicago.

Answer 5: C—the Minnesota Vikings.

FILL-IN-THE-BLANK

These are famous (but commonly misquoted) quotes.

1. "Give me your tired, your poor, your huddled masses yearning to _____ _____ ..." (Emma Lazarus)

A. sing free
B. be free
C. live free
D. breathe free

2. "Alas, poor _____, I knew him _____ ..." (William Shakespeare)

A. Yorick, Horatio
B. Hamlet, Yorick
C. Yorick, well
D. Horatio, well

3. "Music hath charms to soothe the _____ _____ ..." (William Congreve)

A. angry beast
B. savage breast
C. king's armies
D. savage beast

4. "Yesterday, December 7, 1941, a _____ which will live in _____ ..." (Franklin D. Roosevelt)

A. day, infamy
B. tragedy, infamy
C. day, history
D. date, infamy

5. "The _____ of _____ is the root of all evil ..." (from the Bible)

A. love, money
B. money, man
C. want, money
D. want, man

Answer 1: B—grog (he wore a grogram cloak in inclement weather, and was nicknamed Old Grog).

Answer 2: D—Maytag.

Answer 3: C—Seabiscuit.

Answer 4: A—the Northwest Passage.

Answer 5: B—Jed Clampett (as portrayed by Buddy Ebsen in *The Beverly Hillbillies*).

BETWEEN THE BREAD

1. The archipelago once known as the Sandwich Islands is now called:

A. the Bahamas
B. Hawaii
C. Tahiti
D. the Philippines

2. Advertising lore has it that the very first message printed on a "sandwich board" was:

A. "Eat at Joe's"
B. "Will Work for Food"
C. "Repent Now"
D. "Drink Coca-Cola"

3. The Dagwood sandwich became a dictionary entry thanks to Blondie cartoonist Chic Young. The title of which of his earlier strips also became part of our vernacular?

A. "Marvin Milquetoast"
B. "Dumb Dora"
C. "Sad Sack"
D. "Nervous Nellie"

4. In what movie was Jack Nicholson forced to order a chicken salad sandwich with his omelet just to get two slices of wheat toast?

A. *Ironweed*
B. *Easy Rider*
C. *Carnal Knowledge*
D. *Five Easy Pieces*

5. Sandwich glass, known for its ornate floral patterns, is only authentic if it was manufactured in what U.S. state?

A. Pennsylvania
B. Massachusetts
C. West Virginia
D. Vermont

Answer 1: D—breathe free.

Answer 2: A—Yorick, Horatio.

Answer 3: B—savage breast.

Answer 4: D—date, infamy.

Answer 5: A—love, money.

FLAME ON

1. What many believe to be the first fire insurance company in the world began operation around 1670 after a devastating blaze in what city?

A. London
B. Paris
C. Munich
D. Cairo

2. A December 1958 fire at what Chicago school claimed the lives of 90 students and resulted in a complete overhaul of school fire safety laws in the U.S.?

A. Morgan Park Academy
B. St. John's Lutheran
C. Our Lady of the Angels
D. Lincoln Park Secondary

3. What U.S. Supreme Court Justice declared that falsely yelling "fire" in a crowded theater was not protected by First Amendment rights?

A. William H. Moody
B. Oliver Wendell Holmes
C. Salmon P. Chase
D. William Howard Taft

4. July 6, 1944, is still remembered as "the day the clowns cried" due to a tragic circus fire in what northeast city?

A. Philadelphia
B. Trenton
C. Hartford
D. Boston

5. What famous vaudevillian was entertaining onstage when a deadly fire (killing over 600) broke out during a matinee show at Chicago's Iroquois Theatre in 1903?

A. Eddie Cantor
B. George M. Cohan
C. Will Rogers
D. Eddie Foy

Answer 1: B—Hawaii.

Answer 2: A—"Eat at Joe's."

Answer 3: B—"Dumb Dora."

Answer 4: D—*Five Easy Pieces*.

Answer 5: B—Massachusetts.

DRIVEN BY YOU

All questions contain the name of a make of automobile.

1. What frontiersman was appointed Deputy Marshal of Dodge City in 1876, and was later involved in the infamous gunfight at the O.K. Corral?

A. John Ringo
B. Doc Holliday
C. Judge Roy Bean
D. Wyatt Earp

2. Mercedes Ruehl won a Best Supporting Actress Oscar for what film?

A. *Working Girl*
B. *The Fisher King*
C. *Patch Adams*
D. *My Cousin Vinny*

3. For his "Popeye" comic strip, E.C. Segar created a magical animal called a "Jeep" (a name later borrowed by the military). What was the original Jeep's name?

A. Eugene
B. Pee-Wee
C. George
D. Jerry

4. In 1701, French army officer Antoine de la Mothe Cadillac established a settlement in America, which is today known as what city?

A. Baton Rouge
B. Chicago
C. Detroit
D. Boise

5. The son of what famous architect developed the popular interlocking toy known as Lincoln Logs?

A. Charles Rennie Mackintosh
B. Frank Lloyd Wright
C. Eero Saarinen
D. Buckminster Fuller

Answer 1: A—London.

Answer 2: C—Our Lady of the Angels (sprinkler systems and fireproof stairwells became mandatory in schools following this tragedy).

Answer 3: B—Oliver Wendell Holmes.

Answer 4: C—Hartford.

Answer 5: D—Eddie Foy (he was commended for his efforts to keep the crowd calm, but panic ensued).

CHUCK ROAST

1. To which color group does St. Charles Place belong on a standard U.S. Monopoly board?

A. light blue
B. red
C. orange
D. light purple

2. Who portrayed the bespectacled character (and *Hollywood Squares* regular) Charlie Weaver?

A. Cliff Arquette
B. Frank Fontaine
C. Red Skelton
D. Wilford Brimley

3. In 1958, Charlie Starkweather went on a killing spree (eleven victims in five states) with what female accomplice?

A. Susan Atkins
B. Caril Fugate
C. Evelyn Nesbit
D. Myra Hindley

4. In the NATO phonetic alphabet, A-B-C is Alpha, Bravo, Charlie. But in Western Union's alphabet, it's Adams, Boston ... what?

A. Carter
B. Chicago
C. City
D. Cleveland

5. What 1966 novel told the story of a mentally challenged man by the name of Charlie Gordon?

A. *Like Normal People*
B. *The Man Who Loved Clowns*
C. *One Flew Over the Cuckoo's Nest*
D. *Flowers for Algernon*

Answer 1: D—Wyatt Earp.

Answer 2: B—*The Fisher King*.

Answer 3: A—Eugene (the GP—general purpose—Jeep etymology you've heard is partly true, but the "Popeye" strip inspired the word choice).

Answer 4: C—Detroit.

Answer 5: B—Frank Lloyd Wright.

PLEADING THE FIFTH
All about New York City's Fifth Avenue.

1. In 1853, the City of New York purchased 624 acres of land from Fifth Avenue to Eighth Avenue with the intention of developing it into:

A. a racetrack
B. the new U.S. capital
C. a city park
D. a public housing project

2. In 1959, the Guggenheim Museum opened on Fifth Avenue to display the art collection of the late Solomon Guggenheim, who made his fortune trading in what commodity?

A. copper
B. oil
C. silk
D. diamonds

3. In 1940, this New York store moved 20 streets uptown to a location at the corner of Fifth Avenue and 57th Street. The new location was the first fully air-conditioned store. Name it.

A. Gimbel's
B. Saks Fifth Avenue
C. Tiffany & Co.
D. Bloomingdale's

4. P.T. Barnum's Hippodrome opened at the north end of a Fifth Avenue park in 1871. The New York structure has been renovated many times since, and became famous by what name?

A. Carnegie Hall
B. Madison Square Garden
C. The Waldorf-Astoria Hotel
D. Radio City Music Hall

5. In the 1850s, a gentleman named Elisha Otis showcased what new invention at the World's Fair on New York's Fifth Avenue?

A. the reclining chair
B. the electric icebox
C. the alarm clock
D. the elevator

Answer 1: D—light purple.

Answer 2: A—Cliff Arquette.

Answer 3: B—Caril Fugate.

Answer 4: B—Chicago.

Answer 5: D—*Flowers for Algernon.*

PLAYING BRIDGE

1. Madison County, Iowa, is known for its covered bridges (as noted in the Robert James Waller novel) and is also the birthplace of what film star?

A. Clint Eastwood
B. Glenn Ford
C. William Holden
D. John Wayne

2. Which song became synonymous with *The Bridge on the River Kwai*?

A. "Stars and Stripes Forever"
B. "The Colonel Bogey March"
C. "Sharpshooter's March"
D. "Enter the Gladiators"

3. The original London Bridge was purchased by chainsaw magnate Robert McCulloch in 1968 and reconstructed in what U.S. state?

A. Arizona
B. Colorado
C. Nevada
D. California

4. What is the name of the bridge that links Detroit, Michigan, to Windsor, Ontario, and has been North America's #1 international border crossing since 1992?

A. the Mackinac Bridge
B. the Peace Bridge
C. the Bluewater Bridge
D. the Ambassador Bridge

5. In the 1977 motion picture *Saturday Night Fever*, a drunken Barry Miller fell off of which New York bridge?

A. the Queensboro Bridge
B. the Verrazano-Narrows Bridge
C. the Williamsburg Bridge
D. the Brooklyn Bridge

Answer 1: C—a park (the area became Central Park).

Answer 2: A—copper.

Answer 3: C—Tiffany & Co.

Answer 4: B—Madison Square Garden.

Answer 5: D—the elevator.

BE A PEPPER

1. Which of the following was removed from Dr Pepper back in the 1950s?

A. the caffeine
B. the alcohol
C. the period after "Dr"
D. the pepper

2. The numbers 10, 2, and 4 that used to appear in the Dr Pepper logo represented ... what?

A. the ages of the founder's children
B. the best times of day to drink the product
C. the sizes of the drink's cups and bottles
D. the combination to the safe holding the formula

3. What star of the 1981 horror film *An American Werewolf in London* was also a former Dr Pepper spokesman, reportedly inspiring the crew to sing to him at one point, "I'm a werewolf, you're a werewolf ... wouldn't you like to be a werewolf too?"

A. David Soul
B. David Lander
C. David Byrne
D. David Naughton

4. Dr Pepper was first sold in 1885 in which Texas city?

A. Waco
B. Amarillo
C. Galveston
D. Laredo

5. In 1986, Dr Pepper joined forces with what other independent brand of soft drink, forming a new corporation?

A. Royal Crown
B. Nehi
C. 7-Up
D. Canada Dry

Answer 1: D—John Wayne.

Answer 2: B—"The Colonel Bogey March."

Answer 3: A—Arizona.

Answer 4: D—the Ambassador Bridge.

Answer 5: B—the Verrazano-Narrows Bridge.

HEY, BABY

1. What company was the first to sell prepared baby food in glass jars?

A. Gerber
B. Heinz
C. Beech-Nut
D. Carnation

2. What was the first name of the former president of Haiti known as "Baby Doc" Duvalier?

A. François
B. Jean-Claude
C. Bertrand
D. Pierre

3. A baby guinea pig is called what?

A. a pup
B. a leveret
C. a piglet
D. a dray

4. What 1980s coming-of-age film featured a character called Baby?

A. *St. Elmo's Fire*
B. *The Breakfast Club*
C. *Dirty Dancing*
D. *Pretty in Pink*

5. What famous baby graced the cover of the very first issue of *TV Guide* magazine?

A. Pebbles Flintstone
B. John F. Kennedy Jr.
C. Ricky Nelson
D. Desi Arnaz Jr.

Answer 1: C—the period after "Dr."

Answer 2: B—the best times of day to drink the product (according to a medical study).

Answer 3: D—David Naughton.

Answer 4: A—Waco.

Answer 5: C—7-Up.

KICK THE BUCKET

1. Brian Carroll, the guitarist popularly known as Buckethead, joined what rock band in 2000 after attempting a solo career?

A. The Black Crowes
B. Guns N' Roses
C. Mother Love Bone
D. The Cult

2. Benjamin Franklin organized America's very first "bucket brigade," a group whose job it was to:

A. feed the poor
B. stop floods
C. collect taxes
D. put out fires

3. In what year did Ford first offer bucket seats on its automobiles?

A. 1903
B. 1931
C. 1955
D. 1970

4. What actor's portrayal of Charlie Bucket in the 1971 motion picture *Willy Wonka and the Chocolate Factory* was his only feature film credit?

A. Michael Gray
B. Eric Shea
C. Peter Ostrum
D. Lee Montgomery

5. Before it became a song, "The Old Oaken Bucket" was a poem written by what American author?

A. Nathaniel Hawthorne
B. Samuel Woodworth
C. Harriet Beecher Stowe
D. Washington Irving

Answer 1: C—Beech-Nut.

Answer 2: B—Jean-Claude (François was the name of his father, who was known as "Papa Doc").

Answer 3: A—a pup.

Answer 4: C—*Dirty Dancing* (the character's real name was Frances Houseman, and nobody put her in a corner).

Answer 5: D—Desi Arnaz Jr.

HERE'S COOKIN' AT YOU

1. Which salad dressing (comprised of mayonnaise, anchovies, scallions, and garlic) was named after a play?

A. Thousand Island
B. Catalina
C. Green Goddess
D. Hidden Valley Ranch

2. What was the first name of the real Chef Boyardee?

A. Hector
B. Antonio
C. Geno
D. Salvatore

3. When an entree is prepared "en brochette," it is served:

A. sautéed with butter
B. wrapped in bacon
C. in a pastry shell
D. on a skewer

4. Nancy Green, Anna Robinson, and Rosie Hall have all portrayed what food advertising icon?

A. Aunt Jemima
B. Betty Crocker
C. Mrs. Paul
D. Mama Celeste

5. What brand of seasoning was named after a famous prime rib restaurant, originally located in Beverly Hills?

A. Adolph's
B. Mrs. Dash
C. Lawry's
D. Accent

Answer 1: B—Guns N' Roses.

Answer 2: D—put out fires.

Answer 3: A—1903 (the very first Ford models had bucket seats).

Answer 4: C—Peter Ostrum.

Answer 5: B—Samuel Woodworth.

A WHALE OF A TALE

1. Which of these sea creatures is a member of the whale family?

A. pilot whale
B. narwhal
C. killer whale
D. whale shark

2. British-born James Whale was best known for directing which classic Hollywood horror film?

A. *Frankenstein*
B. *The Mummy*
C. *The Wolfman*
D. *Dracula*

3. What constellation is represented by the whale?

A. Puppis
B. Dorado
C. Cetus
D. Ophiuchus

4. What Biblical figure spent three days and nights in the stomach of a whale before being spit out on shore?

A. Joshua
B. Hosea
C. Ezekiel
D. Jonah

5. A young whale is properly known by what name?

A. a calf
B. a spike
C. a fingerling
D. a cub

Answer 1: C—Green Goddess.

Answer 2: A—Hector (last name spelled "Boiardi").

Answer 3: D—on a skewer.

Answer 4: A—Aunt Jemima.

Answer 5: C—Lawry's.

BONE UP

1. The furcula or "wishbone" is actually a bird's:

A. collarbone
B. first rib
C. breast bone
D. humerus

2. What parent company produces Milk-Bone dog biscuits?

A. Heinz
B. Ralston-Purina
C. Del Monte
D. Nabisco

3. When a human bone breaks only on one side, it is called a:

A. simple fracture
B. greenstick fracture
C. burst fracture
D. compound fracture

4. T-Bone and Cleo are the best pals of which literary canine?

A. Lad (from *Lad, a Dog*)
B. Lassle
C. Marmaduke
D. Clifford

5. Which artist recorded the popular 1982 song "Bad to the Bone"?

A. Sammy Hagar
B. Rick Derringer
C. George Thorogood
D. Joe Walsh

Answer 1: B—narwhal (the whale shark is a fish, the other two are dolphins).

Answer 2: A—*Frankenstein*.

Answer 3: C—Cetus.

Answer 4: D—Jonah.

Answer 5: A—a calf.

CHOCK FULL OF CHOCOLATE

1. Which company was the first to offer a Valentine's Day chocolate box?

A. Cadbury
B. Whitman
C. Hershey
D. Godiva

2. *Like Water for Chocolate* was a 1992 film that showcased early 20th century life in which nation of the world?

A. Germany
B. Venezuela
C. Switzerland
D. Mexico

3. What floppy-eared dog puppet used to tell TV audiences that "Nestlé's makes the very best chawk-lit"?

A. Droopy
B. Farfel
C. Ollie
D. Cleo

4. Who wrote the classic young adult novel titled *The Chocolate War*?

A. S.E. Hinton
B. Walter Dean Myers
C. Robert Cormier
D. Paul Zindel

5. What song, originally a British hit for the group Hot Chocolate, became the only #1 American single for the band Stories?

A. "You Sexy Thing"
B. "Emma"
C. "Brother Louie"
D. "Every 1's a Winner"

Answer 1: A—collarbone.

Answer 2: C—Del Monte.

Answer 3: B—greenstick fracture.

Answer 4: D—Clifford.

Answer 5: C—George Thorogood.

HEART TO HEART

1. Born with a faulty heart valve, what humorist wrote about undergoing three open heart surgeries in *I Took a Lickin' and Kept on Tickin'*?

A. Erma Bombeck
B. Bennett Cerf
C. Lewis Grizzard
D. Mike Royko

2. The movie *Heart Like a Wheel* told the story of which drag racing legend?

A. Don Garlits
B. Lucille Lee
C. Bob Glidden
D. Shirley Muldowney

3. The company behind the popular Valentine's Day treats Sweethearts-brand Conversation Hearts also makes which of these confections?

A. Starburst fruit chews
B. Necco wafers
C. Smarties
D. Sno-Caps

4. Joseph Conrad's *Heart of Darkness* was the basis for what classic film of the 1970s?

A. *Mean Streets*
B. *The Deer Hunter*
C. *Badlands*
D. *Apocalypse Now*

5. What deaf-mute was the central character in Carson McCullers's classic novel *The Heart Is a Lonely Hunter*?

A. John Singer
B. Boo Radley
C. Benjy Compson
D. Neeley Nolan

Answer 1: A—Cadbury.

Answer 2: D—Mexico.

Answer 3: B—Farfel.

Answer 4: C—Robert Cormier.

Answer 5: C—"Brother Louie."

CHARACTER FLAWS

Literary characters with unusual names.

1. Evil, hypocritical accountant Uriah Heep appeared in which Charles Dickens novel?

A. *David Copperfield*
B. *Oliver Twist*
C. *Great Expectations*
D. *A Tale of Two Cities*

2. Frontiersman Natty Bumppo was the creation of which author?

A. Jack London
B. John Steinbeck
C. James Fenimore Cooper
D. Robert Louis Stevenson

3. In Harper Lee's Pulitzer Prize–winning novel *To Kill a Mockingbird*, what was Atticus Finch's occupation?

A. doctor
B. banker
C. mayor
D. lawyer

4. Who served as valet to Phileas Fogg in Jules Verne's *Around the World in Eighty Days?*

A. Pluperfect
B. Laissez-Faire
C. Passepartout
D. Savoir-Faire

5. Which Hollywood heartthrob portrayed Ichabod Crane on film in the 1999 Washington Irving adaptation *Sleepy Hollow?*

A. Johnny Depp
B. Leonardo DiCaprio
C. Matt Damon
D. Ben Affleck

Answer 1: C—Lewis Grizzard.

Answer 2: D—Shirley Muldowney.

Answer 3: B—Necco wafers (the company is Necco—the New England Confectionary Company).

Answer 4: D—*Apocalypse Now.*

Answer 5: A—John Singer.

RIGHT BROTHERS

1. What band's 1985 album *Brothers in Arms* was the first album to be fully recorded, mixed, and released in a digital format?

A. Duran Duran
B. Dire Straits
C. The Police
D. U2

2. Which of these was not one of Dostoevsky's *Brothers Karamazov*?

A. Ivan
B. Alexey
C. Sergei
D. Dmitri

3. In 1783, the Montgolfier brothers made the first publicly viewed flight of their hot air balloon in what European country?

A. France
B. Spain
C. the Netherlands
D. Portugal

4. In the 1880s, the Lever Brothers Company introduced what laundry detergent, the first to be packaged and sold under a brand name?

A. Surf
B. Sudsy
C. Safe
D. Sunlight

5. The girl we know as Little Red Riding Hood was called what in the original story by the Brothers Grimm?

A. Little Red Cap
B. Little Red Bonnet
C. Little Red Dress
D. Little Red Apron

Answer 1: A—*David Copperfield.*

Answer 2: C—James Fenimore Cooper.

Answer 3: D—lawyer.

Answer 4: C—Passepartout.

Answer 5: A—Johnny Depp.

IT'S MAGICAL

1. Known for his "World of Magic" show, what magician was making plans for a transcendental meditation theme park at the time of his death?

A. Doug Henning
B. Harry Houdini
C. David Copperfield
D. Harry Blackstone Jr.

2. What animated cat often relied on his Magic Bag of Tricks?

A. Garfield
B. Mr. Jinks
C. Tom
D. Felix

3. By starring in the 1978 film *Magic*, what actor risked being upstaged by a ventriloquist's dummy?

A. Christopher Walken
B. Anthony Hopkins
C. Jack Nicholson
D. Sean Connery

4. What kids' TV show host often enlisted the help of his Magic Drawing Board?

A. Bozo the Clown
B. Captain Kangaroo
C. Mister Rogers
D. Buffalo Bob

5. In the fairy tale "Jack and the Beanstalk," what did Jack trade for the magic beans?

A. a pig
B. a chicken
C. a cow
D. a sack of grain

Answer 1: B—Dire Straits.

Answer 2: C—Sergei.

Answer 3: A—France.

Answer 4: D—Sunlight.

Answer 5: A—Little Red Cap.

GORGEOUS GEORGE

1. Which one of these authors was really named George?

A. George Sand
B. George Eliot
C. George Meredith
D. George Orwell

2. How many American presidents have had the first name George?

A. one
B. two
C. three
D. four

3. George Baker was best known for introducing America to what drawn character(s)?

A. Beetle Bailey
B. Uncle Sam
C. Sad Sack
D. Willy & Joe

4. What George led the NBA in scoring four times?

A. George Gervin
B. George Yardley
C. George Mikan
D. George McGinnis

5. What's the real first name of Culture Club lead singer Boy George?

A. Alan
B. Michael
C. James
D. George

Answer 1: A—Doug Henning.

Answer 2: D—Felix.

Answer 3: B—Anthony Hopkins.

Answer 4: B—Captain Kangaroo.

Answer 5: C—a cow.

NEAR MRS.

1. A "malapropism" (a comical misuse of words) is named after Mrs. Malaprop, a character in what Richard Sheridan play?

A. *St. Patrick's Day*
B. *The Rivals*
C. *The Critic*
D. *The School for Scandal*

2. Mrs. Elva Miller was a Kansas housewife who became famous for:

A. coaching her gymnast daughter to the Olympics
B. providing the voice of the AT&T operator
C. producing her husband's sing-along TV show
D. recording a bad pop music album

3. Jennifer Jason Leigh played the title character in the 1994 film *Mrs. Parker and the Vicious Circle* ... but what Mrs. Parker did the title refer to?

A. bank robber Bonnie Parker
B. accused (and executed) witch Mary Parker
C. author Dorothy Parker
D. Anne Boleyn's sister-in-law Jane Parker

4. The classic novel *Mrs. Mike* told the story of a young Boston girl who married a sergeant in the:

A. French Foreign Legion
B. Royal Canadian Mounted Police
C. U.S. Marine Corps
D. Salvation Army

5. Which actress from TV's *Facts of Life* also appeared in a memorable TV commercial for Mrs. Butterworth's syrup?

A. Mindy Cohn
B. Lisa Whelchel
C. Charlotte Rae
D. Kim Fields

Answer 1: C—George Meredith.

Answer 2: C—three (Washington and the two Bushes).

Answer 3: C—Sad Sack.

Answer 4: A—George Gervin (George Mikan led the league three times).

Answer 5: D—George (full name George Alan O'Dowd).

FATHER DEAR

1. Before he joined the Virginia militia during the French and Indian War, George Washington made his living as a:

A. carpenter
B. banker
C. surveyor
D. lawyer

2. George Washington was a member of which of these fraternal organizations?

A. the Knights of Columbus
B. the Oddfellows
C. the Freemasons
D. the American Legion

3. An avid and experimental farmer, George Washington introduced what animal to the United States?

A. mule
B. ox
C. sheepdog
D. alpaca

4. Which U.S. president officially dedicated the Washington Monument?

A. Rutherford B. Hayes
B. James A. Garfield
C. Grover Cleveland
D. Chester A. Arthur

5. The most popular variety of what vegetable is named after George's wife, Martha Washington?

A. broccoli
B. lettuce
C. asparagus
D. spinach

Answer 1: B—*The Rivals*.

Answer 2: D—recording a bad pop music album (the cult classic *Mrs. Miller's Greatest Hits*).

Answer 3: C—author Dorothy Parker (the "vicious circle" was the Algonquin Round Table).

Answer 4: B—Royal Canadian Mounted Police.

Answer 5: D—Kim Fields (she portrayed Dorothy "Tootie" Ramsey on the sitcom).

WHAT A CROC

1. In what popular arcade video game of the early 1980s did the player attempt to avoid fast moving vehicle traffic and hungry crocodiles?

A. Congo Bongo
B. Jungle Hunt
C. Frogger
D. Donkey Kong

2. "Crocodile birds" are sometimes seen in the wide-open mouths of alligators. For what purpose do they perform this seemingly death-defying stunt?

A. to clean their feet on the croc's tongue
B. to protect themselves from other predators
C. to enjoy the cool shade
D. to pick food from the croc's teeth

3. In what year did Elton John release his hit single "Crocodile Rock"?

A. 1969
B. 1973
C. 1977
D. 1980

4. What was the first name of the title character introduced in the 1986 film *"Crocodile" Dundee*?

A. Michael
B. James
C. Paul
D. Neville

5. Limpopo, also known as the Crocodile River, flows through which continent?

A. Africa
B. North America
C. Australia
D. South America

Answer 1: C—surveyor.

Answer 2: C—the Freemasons.

Answer 3: A—mule.

Answer 4: D—Chester A. Arthur.

Answer 5: C—asparagus.

DOLLED UP

1. What magazine introduced a popular paper doll in 1951 called Betsy?

   A. *Redbook*
   B. *Good Housekeeping*
   C. *Ladies Home Journal*
   D. *McCall's*

2. Although it was a collectible not sold in toy stores, a special-edition 2011 Barbie drew the ire of some parents because the doll included what tiny feature?

   A. a can of Red Bull
   B. a permanent tattoo
   C. thong underwear
   D. a cross necklace

3. The first "anatomically correct" children's doll was Baby Joey, the grandson of which television character?

   A. George Jefferson
   B. Howard Cunningham
   C. Archie Bunker
   D. Cliff Huxtable

4. What doll was patented by John Barton Gurelle in 1915?

A. Raggedy Ann
B. Skookum
C. Kewpie
D. Lucky Penny

5. What company produced the popular soft sculpture dolls called Cabbage Patch Kids until 1989?

A. Mattel
B. Coleco
C. Aurora
D. Hasbro

Answer 1: C—Frogger.

Answer 2: D—to pick food from the croc's teeth.

Answer 3: B—1973.

Answer 4: A—Michael (usually called Mick).

Answer 5: A—Africa (from South Africa to the Indian Ocean).

QUESTIONS ON QUESTION MARKS

1. On the Monopoly board, Chance spaces are indicated by a red or blue question mark. What color are the Chance cards?

A. blue
B. orange
C. green
D. yellow

2. Which song was the biggest hit for the band known as Question Mark & the Mysterians?

A. "16 Candles"
B. "96 Tears"
C. "25 or 6 to 4"
D. "'65 Love Affair"

3. What video game system was first introduced in late 2000 with a promotional blitz focused on a question mark made out of part of its logo?

A. Sony PlayStation 2
B. Nintendo Game Cube
C. Sega Dreamcast
D. Microsoft Xbox

4. The question mark–clad costume of the Riddler was filled by Frank Gorshin on the *Batman* TV show of the 1960s, with the exception of a single episode. Who took his place in that instance?

A. David Wayne
B. John Astin
C. Cesar Romero
D. George Sanders

5. What brand of confection is available in many flavors as listed on its labels, and also occasional ones with question marks that could be any experimental taste sensation?

A. Life Savers
B. SweeTarts
C. Mentos
D. Dum-Dums

Answer 1: D—*McCall's*.

Answer 2: B—a permanent tattoo.

Answer 3: C—Archie Bunker.

Answer 4: A—Raggedy Ann.

Answer 5: B—Coleco.

PHONE HOME

1. What had Alexander Graham Bell spilled on himself in 1876, prompting him to utter the famous words, "Mr. Watson, come here, I need you"?

A. hot tea
B. India ink
C. battery acid
D. lamp oil

2. What Broadway musical featured "The Telephone Song (Going Steady)"?

A. *Bye Bye Birdie*
B. *The Music Man*
C. *Anything Goes*
D. *The Most Happy Fella*

3. Which of the following was NOT a feature of the original Princess Phone?

A. available in pink
B. touch-tone keypad
C. lighted dial
D. no internal bell

4. What sitcom telephone operator connected callers on *Petticoat Junction* and *Green Acres*?

A. Millie
B. Bessy
C. Sarah
D. Clara

5. In the early 1970s, phone pranksters discovered that whistles found in what brand of cereal sounded a tone that enabled them to make free long-distance calls?

A. Cap'n Crunch
B. Honeycomb
C. Alpha-Bits
D. Sugar Crisp

Answer 1: B—orange.

Answer 2: B—"96 Tears."

Answer 3: A—Sony PlayStation 2.

Answer 4: B—John Astin (best known as Gomez from TV's *The Addams Family*).

Answer 5: D—Dum-Dums.

BELL RINGERS

1. Which of these structures does not currently house a bell?

A. the Clock Tower (Big Ben)
B. Independence Hall
C. Notre Dame Cathedral
D. the Leaning Tower of Pisa

2. Written by Frank Dean under the pseudonym Harry Dacre, the song "Daisy Bell" is perhaps better known by what subtitle?

A. "The Band Played On"
B. "Ta-Ra-Ra Boom-De-Ay"
C. "A Bicycle Built for Two"
D. "My Wild Irish Rose"

3. What musical instrument's name means "bells playing" in German?

A. glockenspiel
B. zither
C. heckelphone
D. clavier

4. In 1947, what pilot first broke the supersonic barrier in the Bell X-1 aircraft?

A. Robert Champine
B. Yuri Gagarin
C. John Glenn
D. Chuck Yeager

5. The 1940 Ernest Hemingway novel *For Whom the Bell Tolls* is set during a civil war in what country?

A. Spain
B. the United States
C. Russia
D. Mexico

Answer 1: C—battery acid.

Answer 2: A—*Bye Bye Birdie*.

Answer 3: B—touch-tone keypad.

Answer 4: C—Sarah.

Answer 5: A—Cap'n Crunch.

YOU'VE GOT MAIL

1. Who was the first African-American to be pictured on a U.S. postage stamp?

A. Booker T. Washington
B. Sojourner Truth
C. Langston Hughes
D. George Washington Carver

2. In which U.S. state would you find the zip code 12345?

A. Florida
B. Alaska
C. New York
D. Maine

3. Which group originally recorded "Fly Like an Eagle," a song used in commercials for the U.S. Postal Service?

A. Jefferson Airplane
B. Lynyrd Skynyrd
C. Aerosmith
D. Steve Miller Band

4. To date, who appeared on the biggest-selling commemorative postage stamp in U.S. history?

A. John F. Kennedy
B. Elvis Presley
C. Bugs Bunny
D. Marilyn Monroe

5. From April 1860 to October 1861, mail was carried via Pony Express from St. Joseph, Missouri, to what western state?

A. California
B. Nevada
C. Arizona
D. Oregon

Answer 1: B—Independence Hall (the Liberty Bell is housed in a nearby structure).

Answer 2: C—"A Bicycle Built for Two."

Answer 3: A—glockenspiel.

Answer 4: D—Chuck Yeager.

Answer 5: A—Spain.

MEDICATION NATION

1. The first medication to be sold in the form of water soluble tablets was:

A. sulfa
B. quinine
C. aspirin
D. digitalis

2. What brand was famous for its Little Liver Pills?

A. Dodd's
B. Carter's
C. Doan's
D. Lydia Pinkham

3. The lead singer of which band often appeared as a character called Quay Lude while performing the song "White Punks on Dope"?

A. the Tubes
B. the Clash
C. the Jam
D. the Ramones

4. Who is credited with the discovery of penicillin?

A. Jonas Salk
B. Marie Curie
C. Percy Julian
D. Alexander Fleming

5. What anti-nausea drug, prescribed to pregnant women in the 1960s, what later found to cause severe birth defects in some cases?

A. seldane
B. DES
C. thalidomide
D. halcion

Answer 1: A—Booker T. Washington.

Answer 2: C—New York (Schenectady, to be exact).

Answer 3: D—Steve Miller Band.

Answer 4: B—Elvis Presley.

Answer 5: A—California.

WOOD WORK

1. Fill in the blank, according to David Everett: "Large streams from little fountains flow, _____ oaks from little acorns grow."

A. lofty
B. tall
C. mighty
D. proud

2. Which singer portrayed a fashion model in the 1975 motion picture *Mahogany*?

A. Diana Ross
B. Whitney Houston
C. Natalie Cole
D. Gladys Knight

3. Who was the founder of the John Birch Society?

A. James Thornton
B. Robert Welch
C. Billy Graham
D. John Birch

4. Which television series was set in Walnut Grove, Minnesota?

A. *Northern Exposure*
B. *The Waltons*
C. *Picket Fences*
D. *Little House on the Prairie*

5. What type of animal has long served as the mascot for Fruit Stripe gum?

A. monkey
B. zebra
C. tiger
D. raccoon

Answer 1: C—aspirin.

Answer 2: B—Carter's.

Answer 3: A—the Tubes.

Answer 4: D—Alexander Fleming.

Answer 5: C—thalidomide.

POP MUSIC MONTHS

1. The Four Seasons' hit single "December, 1963" is probably better known by what parenthetical subtitle?

A. "(Baby, Goodbye)"
B. "(Oh, What a Night)"
C. "(Go Away)"
D. "(Don't You Worry 'Bout Me)"

2. The rock group known as April Wine was formed in 1969 in what country?

A. Canada
B. Australia
C. England
D. the Netherlands

3. The 1965 album *December's Children (and Everybody's)* was recorded by what band?

A. the Dave Clark Five
B. the Who
C. the Rolling Stones
D. the Kinks

4. What month fills in the blank in each of these song titles: "_____ in the Rain," "See You in _____," "It Might as Well Rain Until _____."

A. September
B. July
C. October
D. February

5. Guitarist Brian May played with what popular band?

A. Foreigner
B. Styx
C. Journey
D. Queen

Answer 1: B—tall.

Answer 2: A—Diana Ross.

Answer 3: B—Robert Welch.

Answer 4: D—*Little House on the Prairie.*

Answer 5: B—zebra.

BATQUIZ

All questions contain the name of a Batman villain.

1. In a deck of tarot cards, what is the equivalent of the joker?

A. the Harlequin
B. the Jester
C. the Clown
D. the Fool

2. The emperor penguin is the only type of penguin to inhabit which area?

A. Antarctica
B. Australia
C. Arctic Circle
D. Alaska

3. The poison ivy shrub is a relative of what "nutty" plant?

A. peanut
B. almond
C. cashew
D. pecan

4. In *Alice in Wonderland*, which of the following was friend and companion to the Mad Hatter?

A. March Hare
B. Duchess
C. Caterpillar
D. Cheshire Cat

5. Name the archaeologist who discovered King Tut's tomb in 1922.

A. Ruth Benedict
B. Louis Leakey
C. James Breasted
D. Howard Carter

Answer 1: B—"(Oh, What a Night)."

Answer 2: A—Canada.

Answer 3: C—the Rolling Stones.

Answer 4: A—September.

Answer 5: D—Queen.

TEDS & TEDDYS

1. An essential part of the wardrobe of a 1950s "Teddy Boy" in England was:

A. a cummerbund
B. drainpipe trousers
C. white socks
D. a derby hat

2. Ted Cassidy played imposing butler Lurch on TV's *The Addams Family*, along with what other character?

A. Cousin Itt
B. Uncle Fester
C. Thing
D. Cleopatra

3. What actor was born with the name Tadewurz Konopka?

A. Ted McGinley
B. Ted Danson
C. Ted Lange
D. Ted Knight

4. Teddy Roosevelt became the first sitting president to travel to a foreign country when he visited what foreign nation?

A. Canada
B. Panama
C. Cuba
D. Mexico

5. What finally became of Walter "Radar" O'Reilly's teddy bear on the TV series *M*A*S*H*?

A. placed in time capsule
B. destroyed in fire
C. eaten by goat
D. given to orphanage

Answer 1: D—the Fool.

Answer 2: A—Antarctica.

Answer 3: C—cashew.

Answer 4: A—March Hare.

Answer 5: D—Howard Carter.

YOU SAY TOMATO

1. Which of these is not a real type of tomato?

A. cherry tomato
B. apple tomato
C. plum tomato
D. strawberry tomato

2. What actress wrote the 1991 book *Fried Green Tomatoes at the Whistle Stop Cafe*, on which the film *Fried Green Tomatoes* was based?

A. Sally Field
B. Dolly Parton
C. Fannie Flagg
D. Delta Burke

3. Bob the Tomato is a character in what animated children's series?

A. *Mr. Potato Head*
B. *Blue's Clues*
C. *SpongeBob SquarePants*
D. *VeggieTales*

4. In their song "Let's Call the Whole Thing Off," what music-writing duo described two different pronunciations of the word "tomato"?

A. George & Ira Gershwin
B. Richard Rodgers & Lorenz Hart
C. W.S. Gilbert & Arthur Sullivan
D. Alan Jay Lerner & Frederick Loewe

5. What type of clam chowder is made with a tomato-based sauce?

A. New England clam chowder
B. Alaska style clam chowder
C. Eastern Shore clam chowder
D. Manhattan clam chowder

Answer 1: B—drainpipe trousers.

Answer 2: C—Thing.

Answer 3: D—Ted Knight (best known as Ted Baxter on *The Mary Tyler Moore Show*).

Answer 4: B—Panama.

Answer 5: A—placed in time capsule.

HOCKEY TERMS

1. Which of the following Shakespeare works featured a character named Puck?

A. *The Tempest*
B. *Othello*
C. *Hamlet*
D. *A Midsummer Night's Dream*

2. While an art form in hockey, which of these is illegal in basketball?

A. two-on-one break
B. goaltending
C. zone defense
D. blocking shots

3. Which of these actors starred in the 1997 motion picture *Face-Off*?

A. John Goodman
B. John Leguizamo
C. John Travolta
D. John Malkovich

4. When dealing with cakes, what is the difference between icing and frosting?

A. icing has more sugar
B. icing is hardor whon cool
C. icing is applied while the cake is cold
D. there is no difference

5. What hockey term has permeated our everyday language to come to mean any advantageous situation?

A. hat trick
B. high sticking
C. power play
D. penalty shot

Answer 1: B—apple tomato.

Answer 2: C—Fannie Flagg.

Answer 3: D—*VeggieTales*.

Answer 4: A—George & Ira Gershwin.

Answer 5: D—Manhattan clam chowder.

SAY UNCLE

1. What mail-order product, introduced in 1956 by "Uncle Milton" Levine, has sold over 20 million units worldwide?

A. ant farms
B. X-ray specs
C. sea monkeys
D. model rockets

2. What is the subtitle of Harriet Beecher Stowe's classic novel *Uncle Tom's Cabin*?

A. *A Man of Humanity*
B. *The Story of a Slave*
C. *Life Among the Lowly*
D. *Run, Eliza, Run*

3. According to the classic Grateful Dead song, where would you go to hear "Uncle John's Band"?

A. underneath the bridge
B. by the riverside
C. at the big parade
D. anywhere you like

4. What TV series centered on a family that was (for a while, at least) looked after by their curmudgeonly Uncle Charlie?

A. *My Three Sons*
B. *To Rome, With Love*
C. *Family Affair*
D. *Gimme a Break!*

5. In what board game would you find a character known as Rich Uncle Pennybags?

A. Payday
B. Monopoly
C. Life
D. Clue

Answer 1: D—*A Midsummer Night's Dream*.

Answer 2: B—goaltending.

Answer 3: C—John Travolta.

Answer 4: D—there is no difference.

Answer 5: C—power play.

WINNING WORDS

1. What Ivy League university presents the annual Pulitzer Prize journalism awards?

A. Princeton
B. Columbia
C. Yale
D. Harvard

2. The Hugo Awards are given for outstanding literature of what type?

A. mystery
B. science fiction
C. horror
D. true crime

3. The Nobel Prize for Literature is presented annually in what Scandinavian city?

A. Oslo, Norway
B. Copenhagen, Denmark
C. Helsinki, Finland
D. Stockholm, Sweden

4. The Newbery and Caldecott medals are awarded in what field of literature?

A. children's
B. biography
C. religious
D. nonfiction

5. The George Foster Peabody Awards are journalism awards presented each year by what southern school?

A. University of Georgia
B. Florida State University
C. Southern Methodist University
D. Wake Forest University

Answer 1: A—ant farms.

Answer 2: C—*Life Among the Lowly.*

Answer 3: B—by the riverside.

Answer 4: A—*My Three Sons.*

Answer 5: B—Monopoly (Rich Uncle Pennybags was renamed Mr. Monopoly in 1999).

UP THE ANTE (OR ANTI)

1. What the Italians call antipasto, the French call:

A. hors d'oeuvres
B. salade
C. aperitif
D. entier

2. The word "antebellum" means "before war." In the United States, the word is used almost exclusively to refer to which war?

A. the Revolutionary War
B. the War of 1812
C. the Civil War
D. the French and Indian War

3. What was the first commercially available brand of ethylene glycol antifreeze in America?

A. Zerex
B. Quaker State
C. Pennzoil
D. Prestone

4. "Antediluvian" refers to the era before what major Biblical event?

A. the birth of Jesus
B. the delivery of the Ten Commandments
C. the Great Flood
D. the creation of Earth

5. Which of these West Indies locations is not considered part of the Antilles?

A. Puerto Rico
B. the Bahamas
C. Cuba
D. the Virgin Islands

Answer 1: B—Columbia.

Answer 2: B—science fiction.

Answer 3: D—Stockholm, Sweden.

Answer 4: A—children's.

Answer 5: A—University of Georgia.

ANSWER ASAP
More abbreviations and acronyms.

1. If your doctor orders a CBC, what will the nurse do to you?

A. draw your blood
B. put you on a treadmill
C. connect electrodes to you
D. weigh you

2. The "SC" in *SCTV* stands for:

A. Standup Comedy
B. Strictly Canadian
C. Second City
D. South Chicago

3. Where would you usually see the acronym INRI?

A. on a watch face
B. on a crucifix
C. on a slide rule
D. on a prescription bottle

4. If a help-wanted ad specifies GMAW, the employer is looking for what sort of worker?

A. IT specialist
B. HVAC engineer
C. CAD/CAM engineer
D. MIG welder

5. What interjection has its roots in an acronym based on mythological figures?

A. Gadzooks!
B. Egad!
C. Shazam!
D. Eureka!

Answer 1: A—hors d'oeuvres.

Answer 2: C—the Civil War.

Answer 3: D—Prestone.

Answer 4: C—the Great Flood.

Answer 5: B—the Bahamas.

BUG OUT

All about Volkswagen.

1. As it appeared in Volkswagen commercials, what was the meaning of the term "Fahrvergnügen"?

A. long-lasting
B. the people's car
C. driving pleasure
D. German engineering

2. What European automaker was purchased by VW back in 1969?

A. Saab
B. Volvo
C. Fiat
D. Audi

3. Starring an intelligent VW Bug with the number "53" on its side, how many feature films were there total in the original *Herbie, the Love Bug* series?

A. three
B. four
C. five
D. six

4. Which of these was NOT a Volkswagen model?

A. Karmann Ghia
B. Golf
C. Fox
D. Spree

5. A Volkswagen sports model was originally going to be called the Blizzard but instead was given the name Scirocco, which means:

A. a desert wind
B. a snow avalanche
C. an ocean current
D. a lightning-induced fire

Answer 1: A—draw your blood (CBC = complete blood count).

Answer 2: C—Second City.

Answer 3: B—on a crucifix (INRI = Iesus Nazarenus Rex Iudaeorum, meaning "Jesus of Nazareth, King of the Jews").

Answer 4: D—a MIG welder (GMAW = gas metal arc welding).

Answer 5: C—Shazam! (SHAZAM = Solomon, Hercules, Atlas, Zeus, Achilles, Mercury).

LUCK O' THE IRISH

1. Which of these famous writers was NOT born in Ireland?

A. Oscar Wilde
B. William Butler Yeats
C. James Joyce
D. Dylan Thomas

2. Compared to all other breeds of dog, the Irish wolfhound holds which superlative?

A. heaviest
B. oldest
C. tallest
D. hairiest

3. If you are "getting your Irish up," that means you are:

A. dancing
B. on a lucky streak
C. making a toast
D. becoming angry

4. "Irish coffee" is made with what type of alcohol?

A. whiskey
B. crème de menthe
C. schnapps
D. rye

5. First published in 1899, which of these songs is the oldest?

A. "My Wild Irish Rose"
B. "An Irish Lullaby"
C. "When Irish Eyes Are Smiling"
D. "English Muffins and Irish Stew"

Answer 1: C—driving pleasure.

Answer 2: D—Audi.

Answer 3: B—four.

Answer 4: D—Spree.

Answer 5: A—a desert wind.

NORSE CODE

All about Scandinavia.

1. The world's northernmost capital is found in what Scandinavian country?

A. Finland
B. Iceland
C. Denmark
D. Norway

2. What children's literary character hails from Villa Villekulla in Sweden?

A. Hans Brinker
B. Pollyanna
C. Pippi Longstocking
D. Heidi

3. The syndrome often experienced by victims of a hostage situation is named after what Scandinavian city?

A. Stockholm
B. Helsinki
C. Copenhagen
D. Oslo

4. What toy, voted by *Forbes* as the "Toy of the [20th] Century," originated in Denmark in 1932?

A. Slinky
B. Etch A Sketch
C. Lego
D. Mr. Potato Head

5. Which is these countries does NOT contain part of Lapland, a region where the reindeer outnumber the humans and Santa Claus (reportedly) lives during the off-season?

A. Norway
B. Russia
C. Finland
D. Denmark

Answer 1: D—Dylan Thomas (he was born in Wales).

Answer 2: C—tallest.

Answer 3: D—becoming angry.

Answer 4: A—whiskey.

Answer 5: A—"My Wild Irish Rose."

TRICKY DICK

1. What media personality was once a speechwriter for Richard Nixon?

A. Larry King
B. Sam Donaldson
C. Ben Stein
D. Phil Donahue

2. Who composed the 1987 opera *Nixon in China*?

A. John Adams
B. Steve Reich
C. Philip Glass
D. Laurie Anderson

3. In which of these years was Nixon not on the Republican ticket as a candidate for either president or vice president?

A. 1952
B. 1960
C. 1964
D. 1972

4. Like his successors Gerald Ford and Jimmy Carter, Richard Nixon was a member of what branch of the U.S. armed forces?

A. Army
B. Navy
C. Air Force
D. Marines

5. In 1937, Richard Nixon obtained a law degree from what university?

A. Princeton
B. UCLA
C. Duke
D. Northwestern

Answer 1: B—Iceland (the capital is Reykjavík).

Answer 2: C—Pippi Longstocking.

Answer 3: A—Stockholm.

Answer 4: C—Lego.

Answer 5: D—Denmark (besides the three countries listed, Sweden also contains part of Lapland).

GEE, I'M A TREE!

Each question contains the name of a geometric shape.

1. What con man gained fame and made millions in the 1920s using a pyramid scheme?

A. Soapy Smith
B. Frank Abagnale
C. Victor Lustig
D. Carlo Ponzi

2. The "Pentagon Papers" contained secret government information about:

A. the Bay of Pigs invasion
B. the Watergate break-in
C. the bombing of Hiroshima
D. the Vietnam War

3. A 12-sided polygon is known as a:

A. decagon
B. dodecagon
C. heptagon
D. nonagon

4. Henry James's novel *Washington Square* was made into what film (starring Olivia DeHavilland)?

A. *The Heiress*
B. *Lady in a Cage*
C. *My Cousin Rachel*
D. *The Snake Pit*

5. Who was the first European explorer to cross the Arctic Circle?

A. Eric the Red
B. Roald Amundsen
C. Knud the Great
D. Leif Ericson

Answer 1: C—Ben Stein.

Answer 2: A—John Adams.

Answer 3: C—1964 (he was elected vice president in 1952 and 1956, president in 1968 and 1972, and ran for president in 1960).

Answer 4: B—Navy.

Answer 5: C—Duke.

FLY AWAY

1. KLM, the oldest scheduled airline in the world still operating under its original name, is the national airline of what country?

A. Portugal
B. the Netherlands
C. Egypt
D. Belgium

2. What former astronaut once served as chairman of the board of Eastern Airlines?

A. Frank Borman
B. Thomas Stafford
C. Charles Conrad
D. James Lovell

3. The *Enola Gay* dropped the atomic bomb on Hiroshima; what was the name of the plane that dropped the bomb on Nagasaki?

A. *Great Artiste*
B. *Bockscar*
C. *Big Stink*
D. *Spruce Goose*

4. What was the first name of the mysterious skyjacker known as D.B. Cooper?

A. David
B. Don
C. Doug
D. Dan

5. The airport formerly known as Idlewild is now known as:

A. LaGuardia
B. Hartsfield
C. John F. Kennedy
D. Love Field

Answer 1: D—Carlo Ponzi.

Answer 2: D—the Vietnam War.

Answer 3: B—dodecagon.

Answer 4: A—*The Heiress*.

Answer 5: A—Eric the Red.

TWO BITS
All about the number 25.

1. The name of what ancient game is derived from the Hindu word for twenty-five?

A. mancala
B. backgammon
C. pachisi
D. baccarat

2. What famous American landmark bears an inscription from Chapter 25 of the Biblical book of Leviticus?

A. the Statue of Liberty
B. the Tomb of the Unknown Soldier
C. the Washington Monument
D. the Liberty Bell

3. What character's adventures in the 25th century began on CBS radio stations in the year 1932?

A. John Carter
B. Buck Rogers
C. Captain Marvel
D. Flash Gordon

4. What Raymond Chandler character said, "I am so money greedy, that for 25 bucks a day and expenses, mostly gasoline and whisky, I do my thinking myself"?

A. Mike Hammer
B. Sam Spade
C. Philip Marlowe
D. Richard Diamond

5. The 25th Olympiad garnered more nations than had ever participated in any previous Summer Olympic Games. In what city was this event held?

A. Barcelona
B. Atlanta
C. Los Angeles
D. Sydney

Answer 1: B—the Netherlands.

Answer 2: A—Frank Borman.

Answer 3: B—*Bockscar.*

Answer 4: D—Dan (and his initials weren't really D.B.).

Answer 5: C—John F. Kennedy.

DOWN UNDER

1. Which of these uniquely named islands does NOT belong to the Commonwealth of Australia?

A. Kangaroo Island
B. Easter Island
C. Christmas Island
D. Thursday Island

2. What is the capital city of Australia?

A. Sydney
B. Brisbane
C. Canberra
D. Melbourne

3. As dramatized in the film *A Cry in the Night*, a dingo famously snatched baby Azaria Chamberlain from her tent near what Australian landmark?

A. Three Sisters
B. the Great Barrier Reef
C. Ayers Rock
D. Lake Eyre

4. Vegemite, the favorite sandwich spread of Australians, is comprised mainly of:

A. bean curd
B. avocado
C. corn starch
D. brewer's yeast

5. Of the RIAA's 15 top-selling U.S. albums of all time, only one was recorded by an Australian artist. Name this artist.

A. Men at Work
B. Olivia Newton-John
C. AC/DC
D. The Bee Gees

Answer 1: C—pachisi.

Answer 2: D—the Liberty Bell.

Answer 3: B—Buck Rogers.

Answer 4: C—Philip Marlowe.

Answer 5: A—Barcelona.

TAKE A CHANCE

1. Which Monopoly property has a misspelled name?

A. Ventnor Avenue
B. Reading Railroad
C. Marvin Gardens
D. Park Place

2. According to the Monopoly rules, how much money should a player receive for landing on Free Parking?

A. $0
B. $50
C. $100
D. $500

3. What Monopoly color group costs the most to fully purchase and develop?

A. red
B. dark blue
C. orange
D. green

4. When moving forward from "Go," which of these Monopoly board spaces would you encounter first?

A. Community Chest
B. Baltic Avenue
C. Income Tax
D. Chance

5. A Monopoly game comes with an equal number of Chance and Community Chest cards. How many cards are in each of these two sets?

A. 12
B. 16
C. 20
D. 24

Answer 1: B—Easter Island (part of Chile).

Answer 2: C—Canberra.

Answer 3: C—Ayers Rock.

Answer 4: D—brewer's yeast.

Answer 5: C—AC/DC (the album was *Back in Black*).

CELLULAR

1. What maximum-security prison was the site of a week-long riot in 1971?

A. Sing Sing
B. Attica
C. Terminal Island
D. Rahway

2. What literary work by Aleksandr Solzhenitsyn was an in-depth look at the brutal Soviet penal system?

A. *The First Circle*
B. *Cancer Ward*
C. *The Great Terror*
D. *The Gulag Archipelago*

3. What country singer, who once did jail time for picking flowers, recorded a million-selling album at Folsom Prison?

A. Johnny Cash
B. Willie Nelson
C. Merle Haggard
D. Charley Pride

4. What classic film was based on the life of Robert Eliot Burns, a man who escaped from prison and became a successful magazine editor?

A. *Birdman of Alcatraz*
B. *Jailhouse Rock*
C. *I Am a Fugitive From a Chain Gang*
D. *I Want to Live*

5. Devil's Island, once the world's most notorious penal colony, is located off the coast of what country?

A. The Dominican Republic
B. French Guiana
C. Haiti
D. Grenada

Answer 1: C—Marvin Gardens (it should be "Marven Gardens").

Answer 2: A—$0.

Answer 3: D—green ($3920 to purchase and develop to hotels, as opposed to $2750 for the dark blue—the main difference is that there are 3 green properties and only 2 dark blue ones).

Answer 4: A—Community Chest.

Answer 5: B—16.

OPENING LINES

Identify these opening lines.

1. "What can you say about a 25-year-old girl who died?"

A. *Terms of Endearment*
B. *Fear of Flying*
C. *Love Story*
D. *Valley of the Dolls*

2. "Call me Ishmael."

A. *The Sea-Wolf*
B. *The Old Man and the Sea*
C. *Call of the Wild*
D. *Moby-Dick*

3. "Man ... woman ... birth ... death ... infinity ..."

A. *Ben Casey*
B. *Marcus Welby, M.D.*
C. *Dr. Kildare*
D. *Medical Center*

4. "Sing, O goddess, the anger of Achilles, son of Peleus."

A. *Ulysses*
B. *The Iliad*
C. *Beowulf*
D. *The Odyssey*

5. "There's a lady who's sure all that glitters is gold ..."

A. "Love Me Two Times"
B. "Hotel California"
C. "Bohemian Rhapsody"
D. "Stairway to Heaven"

Answer 1: B—Attica.

Answer 2: D—*The Gulag Archipelago.*

Answer 3: A—Johnny Cash.

Answer 4: C—*I Am a Fugitive From a Chain Gang.*

Answer 5: B—French Guiana.

GRAMMAR SCHOOL

1. Adding "ing" to a verb and using it as a noun makes it a:

A. gerund
B. diphthong
C. modifier
D. predicate

2. No, a "schwa" is not the noise one makes after a particularly filling meal. It is:

A. the "at" sign (@)
B. an accent mark
C. an upside-down "e"
D. the paragraph symbol

3. Which of these words is spelled and pronounced the same way in English as it is in Spanish, German, Thai, Chinese, and Farsi?

A. no
B. taxi
C. police
D. visa

4. Which of the following sentences is a pangram?

A. Madam, I'm Adam.
B. Now is the time for all good men to come to the aid of their country.
C. Every good boy does fine.
D. The quick brown fox jumps over the lazy dog.

5. What is the name of the character that can be used in place of the word "and"?

A. caret
B. ampersand
C. octothorpe
D. tilde

Answer 1: C—*Love Story.*

Answer 2: D—*Moby-Dick.*

Answer 3: A—*Ben Casey.*

Answer 4: B—*The Iliad.*

Answer 5: D—"Stairway to Heaven."

CHAIN OF FOOLS

1. Who hit the Top 10 in 1968 with a recording of "The Fool on the Hill"?

A. Gene Chandler
B. the Impressions
C. the Beatles
D. Sergio Mendes

2. The Cardigans, who enjoyed success in the mid-1990s with the radio hit "Lovefool," hail from what European country?

A. Belgium
B. Sweden
C. the Netherlands
D. Scotland

3. Who sang a catchy rendition of "I Ain't Gonna Be Your Fool No More" on a 1963 episode of the animated prime-time TV show *The Flintstones*?

A. Lesley Gore
B. Nancy Sinatra
C. Ann-Margret
D. Eartha Kitt

4. Jewel had a 1997 Top 10 hit with the song "Foolish Games." What is Jewel's last name?

A. Kilcher
B. Spier
C. Rhee
D. Holland

5. Who sang lead vocals on the Elvin Bishop hit "Fooled Around and Fell in Love"?

A. Elvin Bishop
B. Marty Balin
C. Mickey Thomas
D. Stephen Bishop

Answer 1: A—gerund.

Answer 2: C—an upside-down "e" (used as a pronunciation symbol).

Answer 3: B—taxi.

Answer 4: D—The quick brown fox jumps over the lazy dog (contains all the letters of the alphabet).

Answer 5: B—ampersand.

A MEASLY TEST

1. After being exposed to the measles, what astronaut was scrubbed from the Apollo XIII moon mission?

A. John Swigert
B. Fred Haise
C. Ken Mattingly
D. John Young

2. Complete this Lord Byron quote: "Like the measles, _____ is most dangerous when it comes late in life."

A. love
B. wealth
C. fame
D. death

3. In the film *Gone With the Wind*, who lasted only two weeks as Scarlett O'Hara's husband before succumbing to measles?

A. Ashley Wilkes
B. Charles Hamilton
C. Rhett Butler
D. Frank Kennedy

4. During an 1824 trip to Great Britain, King Kamehameha II and his wife died after contracting measles. He was the leader of what kingdom?

A. Swaziland
B. Hawaii
C. Mongolia
D. New Zealand

5. In the episode "Is There a Doctor in the House?," all six kids in the Brady Bunch household came down with the measles. Who was the first to be diagnosed?

A. Jan
B. Bobby
C. Cindy
D. Peter

Answer 1: D—Sergio Mendes (written by Lennon and McCartney, the song was not released as a single by the Beatles).

Answer 2: B—Sweden

Answer 3: C—Ann-Margret.

Answer 4: A—Kilcher.

Answer 5: C—Mickey Thomas (later a member of Jefferson Starship).

A-ONE PANDA TWO

1. Pandas are most closely related to which of these creatures?

A. koalas
B. raccoons
C. chipmunks
D. marmosets

2. In April 1972, China sent two giant pandas to America in honor of then-president Richard Nixon. The male and female lived in a zoo in what city?

A. Washington, D.C.
B. San Diego
C. Atlanta
D. Sacramento

3. On a memorable episode of the TV series *South Park*, a man in a panda suit was used to teach the public about:

A. racial equity
B. drinking and driving
C. sexual harassment
D. endangered species

4. What was the name given to the giant panda cub that was born at the San Diego Zoo on August 21, 1999, viewed by millions over the following years on an Internet Panda Cam?

A. Hua Mei
B. Ying Xin
C. Shi Shi
D. Bai Yun

5. Whose studios produced the Andy Panda series of animated shorts?

A. Walt Disney
B. Jay Ward
C. Max Fleischer
D. Walter Lantz

Answer 1: C—Ken Mattingly.

Answer 2: A—love

Answer 3: B—Charles Hamilton.

Answer 4: B—Hawaii.

Answer 5: D—Peter.

BOAT & SHIP NAMES

1. Who took her very last swim from a boat named *Splendour* back in 1981?

A. Natalie Wood
B. Shirley Bassey
C. Jessica Savitch
D. Carol Wayne

2. What country seized the USS *Pueblo* after accusing its American crew of unlawful spying in 1968?

A. Vietnam
B. Cuba
C. Argentina
D. North Korea

3. What TV neighbors named their ship *Nau-sea* after finding they couldn't agree between the names *Nautical Lady* and *Queen of the Sea*?

A. Ralph Kramden & Ed Norton
B. Fred Flintstone & Barney Rubble
C. Jerry Seinfeld & Cosmo Kramer
D. Ricky Ricardo & Fred Mertz

4. Which of the following was not one of the fabled trio of sister ships that comprised the White Line?

A. *Titanic*
B. *Queen Mary*
C. *Olympic*
D. *Britannica*

5. What Canadian singer wrote about the true-life story of one of the worst disasters in Great Lakes history in the song "The Wreck of the Edmund Fitzgerald"?

A. Paul Anka
B. Bryan Adams
C. Gordon Lightfoot
D. Anne Murray

Answer 1: B—raccoons.

Answer 2: A—Washington, D.C.

Answer 3: C—sexual harassment.

Answer 4: A—Hua Mei.

Answer 5: D—Walter Lantz.

FORD TOUGH

1. Ford Motor Company's headquarters are not located in Detroit, but in what nearby Michigan city?

A. Ann Arbor
B. Monroe
C. Highland Park
D. Dearborn

2. Of the following Hollywood greats, which one has never been nominated for an Academy Award?

A. Michael Ford
B. Glenn Ford
C. John Ford
D. Harrison Ford

3. What is the maiden name of former first lady Betty Ford?

A. Bloomer
B. Archer
C. Jackson
D. Warren

4. Robert Ford shot and killed his cousin on April 3, 1882, in an attempt to claim a $10,000 reward. Who was Ford's cousin?

A. Billy the Kid
B. Ned Kelly
C. Jesse James
D. Sam Bass

5. Whitey Ford won a record 10 World Series games for which major-league baseball team?

A. Pittsburgh Pirates
B. Chicago White Sox
C. New York Yankees
D. St. Louis Cardinals

Answer 1: A—Natalie Wood.

Answer 2: D—North Korea.

Answer 3: B—Fred Flintstone & Barney Rubble.

Answer 4: B—*Queen Mary*.

Answer 5: C—Gordon Lightfoot.

PRESIDENTIAL NICKNAMES

1. Who was the first U.S. president to take the oath of office using a nickname?

A. John Kennedy
B. Bill Clinton
C. Jimmy Carter
D. Teddy Roosevelt

2. What president was known as "Father of the Constitution"?

A. James Madison
B. Thomas Jefferson
C. George Washington
D. John Quincy Adams

3. Which president acquired the nickname "Dutch" at a young age, thanks to a haircut from his mother?

A. Richard Nixon
B. Dwight Eisenhower
C. Gerald Ford
D. Ronald Reagan

4. Zachary Taylor earned what nickname during the Battle of Buena Vista?

A. Old Rough 'n' Ready
B. Unconditional Surrender
C. Old Hickory
D. The Rough Rider

5. Harry Truman was known as "the Haberdasher" because of:

A. his colloquial language
B. his previous occupation
C. his attention to detail
D. his custom-made suits

Answer 1: D—Dearborn.

Answer 2: B—Glenn Ford.

Answer 3: A—Bloomer (Warren was the last name of her first husband).

Answer 4: C—Jesse James.

Answer 5: C—New York Yankees.

AIN'T IT SWEET?

1. What is added to white granulated sugar to make brown sugar?

A. molasses
B. corn syrup
C. vanilla extract
D. caramel

2. In what classic film did Marilyn Monroe portray a character named Sugar Kane Kowalczyk?

A. *Gentleman Prefer Blondes*
B. *The Seven Year Itch*
C. *Some Like It Hot*
D. *Bus Stop*

3. Robert Welch introduced Sugar Daddy and Sugar Babies to the candy world; in 1949, his brother launched what confection (made famous on TV's *Seinfeld*)?

A. Andes Mints
B. Tootsie Rolls
C. Dots
D. Junior Mints

4. Which "Sugar" song did NOT hit number one on the Billboard pop chart?

A. "Sugar Shack"
B. "Sugar Don't Bite"
C. "Sugartime"
D. "Sugar Sugar"

5. Which of these sugar substitutes is made from a sugar derivative known as sucralose?

A. Sugar Twin
B. Sweet'N Low
C. Equal
D. Splenda

Answer 1: C—Jimmy Carter.

Answer 2: A—James Madison.

Answer 3: D—Ronald Reagan.

Answer 4: A—Old Rough 'n' Ready.

Answer 5: B—his previous occupation (he owned a haberdashery shop after serving in World War I).

CAT CALLS

1. If a woman is "grinning like a Cheshire cat," her smile could be described as:

A. insincere
B. mysterious
C. broad
D. forced

2. Besides a protrusion sticking out of a feline's face, a "cat's whisker" is also a type of:

A. antenna
B. guitar string
C. surgical stitch
D. skewer

3. The marsh plants known as "cattails" were once used by Native Americans in New England to make:

A. headdresses
B. pipe cleaners
C. arrow quills
D. hemp rope

4. Which of the following is NOT traditionally available in a "cat's-eye" design?

A. eyeglass frames
B. marbles
C. gemstones
D. sewing needles

5. What American poet wrote: "The fog comes on little cat feet"?

A. Carl Sandburg
B. Walt Whitman
C. T.S. Eliot
D. Edgar Allan Poe

Answer 1: A—molasses.

Answer 2: C—*Some Like It Hot.*

Answer 3: D—Junior Mints.

Answer 4: B—"Sugar Don't Bite."

Answer 5: D—Splenda.

KIDS IN THE HALL

1. The hymn for what branch of the U.S. military begins with the line: "From the halls of Montezuma"?

A. Army
B. Navy
C. Air Force
D. Marine Corps

2. Which of the following was NOT one of the first inductees into the Baseball Hall of Fame in Cooperstown, New York?

A. Ty Cobb
B. Lou Gehrig
C. Walter Johnson
D. Babe Ruth

3. Huntz Hall was a member of what comedic film troupe?

A. the Bowery Boys
B. Our Gang
C. the Ritz Brothers
D. the Three Stooges

4. What actress, an unknown at the time, received a screen credit for *Annie Hall* even though she was onscreen for only a few seconds?

A. Meryl Streep
B. Sigourney Weaver
C. Julia Roberts
D. Mariel Hemingway

5. What acclaimed violinist first appeared at the Royal Albert Hall in 1929 at the tender age of 13?

A. Jascha Heifetz
B. Antonio Stradivarius
C. Yehudi Menuhin
D. Fritz Kreisler

Answer 1: C—broad.

Answer 2: A—antenna.

Answer 3: D—hemp rope.

Answer 4: D—sewing needles.

Answer 5: A—Carl Sandburg.

FEET FIRST

1. What is the name of the funeral home that is central to HBO's hit series *Six Feet Under*?

A. Shady Pines
B. E.J. Mandzuik
C. Fisher & Sons
D. Eternal Rest

2. The expression "having feet of clay," meaning a failing or weakness, originated in:

A. The Bible
B. Aesop's fables
C. Plato's *Republic*
D. Shakespeare's *Julius Caesar*

3. Foot binding was practiced by females in China for over 1,000 years, the intent being to keep the feet tiny enough to fit into three-inch slippers called:

A. song shoes
B. princess shoes
C. golden shoes
D. lotus shoes

4. Which animated matriarch occasionally reflected on her unusually large feet?

A. Wilma Flintstone
B. Marge Simpson
C. Peggy Hill
D. Jane Jetson

5. A tetrapod is a creature with how many feet?

A. two
B. four
C. six
D. eight

Answer 1: D—Marine Corps.

Answer 2: B—Lou Gehrig.

Answer 3: A—the Bowery Boys.

Answer 4: B—Sigourney Weaver.

Answer 5: C—Yehudi Menuhin.

IT'S ALL "GOOD"

1. What hand-operated instrument was used to great effect to produce space-like sounds in the Beach Boys hit single "Good Vibrations"?

A. electro-theremin
B. synthesizer
C. saw
D. pan flute

2. What explorer was the first European to record a circumnavigation of the Cape of Good Hope, near the southernmost point of Africa?

A. Jacques Cartier
B. Ferdinand Magellan
C. John Davis
D. Bartolomeu Dias

3. Which of these "Good" things appeared on the market first?

A. Good & Plenty candy
B. *Good Housekeeping* magazine
C. Goodyear tires
D. Good Humor ice cream bars

4. The parable of the Good Samaritan appears in which of these Biblical Gospels?

A. Matthew
B. Mark
C. Luke
D. John

5. Of the following 1990s movies, which one was NOT nominated for an Academy Award for Best Picture?

A. *A Few Good Men*
B. *One Good Cop*
C. *Good Will Hunting*
D. *As Good As It Gets*

Answer 1: C—Fisher & Sons.

Answer 2: A—The Bible (Daniel in the Old Testament).

Answer 3: D—lotus shoes.

Answer 4: C—Peggy Hill (from *King of the Hill*).

Answer 5: B—four.

A TAXING TEST

1. Which early sitcom star refused to perform a script in which he cheated on his income tax, since he felt it would make him look like a bad American?

A. Jackie Gleason
B. Danny Thomas
C. Desi Arnaz
D. Dick Van Dyke

2. In 1992, what famous person paid income tax for the first time ever?

A. Queen Elizabeth II
B. Bill Gates
C. Arnold Schwarzenegger
D. George Herbert Walker Bush

3. After her housekeeper testified she heard her say that "only the little people pay taxes," who was sentenced to four years in prison when found guilty of evasion?

A. Ivana Trump
B. Martha Stewart
C. Leona Helmsley
D. Tammy Faye Bakker

4. Which Constitutional amendment, ratified in 1913, gave Congress the power to levy tax on personal incomes?

A. Fourteenth
B. Sixteenth
C. Eighteenth
D. Twentieth

5. In 1973, who resigned as U.S. vice president after he pleaded "no contest" to charges of not claiming income he received while he was the governor of Maryland?

A. Gerald Ford
B. Nelson Rockefeller
C. Richard Nixon
D. Spiro Agnew

Answer 1: A—electro-theremin.

Answer 2: D—Bartolomeu Dias.

Answer 3: B—*Good Housekeeping* magazine (in 1885).

Answer 4: C—Luke.

Answer 5: B—*One Good Cop.*

BASKET CASES
Trivia about NBA team names.

1. When the Lakers moved to Los Angeles, they kept the team name even though it was more appropriate to their original home, which was:

A. Buffalo
B. Minneapolis
C. Detroit
D. Salt Lake City

2. In 1987, what newly franchised NBA team was almost named the Spirit until the public cried "foul" and voted for a new name?

A. the Hornets
B. the Mavericks
C. the Magic
D. the Raptors

3. What city's ABA team was called the Rockets, but had to change their name when they joined the NBA in 1974 (since the NBA already had the Houston Rockets)?

A. San Diego
B. Orlando
C. Richmond
D. Denver

4. The NBA franchise formerly known as the Rochester Royals now play basketball in which state?

A. California
B. Texas
C. Ohio
D. Florida

5. In 1961 they were the Chicago Packers, but they've changed location and/or team names five times since then. They're now known as:

A. the Atlanta Hawks
B. the Washington Wizards
C. the Los Angeles Clippers
D. the Chicago Bulls

Answer 1: C—Desi Arnaz.

Answer 2: A—Queen Elizabeth II.

Answer 3: C—Leona Helmsley.

Answer 4: B—Sixteenth.

Answer 5: D—Spiro Agnew.

ISLANDERS

1. What suave actor spent six years welcoming visitors to ABC's original *Fantasy Island*?

A. Cesar Romero
B. Fernando Lamas
C. Antonio Banderas
D. Ricardo Montalbán

2. Residents of which island are primarily descendants of HMS *Bounty* mutineer Fletcher Christian?

A. Guam
B. Pitcairn
C. Bermuda
D. Fiji

3. The Thousand Islands (for which the salad dressing is named) are located in what body of water?

A. St. Lawrence River
B. Lake Ontario
C. Niagara River
D. Long Island Sound

4. Born Farouk Bulsara, the lead singer of what rock band was born on the island of Zanzibar off the coast of present-day Tanzania?

A. the Police
B. Queen
C. Red Hot Chili Peppers
D. Led Zeppelin

5. What establishment has been selling its "world famous" hot dogs at New York's Coney Island since 1916?

A. Stillwell's
B. Leo's
C. Feldman's
D. Nathan's

Answer 1: B—Minneapolis.

Answer 2: A—the Hornets.

Answer 3: D—Denver (their name was changed to the Nuggets).

Answer 4: A—California (where they became known as the Sacramento Kings).

Answer 5: B—the Washington Wizards (after the Chicago Packers, they were the Chicago Zephyrs, the Baltimore Bullets, the Capital Bullets, the Washington Bullets, and the Washington Wizards).

OUR DAILY BREAD

1. In the 1940s, vitamin-enriched bread was introduced in the United States, which helped to eliminate what disease?

A. beriberi
B. rickets
C. typhoid fever
D. cholera

2. Who coined the phrase "Is it bigger than a breadbox?" as a panelist on the TV game show *What's My Line?*

A. Bennett Cerf
B. Henry Morgan
C. Steve Allen
D. Soupy Sales

3. If you are hit in the "breadbasket," you've sustained a blow to what part of the body?

A. the chest
B. the stomach
C. the kidney
D. the throat

4. U.S. bread prices soared after which president pledged 25 million tons of grain to the struggling Soviet Union?

A. Jimmy Carter
B. Lyndon Johnson
C. Richard Nixon
D. Gerald Ford

5. Name the only song that soft-rock band Bread took to the top of the U.S. pop chart.

A. "If"
B. "Everything I Own"
C. "Make It With You"
D. "Baby, I'm-A Want You"

Answer 1: D—Ricardo Montalbán.

Answer 2: B—Pitcairn.

Answer 3: A—St. Lawrence River.

Answer 4: B—Queen (he became known as Freddie Mercury).

Answer 5: D—Nathan's.

IT'S INSTRUMENTAL

1. In terms of decibels, what is normally the loudest instrument in a symphony orchestra?

A. trumpet
B. French horn
C. tuba
D. trombone

2. What musical instrument is sometimes called a "sweet potato"?

A. bagpipes
B. concertina
C. ocarina
D. harmonica

3. What whimsical work was written by Sergei Prokofiev to introduce children to the instruments of the orchestra?

A. *Tales of an Old Grandmother*
B. *Peter and the Wolf*
C. *Dreams*
D. *The Fiery Angel*

4. Which of the following is NOT considered a percussion instrument?

A. clavichord
B. glockenspiel
C. xylophone
D. timpani

5. Jazz musicians sometimes refer to which instrument as a "licorice stick"?

A. saxophone
B. piano
C. clarinet
D. double bass

Answer 1: A—beriberi (a thiamine deficiency).

Answer 2: C—Steve Allen.

Answer 3: B—the stomach.

Answer 4: C—Richard Nixon.

Answer 5: C—"Make It With You."

WILD CATS

1. The offspring of a male lion and a female tiger is known by what name?

A. liger
B. tigress
C. tiglon
D. ligron

2. The entrance to what New York City landmark is adorned by a pair of beautiful lion sculptures?

A. Ellis Island
B. Empire State Building
C. Metropolitan Opera House
D. Public Library

3. Three of the following are different names for the same type of cat; one is unique. Which one stands alone?

A. cougar
B. puma
C. bobcat
D. mountain lion

4. In the *Tarzan* motion pictures, Cheeta (also commonly spelled "Cheetah") was not actually a cheetah, but what type of animal?

A. elephant
B. wild boar
C. chimpanzee
D. parrot

5. What wild feline's name is actually Guarani for "dog"?

A. jaguar
B. leopard
C. ocelot
D. lynx

Answer 1: D—trombone.

Answer 2: C—ocarina.

Answer 3: B—*Peter and the Wolf*.

Answer 4: A—clavichord.

Answer 5: C—clarinet.

GO MARCHING IN

1. Which of these "saintly" actresses portrayed the first character to die on the 1960s live-action *Batman* TV series?

A. Susan St. James
B. Jill St. John
C. Buffy St. Marie
D. Diana St. Clair

2. What entertainer founded St. Jude's Research Hospital as a result of a pledge he made while still struggling in show business?

A. Sid Caesar
B. Jack Benny
C. Milton Berle
D. Danny Thomas

3. In 1825, the Fifth Infantry Regiment of the U.S. Army completed what fort in St. Paul, Minnesota?

A. Fort Snelling
B. Fort Erie
C. Fort Wayne
D. Fort Issimo

4. What playwright's *Saint Joan* was based on the life of Joan of Arc?

A. James Joyce
B. Eugene O'Neill
C. George Bernard Shaw
D. Arthur Miller

5. Which of these NFL teams was awarded its franchise on All Saints' Day (November 1) in 1966?

A. New Orleans Saints
B. Minnesota Vikings
C. Seattle Seahawks
D. Miami Dolphins

Answer 1: A—liger (a female lion and male tiger can produce a tiglon).

Answer 2: D—Public Library (on Fifth Avenue).

Answer 3: C—bobcat.

Answer 4: C—chimpanzee.

Answer 5: A—jaguar.

NURSERY RHYMES

1. On what thoroughfare does the Muffin Man live?

A. Crooked Road
B. Carnaby Street
C. Drury Lane
D. Pie Corner

2. In "The Farmer in the Dell," what does the child take?

A. a nurse
B. the cat
C. a book
D. his time

3. Whose wife could eat no lean?

A. Jack Horner
B. Jumping Jack
C. Jack Sprat
D. Tommy Tucker

4. How much did the pieman charge Simple Simon for a sample?

A. a sixpence
B. two bits
C. a farthing
D. a penny

5. "Oranges and lemons" say the bells of:

A. St. Swithins
B. St. Clemens
C. St. Bremens
D. St. Simmons

Answer 1: B—Jill St. John (in the role of Molly, the Riddler's assistant, in the series' premiere episode).

Answer 2: D—Danny Thomas.

Answer 3: A—Fort Snelling.

Answer 4: C—George Bernard Shaw.

Answer 5: A—New Orleans Saints.

THE FRIEND-LY QUIZ

1. What motivational guru's *How to Win Friends and Influence People* became a best-selling book?

A. Dale Carnegie
B. Wayne Dyer
C. Norman Vincent Peale
D. Tony Robbins

2. "Friendship," the classic Cole Porter tune, was originally featured in what musical?

A. *Anything Goes*
B. *Kiss Me, Kate*
C. *High Society*
D. *DuBarry Was a Lady*

3. "Friends of Bill W." is another name for:

A. Weight Watchers
B. Alcoholics Anonymous
C. Oddfellows
D. Big Brothers

4. What Shakespeare work includes the line, "Friends, Romans, countrymen, lend me your ears"?

A. *Othello*
B. *Julius Caesar*
C. *Antony & Cleopatra*
D. *King Lear*

5. What derby-wearing, cigar-smoking spirit is the comic book nemesis of Casper, the Friendly Ghost?

A. Nightmare
B. Hot Stuff
C. Spooky
D. Tuff Guy

Answer 1: C—Drury Lane.

Answer 2: A—a nurse.

Answer 3: C—Jack Sprat.

Answer 4: D—a penny.

Answer 5: B—St. Clemens.

OOH, THE COLORS

1. According to the 1973 motion picture, "Soylent Green is ...," what?

A. futile
B. freedom
C. people
D. the answer

2. Which of these types of whales is the largest?

A. blue whale
B. white whale
C. black whale
D. gray whale

3. Blue curaçao is flavored with laraha, a fruit that's a relative of what better-known fruit?

A. blueberry
B. plum
C. cherry
D. orange

4. In 1978, what terrorist group kidnapped and murdered former Italian prime minister Aldo Moro?

A. Black Sunday
B. Blue Ribbon Coalition
C. Red Brigade
D. Bonnie Blue Society

5. Which of these colorful tunes was NOT a hit for Bobby Vinton?

A. "Red Roses for a Blue Lady"
B. "Blue on Blue"
C. "Roses Are Red"
D. "Blue Velvet"

Answer 1: A—Dale Carnegie.

Answer 2: D—*DuBarry Was a Lady*.

Answer 3: B—Alcoholics Anonymous.

Answer 4: B—*Julius Caesar*.

Answer 5: C—Spooky.

WHEN "PUSH" COMES TO SHOVE

1. In what classic children's book would you find a creature called a Pushmi-Pullyu?

A. *The Secret Garden*
B. *Dr. Dolittle*
C. *Where the Wild Things Are*
D. *The Jungle Book*

2. Who founded an African-American assistance program known as "Operation: PUSH" in 1971?

A. H. Rap Brown
B. Al Sharpton
C. Stokely Carmichael
D. Jesse Jackson

3. What Oscar-winning actor was the executive producer of the offbeat ABC mystery series *Push, Nevada*?

A. Ben Affleck
B. Kevin Spacey
C. Chris Cooper
D. Cuba Gooding Jr.

4. What company introduced the first radio with push-button tuning in 1927?

A. RCA
B. Emerson
C. Zenith
D. General Electric

5. What character used to push Ironside around (in his wheelchair, that is) on the TV detective series of the same name?

A. Steve Keller
B. Mark Sanger
C. Pete Ryan
D. Ed Brown

Answer 1: C—people.

Answer 2: A—blue whale.

Answer 3: D—orange (the blue coloring is artificial).

Answer 4: C—Red Brigade.

Answer 5: A—"Red Roses for a Blue Lady" (a 1965 hit for Burt Kaempfert and Vic Dana).

THE "MAN" SHOW

1. The Portuguese man-of-war is a type of:

A. sailboat
B. mosquito
C. jellyfish
D. drum

2. The first Rolling Stones song to hit the British top 20 was a rendition of what Lennon-McCartney song?

A. "Baby, You're a Rich Man"
B. "Nowhere Man"
C. "I Wanna Be Your Man"
D. "Taxman"

3. What is the alter ego of the superhero known as the Amazing Spider-Man?

A. Tony Stark
B. Peter Parker
C. Britt Reid
D. Bruce Wayne

4. The Broadway musical *Man of La Mancha* was based on which novel?

A. *Arrowsmith*
B. *Silas Marner*
C. *The Last of the Mohicans*
D. *Don Quixote*

5. What baseball great was nicknamed the Iron Man?

A. Cal Ripken Jr.
B. Al Kaline
C. Nolan Ryan
D. Rod Carew

Answer 1: B—*Dr. Dolittle.*

Answer 2: D—Jesse Jackson.

Answer 3: A—Ben Affleck.

Answer 4: C—Zenith.

Answer 5: B—Mark Sanger.

THE RENOWN OF BROWN

1. The Ivy League school known as Brown University is located in which U.S. state?

A. Massachusetts
B. Connecticut
C. New York
D. Rhode Island

2. Apple Brown Betty is a dessert comprised of apples and:

A. molasses
B. brown sugar
C. chocolate
D. dark corn syrup

3. The 1954 Supreme Court decision *Brown vs. Board of Education* overturned what famous ruling?

A. *Plessy vs. Ferguson*
B. *Roe vs. Wade*
C. *Dred Scott vs. Sanford*
D. *Scopes vs. State*

4. On the sitcom *I Love Lucy*, Lucy's actions while dining at Hollywood's Brown Derby caused what actor to be hit in the face with a pie?

A. Harpo Marx
B. William Holden
C. Rock Hudson
D. Cornel Wilde

5. Hall of Fame running back Jim Brown played his entire pro career for which NFL team?

A. Pittsburgh Steelers
B. Los Angeles Rams
C. Cleveland Browns
D. Green Bay Packers

Answer 1: C—jellyfish.

Answer 2: C—"I Wanna Be Your Man."

Answer 3: B—Peter Parker.

Answer 4: D—*Don Quixote*.

Answer 5: A—Cal Ripken Jr.

THE GANGSTER FIVE

1. Notorious gangster Al Capone was eventually arrested and convicted of what charge?

A. racketeering
B. tax evasion
C. illegal gambling
D. bigamy

2. What infamous bank robber appeared as a character in the Coen brothers' 2000 film, *O Brother, Where Art Thou?*

A. Alvin "Creepy" Karpis
B. "Baby Face" Nelson
C. "Ma" Barker
D. "Machine Gun" Kelly

3. John Dillinger was gunned down by the FBI in front of what Chicago movie theater?

A. Biograph
B. Bijou
C. Oneida
D. Alhambra

4. "Bugsy" Siegel, who founded modern Las Vegas with the construction of the Flamingo, preferred to be addressed by his real first name, which was:

A. Bill
B. Barney
C. Bob
D. Ben

5. What folk singer's song "Pretty Boy Floyd" told the story of gangster Charles Arthur Floyd?

A. Pete Seeger
B. Alan Lomax
C. Woody Guthrie
D. Tim Buckley

Answer 1: D—Rhode Island.

Answer 2: B—brown sugar.

Answer 3: A—*Plessy vs. Ferguson.*

Answer 4: B—William Holden.

Answer 5: C—Cleveland Browns.

EYE'LL BE SEEING YOU

1. Which of these made its debut on October 20, 1951?

A. the CBS eye logo
B. Birdseye frozen foods
C. the first eye bank
D. the hit single "Bette Davis Eyes"

2. What part of the eye is damaged by glaucoma?

A. iris
B. pupil
C. retina
D. optic nerve

3. Who sang the title song for the 1978 suspense film *Eyes of Laura Mars*?

A. Linda Ronstadt
B. Barbra Streisand
C. Carly Simon
D. Judy Collins

4. Prior to his execution, what convicted killer made arrangements to donate his corneas after he was put to death?

A. Ted Bundy
B. Richard Speck
C. Gary Gilmore
D. John Wayne Gacy

5. What is the source of the quote: "It is easier for a camel to go through the eye of a needle, than for a rich man to enter into the kingdom of God"?

A. The Koran
B. *The Iliad*
C. *The Tempest*
D. The Bible

Answer 1: B—tax evasion.

Answer 2: B—"Baby Face" Nelson (who in the movie, as in real life, demanded that he be referred to as George).

Answer 3: A—Biograph.

Answer 4: D—Ben.

Answer 5: C—Woody Guthrie.

THE "FIFTH" ELEMENT

1. Who was the fifth president of the United States?

A. James Knox Polk
B. James Madison
C. James Monroe
D. James Garfield

2. Which of these Supreme Court cases did NOT involve a major judgment concerning the Fifth Amendment?

A. *Ullmann vs. United States*
B. *Gideon vs. Wainwright*
C. *Bolling vs. Sharpe*
D. *Miranda vs. Arizona*

3. How many members were there in the popular 1960s–'70s vocal group known as the Fifth Dimension?

A. three
B. five
C. seven
D. nine

4. What New York Yankees pitcher hurled the first perfect game in World Series history in the fifth game of the 1956 Fall Classic?

A. Whitey Ford
B. Bob Turley
C. Don Larsen
D. Allie Reynolds

5. What 20th-century European leader was referred to as the first president of the Fifth Republic?

A. Charles de Gaulle
B. Thomas Masaryk
C. Benito Mussolini
D. Francisco Franco

Answer 1: A—the CBS eye logo.

Answer 2: D—optic nerve.

Answer 3: B—Barbra Streisand (the film was produced by her then-squeeze Jon Peters).

Answer 4: C—Gary Gilmore.

Answer 5: D—The Bible.

A SWAN DIVE

1. *The Trumpet of the Swan* is a children's book by which author?

A. E.B. White
B. Anna Sewell
C. Roald Dahl
D. A.A. Milne

2. A male swan is called a:

A. cockerel
B. cob
C. drake
D. cygnet

3. The lagoon in what American city's Public Garden has offered rides in swan-shaped pedal-boats since 1877?

A. Savannah
B. Atlantic City
C. Charleston
D. Boston

4. What Russian composer wrote the ballet *Swan Lake*?

A. Rachmaninov
B. Moussorgsky
C. Borodin
D. Tchaikovsky

5. What Greek mythological god appeared to Leda in the form of a swan, after which she produced eggs that hatched Castor, Clytemnestra, Polydeuces, and Helen?

A. Zeus
B. Hercules
C. Poseidon
D. Atlas

Answer 1: C—James Monroe.

Answer 2: B—*Gideon vs. Wainwright* (this case concerned the Fourteenth Amendment).

Answer 3: B—five.

Answer 4: C—Don Larsen.

Answer 5: A—Charles de Gaulle.

ANSWERSS!

Each answer ends with a double-S.

1. Hyperopia is the scientific name for what eye condition?

A. night blindness
B. colorblindness
C. nearsightedness
D. farsightedness

2. Which of these early '80s films did NOT revolve around the life of a teenager?

A. *Risky Business*
B. *Class*
C. *Reckless*
D. *Breathless*

3. "I never saw a purple cow" is the beginning of a poem by what author?

A. Harold Ross
B. Gelett Burgess
C. Johann Wyss
D. Dr. Seuss

4. Which of these musical groups recorded the hit song "Our House"?

A. Kiss
B. Looking Glass
C. Madness
D. Ohio Express

5. What British tabloid bills itself as "The World's Greatest Newspaper"?

A. *Daily Express*
B. *People's Address*
C. *Free Press*
D. *News Access*

Answer 1: A—E.B. White (best known as the author of *Charlotte's Web*).

Answer 2: B—cob.

Answer 3: D—Boston.

Answer 4: D—Tchaikovsky.

Answer 5: A—Zeus.

SOUTHERN-FRIED TRIVIA

1. In the original draft of Margaret Mitchell's novel *Gone With the Wind*, what was southern belle Scarlett O'Hara's first name?

A. Ruby
B. Pansy
C. Violet
D. Rosemary

2. Which one of these universities is NOT located in the south?

A. Vanderbilt
B. Lehigh
C. Rice
D. Clemson

3. What music star was awarded a fur coat by the makers of Southern Comfort for showcasing their brand of alcohol on stage so often?

A. Janis Joplin
B. Hank Williams Jr.
C. Michael Anthony
D. Jim Morrison

4. What southern state has changed the design of its flag not once, but twice since the new millennium?

A. South Carolina
B. Louisiana
C. Kentucky
D. Georgia

5. Which one of TV's *Designing Women* was NOT born in the south?

A. Jean Smart (Charlene)
B. Dixie Carter (Julia)
C. Annie Potts (Mary Jo)
D. Delta Burke (Suzanne)

Answer 1: D—farsightedness.

Answer 2: D—*Breathless*.

Answer 3: B—Gelett Burgess.

Answer 4: C—Madness.

Answer 5: A—*Daily Express*.

PULLING THE WOOL

1. The Golden Fleece was a treasure sought by:

A. Ulysses
B. Sinbad the Sailor
C. Rumpelstiltskin
D. Jason and the Argonauts

2. What emollient is derived from sheep's wool?

A. lanolin
B. aloe vera
C. jojoba
D. castor oil

3. If one is described as "dyed in the wool," it means that he is:

A. recently converted
B. complete and unchangeable
C. masquerading as something he's not
D. hesitant and indecisive

4. Which member of the Monkees commonly sported a wool hat?

A. Mike Nesmith
B. Peter Tork
C. Davy Jones
D. Micky Dolenz

5. Alpacas, known for their soft, strong wool (and the late-night TV commercials promoting them), are native to which continent?

A. Australia
B. Europe
C. South America
D. Africa

Answer 1: B—Pansy.

Answer 2: B—Lehigh (located in Pennsylvania).

Answer 3: A—Janis Joplin.

Answer 4: D—Georgia.

Answer 5: A—Jean Smart (born in Washington state).

CONTROVERSIAL COVERS

1. What actress raised eyebrows when she posed nude (and seven months pregnant) on the cover of a 1991 issue of *Vanity Fair*?

A. Cher
B. Demi Moore
C. Jennifer Aniston
D. Drew Barrymore

2. A 1993 issue of what magazine drew some criticism for an Art Spiegelman cover depicting a male Hasidic Jew kissing an African-American woman?

A. *Atlantic Monthly*
B. *Elle*
C. *The New Yorker*
D. *Harper's*

3. The August 26, 1989, cover of *TV Guide* used some photographic trickery (without permission) when it placed Oprah Winfrey's head on whose body?

A. Kathleen Turner
B. Whitney Houston
C. Sophia Loren
D. Ann-Margret

4. What musical group created quite a ruckus with a 2003 appearance on the cover of *Entertainment Weekly* magazine clad in nothing but a little bit of ink?

A. Matchbox 20
B. Blue Man Group
C. The Dixie Chicks
D. Linkin Park

5. What magazine caught flak in 1994 when it darkened O.J. Simpson's mug shot before placing it on the cover?

A. *Time*
B. *U.S. News & World Report*
C. *People*
D. *Newsweek*

Answer 1: D—Jason and the Argonauts.

Answer 2: A—lanolin.

Answer 3: B—complete and unchangeable.

Answer 4: A—Mike Nesmith.

Answer 5: C—South America.

EAGER BEAVERS

1. A "beaver" was an attachment to what piece of human armor?

A. helmet
B. backplate
C. shield
D. solleret (shoe)

2. Which of these was NOT the nickname of a character on TV's original *Leave It to Beaver*?

A. Lumpy
B. Carly
C. Tooey
D. Whitey

3. What type of natural perfume comes from beavers?

A. musk
B. civet
C. ambergris
D. castor

4. Bucky Beaver was a cartoon character on TV commercials who promoted Ipana, which was a brand of:

A. shoes
B. toothpaste
C. detergent
D. chainsaw

5. Which U.S. state is sometimes referred to as the Beaver State?

A. Minnesota
B. New Hampshire
C. Oregon
D. West Virginia

Answer 1: B—Demi Moore.

Answer 2: C—*The New Yorker*.

Answer 3: D—Ann-Margret.

Answer 4: C—The Dixie Chicks.

Answer 5: A—*Time*.

THE WALLY QUIZ

1. A few segments of Hadrian's Wall still stand in what European country?

A. Great Britain
B. Italy
C. France
D. Greece

2. Bob Geldof, star of the 1982 film version of *Pink Floyd: The Wall*, is probably best known for his work in:

A. ending Apartheid
B. children's literature
C. organizing Live Aid
D. promoting recycling

3. New York's Wall Street was named when a wall was built there for what purpose?

A. to retain topsoil for farming
B. protection from storms
C. to divide religious areas
D. defense from attack

4. In the 1530s, Michelangelo began work on what huge fresco on the wall of the Sistine Chapel?

A. *The Creation of Adam*
B. *The Last Judgment*
C. *Ignudi*
D. *God Separating Light from Darkness*

5. How many openings were there in the Berlin Wall?

A. none
B. one
C. two
D. three

Answer 1: A—helmet (the name applied to both the visor and the protective cover for the lower jaw).

Answer 2: B—Carly.

Answer 3: D—castor.

Answer 4: B—toothpaste.

Answer 5: C—Oregon.

FAKE FAST FOOD

All about fictional fast food restaurants that appeared in films.

1. Lester Burnham has trouble convincing the manager at Mr. Smiley's fast food restaurant that he has the experience necessary for employment there.

A. *Dogma*
B. *Big Daddy*
C. *American Beauty*
D. *Pulp Fiction*

2. An older woman, Nora Baker, works at a fast food burger joint and falls in love with a young widower who works as an advertising executive.

A. *White Palace*
B. *Alice Doesn't Live Here Anymore*
C. *Five Easy Pieces*
D. *Thelma & Louise*

3. Bill Foster finds that the Whammy Burger stopped serving breakfast three minutes ago, then complains that his burger doesn't look like the picture on the menu.

A. *Fast Times at Ridgemont High*
B. *Falling Down*
C. *As Good As It Gets*
D. *Gone Fishin'*

4. Two young friends who work in fast food join forces to try to thwart the threat of the new Mondo Burger restaurant that has opened across the street.

A. *Harry & the Hendersons*
B. *Frankie & Johnny*
C. *Mystic Pizza*
D. *Good Burger*

5. A fast food location named McDowell's uses golden arcs, not golden arches—and plain buns, not sesame seed buns—to keep one step ahead of McDonald's lawyers.

A. *The Thief Who Came to Dinner*
B. *Coming to America*
C. *Hamburger, the Motion Picture*
D. *Diner*

Answer 1: A—Great Britain.

Answer 2: C—organizing Live Aid (he was also the lead singer of the Boomtown Rats, best known for their song "I Don't Like Mondays").

Answer 3: D—defense from attack.

Answer 4: B—*The Last Judgment*.

Answer 5: C—two (both heavily guarded).

ANCHORS AWEIGH

1. What admiral of the American Revolution is considered to be the father of the U.S. Navy?

A. David G. Farragut
B. John Paul Jones
C. James Lawrence
D. William Halsey

2. What group had a 1979 hit with the single "In the Navy"?

A. Sister Sledge
B. Peaches & Herb
C. Men at Work
D. the Village People

3. Which of these late-20th-century U.S. presidents did NOT serve in the Navy?

A. Ronald Reagan
B. Jimmy Carter
C. Gerald Ford
D. Richard Nixon

4. On TV's *McHale's Navy*, what was the first name of the title character?

A. Quinton
B. Cameron
C. Quincy
D. Calvin

5. What former fashion editor became a spokesperson for Old Navy clothing in print ads and TV commercials before dying in 2001?

A. Anna Wintour
B. Diana Vreeland
C. Elsa Klensch
D. Carrie Donovan

Answer 1: C—*American Beauty.*

Answer 2: A—*White Palace.*

Answer 3: B—*Falling Down.*

Answer 4: D—*Good Burger.*

Answer 5: B—*Coming to America.*

HEADED NORTH

1. The African nation formerly known as Northern Rhodesia is now known as:

A. Zaire
B. Zimbabwe
C. Zululand
D. Zambia

2. A person from North Carolina is properly known as a:

A. North Caroliner
B. North Carolean
C. North Carolinian
D. North Caroler

3. What rank did Oliver North ultimately achieve in the U.S. Marine Corps?

A. Lieutenant Colonel
B. Major
C. Brigadier General
D. Field Marshal

4. Which of the following is true about the North Pole?

A. it is claimed by Russia
B. it does not lie on land
C. it is home to two species of penguin
D. none of the above

5. Which one of these "North" motion pictures was nominated for an Academy Award?

A. *North Dallas Forty*
B. *North by Northwest*
C. *North of the Great Divide*
D. *North to Alaska*

Answer 1: B—John Paul Jones.

Answer 2: D—the Village People.

Answer 3: A—Ronald Reagan.

Answer 4: A—Quinton.

Answer 5: D—Carrie Donovan.

OH, LORD

1. *Lord of the Dance* star Michael Flatley was born in what country?

A. Spain
B. the U.S.
C. Australia
D. Ireland

2. Little Lord Fauntleroy suits are generally associated with what fabric?

A. velvet
B. gabardine
C. wool
D. tweed

3. Who was elected as leader of the boys at the beginning of William Golding's novel *Lord of the Flies*?

A. Piggy
B. Jack
C. Ralph
D. Simon

4. George Harrison was sued for plagiarism because his hit song "My Sweet Lord" closely resembled what other tune?

A. "Baby, It's You"
B. "He's So Fine"
C. "Our Day Will Come"
D. "Be My Baby"

5. In what decade were the books of J.R.R. Tolkien's *Lord of the Rings* trilogy first published?

A. the 1830s
B. the 1870s
C. the 1910s
D. the 1950s

Answer 1: D—Zambia.

Answer 2: C—North Carolinian.

Answer 3: A—Lieutenant Colonel.

Answer 4: B—it does not lie on land.

Answer 5: B—*North by Northwest*.

BORDERLINE

Find the correct state for each clue. A river crossing is considered a border.

1. New Hampshire, New York, and Massachusetts are the three states that border which state?

A. New Jersey
B. Vermont
C. Connecticut
D. Maine

2. Idaho, North Dakota, South Dakota, and Wyoming are the four states that border which state?

A. Minnesota
B. Colorado
C. Montana
D. Oregon

3. Georgia, South Carolina, Tennessee, and Virginia are the four states that border which state?

A. Kentucky
B. Maryland
C. Alabama
D. North Carolina

4. Illinois, Iowa, Michigan, and Minnesota are the four states that border which state?

A. Wisconsin
B. Ohio
C. Indiana
D. Missouri

5. Maryland, New Jersey, and Pennsylvania are the three states that border which state?

A. Virginia
B. Connecticut
C. Delaware
D. West Virginia

Answer 1: B—the U.S.

Answer 2: A—velvet.

Answer 3: C—Ralph.

Answer 4: B—"He's So Fine."

Answer 5: D—the 1950s.

YES, WE HAVE NO ...

1. A banana seat would most likely be found on which of these contraptions?

A. hot-air balloon
B. kayak
C. chaise longue
D. bicycle

2. Bananas are known for being a good source of potassium. Which of the following is the chemical symbol for potassium?

A. Pm
B. K
C. Ag
D. P

3. Who cowrote, directed, and starred in the 1971 motion picture *Bananas*?

A. Mel Brooks
B. Robert Redford
C. Woody Allen
D. Alan Alda

4. Which of these made occasional appearances on TV's *Captain Kangaroo*?

A. Bananas in Pajamas
B. Banana Man
C. the Banana Splits
D. Banana Fontana

5. In the 1970s and '80s, Bananas and Dynamite were two _____ popular with school-age children.

A. rock bands
B. cartoons
C. magazines
D. video games

Answer 1: B—Vermont.

Answer 2: C—Montana.

Answer 3: D—North Carolina.

Answer 4: A—Wisconsin.

Answer 5: C—Delaware.

FIRST "AID"

1. What author wrote *The Electric Kool-Aid Acid Test*?

A. Tom Wolfe
B. Jack Kerouac
C. Ken Kesey
D. Neal Cassady

2. The Federal Aid Highway Act marked the introduction of the:

A. national 55 mph speed limit
B. uniform road signage requirement
C. sale of unleaded gasoline
D. interstate highway system

3. What American president signed the bill that began Medicaid benefits?

A. Harry Truman
B. Franklin Roosevelt
C. Lyndon Johnson
D. Herbert Hoover

4. In 1950, what company introduced the first transistor-based hearing aid?

A. Zenith
B. General Electric
C. Sylvania
D. Tandy

5. Two concerts took place for the Live Aid benefit on July 13, 1985—one was in London, England, and the other occurred in:

A. Washington, D.C.
B. Philadelphia
C. New York City
D. Los Angeles

Answer 1: D—bicycle.

Answer 2: B—K (for "kalium," the neo-Latin word for potassium, derived from Arabic "al-qali," a kind of ash).

Answer 3: C—Woody Allen.

Answer 4: B—Banana Man.

Answer 5: C—magazines (offered by Scholastic Books).

LADYLIKE

1. The musical *My Fair Lady* was based on what classic play?

A. *Our Town*
B. *Cyrano de Bergerac*
C. *Pygmalion*
D. *Romeo and Juliet*

2. Each of the following artists recorded a hit song with the same title—"Lady"—but who recorded the only one of them that reached #1 on the pop chart?

A. Kenny Rogers
B. Styx
C. Little River Band
D. Jack Jones

3. What was the real first name of the First Lady known as Mamie Eisenhower?

A. Margaret
B. Madeline
C. Maureen
D. Mary

4. The Lady Byng Memorial Trophy is awarded annually to the NHL player that earns what superlative?

A. Leading Scorer
B. Rookie of the Year
C. Most Gentlemanly
D. Outstanding Defenseman

5. Although it's not mentioned in the Shakespeare play, what was the given name of Lady Macbeth, the 11th-century wife of the King of Scotland?

A. Hounshed
B. Gruoch
C. Penelope
D. Marie-Christine

Answer 1: A—Tom Wolfe.

Answer 2: D—interstate highway system.

Answer 3: C—Lyndon Johnson.

Answer 4: A—Zenith.

Answer 5: B—Philadelphia.

HI-YO, DINOSAUR

1. In what period of the Mesozoic era did dinosaurs first appear?

A. Jurassic
B. Cretaceous
C. Triassic
D. Cambrian

2. In 1995, what former NBA star became co-owner of the expansion Toronto Raptors (the first major league sports team to be named after a dinosaur)?

A. Isiah Thomas
B. Magic Johnson
C. Oscar Robertson
D. Dominique Wilkins

3. What fictional type of dinosaur was Dino, the family pet on *The Flintstones*?

A. dogosaurus
B. rabosaurus
C. snorkasaurus
D. purplesaurus

4. "Pterodactyl" is based on a Greek phrase meaning:

A. sky lizard
B. fire water
C. three horns
D. wing finger

5. Who was the lead singer of the rock band known as T. Rex?

A. Gary Glitter
B. Marc Bolan
C. Phil Lynott
D. Tim Buckley

Answer 1: C—*Pygmalion*.

Answer 2: A—Kenny Rogers.

Answer 3: D—Mary.

Answer 4: C—Most Gentlemanly.

Answer 5: B—Gruoch.

BODY LANGUAGE

1. On which of the following parts of the human body would you find whorls and arches?

A. scalp
B. fingers
C. nose
D. ears

2. Which joint type can be found inside the human skull?

A. suture
B. sliding
C. ball-and-socket
D. hinge

3. Which of the following is NOT one of the "taste areas" on the human tongue?

A. sour
B. bitter
C. salty
D. spicy

4. Which of these body parts can be used to trigger the gag reflex?

A. uvula
B. coccyx
C. pharynx
D. epiglottis

5. In what part of the human body would you find the fissure of Rolando?

A. small intestine
B. heart
C. liver
D. brain

Answer 1: C—Triassic.

Answer 2: A—Isiah Thomas.

Answer 3: C—snorkasaurus.

Answer 4: D—wing finger.

Answer 5: B—Marc Bolan.

BIG SKY

1. Montana contains only two National Parks, one of which—Yellowstone National Park, the nation's oldest—is located mostly in neighboring Wyoming. What is Montana's other National Park?

A. Wind Cave
B. Glacier
C. Grand Teton
D. Big Horn Canyon

2. What fast food chain once offered a sizeable sandwich known as the Big Montana?

A. Subway
B. KFC
C. Arby's
D. Wendy's

3. Which notoriously famous union leader was born in Montana?

A. Tony Boyle
B. Eugene V. Debs
C. George Meany
D. Walter Reuther

4. Bob Montana was an artist best known for inventing which of these popular comic book characters?

A. Dick Tracy
B. Archie
C. Pogo
D. Richie Rich

5. In what state was NFL Hall of Fame quarterback Joe Montana born?

A. California
B. Montana
C. Indiana
D. Pennsylvania

Answer 1: B—fingers.

Answer 2: A—suture.

Answer 3: D—spicy.

Answer 4: A—uvula.

Answer 5: D—brain.

FIVE ON TEN

1. Which of the following decapods (ten-legged sea creatures) is NOT a crustacean?

A. crab
B. shrimp
C. cuttlefish
D. lobster

2. According to the Biblical book of Exodus, which is the first of the Ten Commandments?

A. "Remember the Sabbath Day, to keep it holy"
B. "Thou shalt not kill"
C. "Thou shalt have no other gods before me"
D. "Thou shalt not steal"

3. The "Hollywood Ten" was/were:

A. major early-20th-century film studios
B. a 1940s gang that terrorized L.A.
C. suspected Communists
D. the first multiplex theater in the U.S.

4. Nadia Comaneci scored a "perfect ten" seven times in the 1976 Olympics. What other gymnast scored a 10 twice in those same games?

A. Nelli Kim
B. Shannon Miller
C. Ludmilla Turisheva
D. Olga Korbut

5. Which of these scouting groups is designed for ten-year-old kids?

A. Tiger Scouts
B. Cub Scouts
C. Boy Scouts
D. Eagle Scouts

Answer 1: B—Glacier.

Answer 2: C—Arby's.

Answer 3: A—Tony Boyle.

Answer 4: B—Archie.

Answer 5: D—Pennsylvania.

IT'S CLOUDY

1. "I wandered lonely as a cloud ..." is the opening line of which William Wordsworth poem?

A. "Eve of St. Mark"
B. "A Birthday"
C. "The Chinese Nightingale"
D. "Daffodils"

2. What type of cloud can form a funnel, giving birth to a tornado?

A. cumulonimbus
B. stratus
C. nimbus
D. altocumulus

3. The Oort Cloud is made up of:

A. ozone
B. volcanic ash
C. comets
D. water mist

4. What American auto maker produced a car known as the Cirrus?

A. Chevrolet
B. Chrysler
C. Cadillac
D. Mercury

5. Born Byron Elsworth Barr in St. Paul, Minnesota, what actor won an Oscar for his role as Rocky in *They Shoot Horses, Don't They?*

A. Red Buttons
B. Bruce Dern
C. Gig Young
D. Al Lewis

Answer 1: C—cuttlefish.

Answer 2: C—"Thou shalt have no other gods before me."

Answer 3: C—suspected Communists.

Answer 4: A—Nelli Kim.

Answer 5: B—Cub Scouts.

PEOPLE IN PARIS

1. Who was the first American artist to have a painting on display in the Louvre?

A. James Whistler
B. Grandma Moses
C. Andrew Wyeth
D. Georgia O'Keeffe

2. What bandleader was en route to Paris to play a concert for the Allied troops when his plane disappeared?

A. Guy Lombardo
B. Jimmy Dorsey
C. Glenn Miller
D. Kay Kyser

3. What TV character's venture to Paris resulted in her wearing a burlap dress, being busted for counterfeiting, and putting ketchup on snails?

A. Fran Fine
B. Lucy Ricardo
C. Samantha Stevens
D. Louise Jefferson

4. Who was the first woman to be entombed at the Pantheon on her own merit?

A. Charlotte Corday
B. Marie Antoinette
C. Josephine Bonaparte
D. Marie Curie

5. In a speech made in Paris, what American president said: "I do not think it altogether inappropriate to introduce myself to this audience ..."?

A. Dwight Eisenhower
B. Lyndon Johnson
C. John Kennedy
D. Harry Truman

Answer 1: D—"Daffodils."

Answer 2: A—cumulonimbus.

Answer 3: C—comets.

Answer 4: B—Chrysler.

Answer 5: C—Gig Young.

GOPHER BROKE

1. The gopher is a member of what order of mammals?

A. insectivores
B. rodents
C. edentates
D. lagomorphs

2. Fred Grandy, known for his role as Gopher on TV's original *Love Boat*, served four terms as a U.S. Representative from his home state of:

A. Iowa
B. Illinois
C. Idaho
D. Indiana

3. In baseball, a "gopher pitch" is another name for:

A. a pitch using an illegally scuffed baseball
B. a pitch hit for a home run
C. a pitch that hits a batter
D. a pitch that bounces off the ground/plate

4. The Gopher State is among what U.S. state's many nicknames?

A. Pennsylvania
B. Arkansas
C. Minnesota
D. North Dakota

5. In the early days of the Internet, what was the nickname used to reference the program that searched Gopher menus to find information on the Internet?

A. Archie
B. Betty
C. Moose
D. Veronica

Answer 1: A—James Whistler (the work was *Arrangement in Grey and Black No. 1*, commonly known as *Whistler's Mother*).

Answer 2: C—Glenn Miller.

Answer 3: B—Lucy Ricardo.

Answer 4: D—Marie Curie.

Answer 5: C—John Kennedy (he continued: "I am the man who accompanied Jacqueline Kennedy to Paris, and I have enjoyed it").

THE YEAR 1973

1. Marvin Hamlisch's arrangement of Scott Joplin's "The Entertainer" was the theme song for what 1973 motion picture?

A. *The Exorcist*
B. *Paper Moon*
C. *American Graffiti*
D. *The Sting*

2. What TV network premiered the first "teletext" system (the precursor of closed captioning) in 1973?

A. BBC
B. PBS
C. ABC
D. TV Globo

3. Augusto Pinochet took power in Chile in September 1973 when what president was overthrown?

A. Ricardo Lagos
B. Salvadore Allende
C. Jorge Alessandria
D. Ramon Freire

4. In October 1973, kidnappers cut off the ear of what multimillionaire's grandson and mailed it to a newspaper to dispel rumors of a hoax?

A. John D. Rockefeller
B. H.L. Hunt
C. J. Paul Getty
D. William Randolph Hearst

5. What TV series was abruptly cancelled by NBC after 14 seasons and aired its final episode on January 16, 1973?

A. *Bonanza*
B. *The Ed Sullivan Show*
C. *Gunsmoke*
D. *The FBI*

Answer 1: B—rodents.

Answer 2: A—Iowa.

Answer 3: B—a pitch hit for a home run.

Answer 4: C—Minnesota.

Answer 5: D—Veronica.

POOR PLUTO

1. Scientists have concluded that the surface of the dwarf planet Pluto Is made largely of what type of frozen gas?

A. helium
B. ammonia
C. methane
D. argon

2. What is the only planet that—like Pluto—orbits the Sun in a markedly inclined pattern?

A. Mercury
B. Jupiter
C. Uranus
D. Mars

3. Every zodiac sign is ruled by a corresponding celestial body. Traditionally, what sign of the zodiac is ruled by Pluto?

A. Scorpio
B. Aquarius
C. Virgo
D. Sagittarius

4. In what year did Pluto cross the orbit of Neptune, putting it back into its common spot as the most distant planet in the solar system (back when it was still a regular planet)?

A. 1982
B. 1987
C. 1993
D. 1999

5. What is the name of the largest known satellite of Pluto?

A. Titania
B. Charon
C. Rhea
D. Triton

Answer 1: D—*The Sting.*

Answer 2: A—BBC.

Answer 3: B—Salvadore Allende.

Answer 4: C—J. Paul Getty.

Answer 5: A—*Bonanza.*

ON YOUR TOES

1. Toeshoes, which enable ballerinas to stand on tiptoe, are also called:

A. pointe shoes
B. character shoes
C. ballet slippers
D. jazz shoes

2. *Bells on Their Toes* was the sequel to what bestseller about the Gilbreth family?

A. *Life With Father*
B. *Meet Me in St. Louis*
C. *Cheaper by the Dozen*
D. *Please Don't Eat the Daisies*

3. Which of the following is an edentate, an order of animals that includes the three-toed sloth?

A. koala bear
B. raccoon
C. spider monkey
D. armadillo

4. British sitcom character Albert Steptoe was known by what name when a U.S. version of his series hit the airwaves?

A. George Jefferson
B. James Evans
C. Fred Sanford
D. Cliff Huxtable

5. What was the real name of "Tip-Toe Thru' the Tulips With Me" crooner Tiny Tim?

A. Paul Gadd
B. Reginald Dwight
C. Chaim Weitz
D. Herbert Khaury

Answer 1: C—methane.

Answer 2: A—Mercury.

Answer 3: A—Scorpio (also partially ruled by Mars).

Answer 4: D—1999.

Answer 5: B—Charon.

YELLOW THERE

1. "The Man in the Yellow Hat" can be found in books that feature what children's literary character?

A. Babar the Elephant
B. Paddington Bear
C. Curious George
D. Peter Rabbit

2. Besides Texas, what other U.S. state is mentioned in the lyrics of the song "The Yellow Rose of Texas"?

A. Tennessee
B. Kentucky
C. Mississippi
D. Missouri

3. The insect known as the yellow jacket is a type of:

A. wasp
B. bee
C. hornet
D. mosquito

4. Which of the following was NOT featured in the 1968 animated Beatles motion picture *Yellow Submarine*?

A. Blue Meanies
B. Screaming Yellow Zonkers
C. Snapping Turtle Turks
D. Butterfly Stompers

5. Yellowknife was the first city in what area of Canada?

A. Yukon Territory
B. Labrador
C. the Maritimes
D. Northwestern Territories

Answer 1: A—pointe shoes.

Answer 2: C—*Cheaper by the Dozen*.

Answer 3: D—armadillo.

Answer 4: C—Fred Sanford (*Steptoe & Son* was previously a BBC radio and TV show).

Answer 5: D—Herbert Khaury.

IT'S A FAMILY AFFAIR

1. Who was the only son born to Henry Ford, founder of the automotive dynasty that bears his name?

A. Benson
B. Edsel
C. Henry II
D. William

2. What prominent Italian family, a dominant force in Florentine politics for two and a half centuries, includes two popes in its lineage?

A. Canevaro
B. Visconti
C. Ricasoli
D. Medici

3. Three members of the Kennedy family have perished in plane crashes: Joe Jr., John Jr., and Kathleen, who was known by what family nickname?

A. Kleen
B. Kitty
C. Kick
D. Kiki

4. In a famous but tragic story, brothers Joe, Frank, Albert, Madison, and George Sullivan each enlisted in the U.S. Navy in 1937 and were all aboard what Navy ship when it was torpedoed in 1942?

A. *Hornet*
B. *Batfish*
C. *Yorktown*
D. *Juneau*

5. Which of the following Jackson family members uses his/her real first name?

A. Tito
B. Marlon
C. Jackie
D. Rebbie

Answer 1: C—Curious George.

Answer 2: A—Tennessee.

Answer 3: A—wasp.

Answer 4: B—Screaming Yellow Zonkers.

Answer 5: D—Northwestern Territories.

CATCHIN' A COLT

1. An ungelded male horse is known as a colt until it reaches what age?

A. three
B. four
C. five
D. six

2. In what year did the NFL's Baltimore Colts move west to Indianapolis?

A. 1976
B. 1980
C. 1984
D. 1988

3. A subcompact car known as the Colt was sold under which one of these automotive nameplates?

A. Dodge
B. Mercury
C. Pontiac
D. Chevrolet

4. During World War I, what future five-star general took his first commanding post in charge of Camp Colt in Gettysburg, Pennsylvania?

A. George Marshall
B. Dwight Eisenhower
C. Omar Bradley
D. Douglas MacArthur

5. He developed the first practical revolver, and his name was immortalized in the company he founded, Colt Firearms. What was this gunsmith's first name?

A. Harlan
B. Jacob
C. Walter
D. Samuel

Answer 1: B—Edsel.

Answer 2: D—Medici.

Answer 3: C—Kick.

Answer 4: D—*Juneau.*

Answer 5: B—Marlon (Tito's real name is Toriano Adaryll, Jackie's is Sigmund Esco, and Rebbie was Maureen Reilette).

JOKING AROUND
All about jokers in pop culture.

1. What TV game show host was the emcee for *The Joker's Wild* for twelve years through 1984?

A. Allen Ludden
B. Jack Barry
C. Bill Cullen
D. Wink Martindale

2. Matthew Modine portrayed the role of Private Joker in what military motion picture of the 1980s?

A. *Full Metal Jacket*
B. *Hamburger Hill*
C. *Platoon*
D. *Heartbreak Ridge*

3. According to the lyrics of the Steve Miller Band's hit single "The Joker," some people call him by what name?

A. Patrick
B. Francis
C. Carlton
D. Maurice

4. In a deck of Bicycle brand playing cards, what type of character is depicted riding a bicycle on the Joker cards?

A. a king
B. a jester
C. a bear
D. a knave

5. What color was the hair of the *Batman* villain known as the Joker, as portrayed by Cesar Romero on the 1960s TV series and Jack Nicholson in the 1989 feature film?

A. orange
B. red
C. green
D. blue

Answer 1: C—five.

Answer 2: C—1984.

Answer 3: A—Dodge (and also as both Plymouth and Mitsubishi).

Answer 4: B—Dwight Eisenhower.

Answer 5: D—Samuel.

BENELUX

1. Which of these international organizations is headquartered in Brussels, Belgium?

A. NATO
B. EFTA
C. OAS
D. WHO

2. What rock legend bought a guitar and formed his first band (the Quarrymen) after hearing Lonnie Donegan's "Rock Island Line" on Radio Luxembourg?

A. Pete Townshend
B. David Bowie
C. John Lennon
D. Elton John

3. In what Dutch museum would you find Rembrandt's masterpiece *The Night Watch*?

A. Mauritshuis
B. Rembrandt House
C. Van Gogh Museum
D. Rijksmuseum

4. Which of these is NOT one of the three official languages of Belgium?

A. English
B. German
C. Dutch
D. French

5. All of the following beers are brewed in Holland, except:

A. Amstel
B. Heineken
C. Grolsch
D. Rheingold

Answer 1: B—Jack Barry.

Answer 2: A—*Full Metal Jacket.*

Answer 3: D—Maurice.

Answer 4: A—a king.

Answer 5: C—green.

REACHING A PEAK

1. In what U.S. state would you find Pikes Peak?

A. Montana
B. Washington
C. Utah
D. Colorado

2. A "peak flow meter" is a device most commonly used by a person suffering from which of these physical ailments?

A. diabetes
B. angina
C. asthma
D. epilepsy

3. Peak toothpaste was the first national brand to contain:

A. fluoride
B. baking soda
C. mouthwash
D. peroxide

4. What British author's *Peveril of the Peak* was first published in 1822?

A. Sir Walter Scott
B. George Eliot
C. William Makepeace Thackeray
D. Elizabeth Gaskell

5. The 1997 motion picture *Dante's Peak* tells the story of a town that is threatened by:

A. rock slides
B. ghosts
C. a volcano
D. wild animals

Answer 1: A—NATO.

Answer 2: C—John Lennon.

Answer 3: D—Rijksmuseum.

Answer 4: A—English.

Answer 5: D—Rheingold.

WHAT'S UP, DOC?

1. What was the first foot product invented by Dr. William Mutthius Scholl?

A. soft stockings
B. cushioned insoles
C. corn pads
D. arch supports

2. What was the name of the first professional basketball team for which Julius "Dr. J" Erving played?

A. New Jersey Nets
B. Virginia Squires
C. Boston Celtics
D. Philadelphia 76ers

3. What feel-good author is known as "Doctor Love"?

A. Dale Carnegie
B. Leo Buscaglia
C. Zig Ziglar
D. Wayne Dyer

4. What Greek god is the first mentioned in the Hippocratic Oath, a version of which is still used today by medical students?

A. Hermes
B. Zeus
C. Apollo
D. Hephaestus

5. What is the real first name of the former late-night TV band leader Doc Severinsen?

A. Carl
B. Rodney
C. William
D. Doug

Answer 1: D—Colorado.

Answer 2: C—asthma.

Answer 3: B—baking soda.

Answer 4: A—Sir Walter Scott.

Answer 5: C—a volcano.

JUNE OH!

1. A June bug is what type of insect?

A. a beetle
B. a grasshopper
C. a fly
D. a moth

2. What is the traditional beverage served at annual Juneteenth events (which celebrate the end of slavery in America)?

A. buttermilk
B. apple cider
C. white wine
D. red soda pop

3. The 1990 motion picture *Henry & June* was the first major studio film:

A. in which Uma Thurman appeared
B. to be given the NC-17 rating
C. made available in DVD format
D. banned by Blockbuster Video

4. Which of the following was NOT the code name of one of the beaches landed upon by Allied troops on June 6, 1944 (otherwise known as D-Day)?

A. Janus
B. Sword
C. Omaha
D. Gold

5. What was the maiden name of *Leave It to Beaver* TV mom June Cleaver?

A. Brown
B. Collins
C. Bronson
D. Carter

Answer 1: D—arch supports.

Answer 2: B—Virginia Squires (of the American Basketball Association).

Answer 3: B—Leo Buscaglia.

Answer 4: C—Apollo.

Answer 5: A—Carl.

YOU'RE SOAKING IN IT!

1. What brand of soap got its name in the late 19th century when Harley Procter (of Procter & Gamble) read the 45th Psalm while attending church?

A. Joy
B. Swan
C. Ivory
D. Dove

2. What U.S. city is home to the annual All-American Soap Box Derby?

A. Indianapolis, Indiana
B. Rockford, Illinois
C. Akron, Ohio
D. Pittsburgh, Pennsylvania

3. What color is soapstone when it is first mined?

A. blue
B. white
C. pink
D. green

4. Which of these business legends started his professional career as a soap salesman?

A. King Gillette
B. Edward J. Noble
C. Ray Kroc
D. William Wrigley

5. Which of the following actors was the only one to regularly appear on a TV series before joining ABC's controversial comedy *Soap*?

A. Billy Crystal
B. Richard Mulligan
C. Robert Guillaume
D. Katherine Helmond

Answer 1: A—beetle.

Answer 2: D—red soda pop (some theorize that it represents the blood shed for the cause).

Answer 3: B—to be given an NC-17 rating (the MPAA has since gone back and rerated several older films using this designation).

Answer 4: A—Janus.

Answer 5: C—Bronson.

POOL YOUR RESOURCES

1. In the game of 9-ball, the pool balls are initially placed in a grouping of what shape?

A. hourglass
B. diamond
C. circle
D. triangle

2. Which of these materials is commonly used on the tips of pool cue sticks?

A. leather
B. sponge
C. rubber
D. felt

3. Which of the following descriptions of numbered pocket billiard balls is NOT correct?

A. the 1 ball is yellow
B. the 2 ball is blue
C. the 3 ball is red
D. the 4 ball is orange

4. What's the total weight of a full standard set of billiard balls (numbered 1 through 15, including the cue ball)?

A. 6 pounds
B. 9 pounds
C. 12 pounds
D. 15 pounds

5. What is the length-to-width ratio of a regulation pool table?

A. 3:2
B. 2:1
C. 5:2
D. 3:1

Answer 1: C—Ivory.

Answer 2: C—Akron, Ohio.

Answer 3: A—blue.

Answer 4: D—William Wrigley.

Answer 5: B—Richard Mulligan (he starred in the short-lived sitcom *The Hero* in 1966, but is perhaps best known as Harry on TV's *Empty Nest*).

EVERYTHING'S ARCHIE

1. What was the name of the high school attended by Archie Andrews and his comic-book buddies?

A. Westside
B. Forest Lawn
C. Taft
D. Riverdale

2. The late Dr. Archie Carr, zoology professor at the University of Florida, was an authority and activist dedicated to which of these endangered animals?

A. sea turtles
B. crocodiles
C. pumas
D. whooping cranes

3. Archie Griffin was the first to win what sports award in two consecutive years?

A. Cy Young Award
B. NBA All-Star MVP
C. Heisman Trophy
D. NHL Coach of the Year

4. He later had the surname Bunker, but what was the last name of Archie in the original pilot for the TV sitcom *All in the Family*?

A. Thomas
B. Justice
C. Hall
D. Barber

5. In the 2001 motion picture *Dr. Dolittle 2*, what type of animal was Archie?

A. bear
B. weasel
C. dog
D. beaver

Answer 1: B—diamond.

Answer 2: A—leather.

Answer 3: D—the 4 ball is orange (the 4 ball is usually purple, though is sometimes pink; the 5 ball is orange).

Answer 4: A—6 pounds (each of the 16 balls, including the cue ball, weighs 6 ounces).

Answer 5: B—2:1 (a regulation table is twice as long as it is wide).

CHICKEN OUT

1. The disease we call chickenpox is more properly known as:

A. rubella
B. cytomegalovirus
C. varicella
D. rubeola

2. The loose skin hanging from the neck of a chicken is known as a:

A. comb
B. wattle
C. talon
D. gizzard

3. In the book and the TV miniseries *Roots*, which character had a son named Chicken George?

A. Kizzy
B. Fanta
C. Bell
D. Malizy

4. What is the correct name for a female chicken between eight weeks and one year old?

A. chick
B. pullet
C. hen
D. capon

5. Nick Park and Peter Lord, the animators responsible for the 2000 motion picture *Chicken Run*, were also the creators of which of these popular duos?

A. Beavis & Butt-head
B. Pinky & the Brain
C. Wallace & Gromit
D. Ren & Stimpy

Answer 1: D—Riverdale.

Answer 2: A—sea turtles.

Answer 3: C—Heisman Trophy.

Answer 4: B—Justice (the show's first pilot was titled *Justice for All*).

Answer 5: A—bear.

IMPERIAL-ISM

1. Opened in 1765, the Imperial Menagerie in Vienna, Austria, was the world's first modern.

A. toy store
B. agricultural school
C. public zoo
D. wax museum

2. Prince Imperial Louis was a descendant of which of these European leaders?

A. Canute
B. Hadrian
C. George III
D. Napoleon

3. What auto manufacturer introduced a luxury model known as the Imperial in 1926?

A. Chrysler
B. Lincoln
C. Studebaker
D. Cadillac

4. What singer's backing group was known as the Imperials?

A. Little Roger
B. Little Anthony
C. Little Richard
D. Little Steven

5. The York Imperial is a popular type of which of these fruits?

A. apple
B. plum
C. cherry
D. pear

Answer 1: C—varicella.

Answer 2: B—wattle.

Answer 3: A—Kizzy.

Answer 4: B—pullet.

Answer 5: C—Wallace & Gromit.

IN THE MIDDLE

1. Which of these countries is NOT part of the area known as the Middle East?

A. Qatar
B. Lebanon
C. Bhutan
D. Yemen

2. Which of these is the proper medical term for the middle finger?

A. medius
B. phalanx
C. manus
D. pollex

3. Which of these book series is set in a location known as Middle-earth?

A. *The Hitchhiker's Guide to the Galaxy*
B. *Dune*
C. *The Lord of the Rings*
D. *A Song of Ice and Fire*

4. Which of these presidents had the middle name Alan?

A. James Garfield
B. Zachary Taylor
C. Grover Cleveland
D. Chester Arthur

5. Which of these boxing classes is heavier than a middleweight?

A. lightweight
B. cruiserweight
C. bantamweight
D. welterweight

Answer 1: C—public zoo.

Answer 2: D—Napoleon.

Answer 3: A—Chrysler.

Answer 4: B—Little Anthony.

Answer 5: A—apple.

"DC" UNITED

1. In the DC series of planes, introduced in 1933 with the DC-1, the letters DC stand for:

A. Delta Charter
B. Dutch Canadian
C. Daley Corporation
D. Douglas Commercial

2. Who is popularly credited with inventing the first DC (direct current) motor back in 1837?

A. Thomas Davenport
B. Charles Steinmetz
C. Nikola Tesla
D. William Stanley

3. Which of these is NOT a DC Comic Book character?

A. Wonder Woman
B. the Green Lantern
C. the Sub-Mariner
D. Swamp Thing

4. In November 2000, what phrase started appearing on license plates in Washington, D.C.?

A. Don't Tread on Me
B. Join or Die
C. Taxation Without Representation
D. Give Me Liberty

5. What's the last name of the siblings that share guitar-playing duties for the heavy metal band known as AC/DC?

A. Johnson
B. Young
C. Rudd
D. Scott

Answer 1: C—Bhutan.

Answer 2: A—medius.

Answer 3: C—*The Lord of the Rings*.

Answer 4: D—Chester Arthur.

Answer 5: B—cruiserweight.

FIRST?

A set of five nostalgic foursomes from the 20th century.

1. Which U.S. president appears on the far left at Mount Rushmore?

A. Thomas Jefferson
B. Abraham Lincoln
C. Theodore Roosevelt
D. George Washington

2. Which Pac-Man ghost appears first on the arcade game's list?

A. Bashful (Inky)
B. Speedy (Pinky)
C. Shadow (Blinky)
D. Pokey (Clyde)

3. On the *Abbey Road* album cover, which member of the Beatles is on the far left?

A. George Harrison
B. John Lennon
C. Paul McCartney
D. Ringo Starr

4. In TV commercials, what was the first mentioned of the four original types of Lucky Charms marshmallow bits?

A. green clovers
B. orange stars
C. pink hearts
D. yellow moons

5. In the opening scene of the credits for *The Brady Bunch*, which of the females appears in the upper left?

A. Carol
B. Marcia
C. Jan
D. Cindy

Answer 1: D—Douglas Commercial.

Answer 2: A—Thomas Davenport.

Answer 3: C—the Sub-Mariner (a Marvel superhero).

Answer 4: C—Taxation Without Representation (the plates protest Washington, D.C.'s nonvoting status in Congress despite the district being subject to all U.S. taxes).

Answer 5: B—Young (Angus & Malcolm).

WELCOME TO MARY-LAND

1. A Bloody Mary is a cocktail made with tomato juice and what type of alcohol?

A. ouzo
B. gin
C. vodka
D. rum

2. Queen Mary of England made her reputation by trying to rid her country of what segment of the population?

A. astronomers
B. Protestants
C. Scots
D. unmarried women

3. In which of these team sports might you see a game-ending play widely referred to as a Hail Mary?

A. ice hockey
B. baseball
C. soccer
D. football

4. "Cross-Eyed Mary" was a song first recorded by which of these bands?

A. Jethro Tull
B. Soundgarden
C. Genesis
D. Squirrel Nut Zippers

5. Known as Typhoid Mary, what job did Mary Mallon take that led to her causing scores of persons to become infected with the disease?

A. cook
B. prostitute
C. nurse
D. teacher

Answer 1: D—George Washington.

Answer 2: C—Shadow (Blinky).

Answer 3: A—George Harrison.

Answer 4: C—pink hearts.

Answer 5: B—Marcia.

KICK THE HABIT

1. According to the song, you can "get your kicks" on what famous roadway?

A. Sunset Strip
B. Ventura Highway
C. Route 66
D. Hollywood Boulevard

2. As of 2011, which of the following kickers is NOT tied for the longest field goal in NFL history (63 yards)?

A. Sebastian Janikowski
B. Morten Andersen
C. Jason Elam
D. Tom Dempsey

3. Richard Nixon told the press "you won't have Nixon to kick around" after he lost the California gubernatorial race to what opponent?

A. Earl Warren
B. Leland Stanford
C. Ronald Reagan
D. Edmund Brown

4. In the arcade video game known as Kickman, what device was used to transport the kicking clown across the screen?

A. a unicycle
B. a skateboard
C. a tiny car
D. a pair of roller skates

5. What was the first name of Mrs. O'Leary, whose cow allegedly started the Great Chicago Fire when she kicked over a burning lamp?

A. Maggie
B. Kate
C. Colleen
D. Millie

Answer 1: C—vodka.

Answer 2: B—Protestants.

Answer 3: D—football.

Answer 4: A—Jethro Tull.

Answer 5: A—cook.

BUILDING BLOCKS

1. The name of the building known as the Taj Mahal means:

A. crown palace
B. beautiful tomb
C. living stones
D. four promises

2. Which of the following states can NOT be seen from the top of New York City's Empire State Building (even on a clear day)?

A. New Jersey
B. Connecticut
C. Pennsylvania
D. New Hampshire

3. The Hall of Mirrors is the largest room in what famous structure?

A. Palace of Versailles
B. Leaning Tower of Pisa
C. Eiffel Tower
D. Buckingham Palace

4. The company that built Toronto's CN Tower is Canadian National _____.

A. Engineering
B. Bank
C. Railway
D. Broadcasting

5. When the Petronas Twin Towers were completed in 1998, they became the world's tallest buildings. They're located in Kuala Lumpur in what Southeast Asian nation?

A. Indonesia
B. Philippines
C. Malaysia
D. Singapore

Answer 1: C—Route 66.

Answer 2: B—Morten Andersen.

Answer 3: D—Edmund Brown.

Answer 4: A—a unicycle.

Answer 5: B—Kate.

MURPHY'S LAW

1. A Murphy bed is also known as a:

A. bunk bed
B. hammock
C. waterbed
D. foldaway bed

2. What West Coast city was home to Jack Murphy Stadium (now known as Qualcomm Stadium)?

A. San Francisco
B. Seattle
C. San Diego
D. Los Angeles

3. In the film series of the same name, the character named Alex J. Murphy was better known as:

A. *The Karate Kid*
B. *RoboCop*
C. *Mad Max*
D. *The Terminator*

4. Dale Murphy was a two-time Most Valuable Player in what professional team sport?

A. basketball
B. hockey
C. football
D. baseball

5. What Irish Nobel Prize–winning author wrote the 1938 novel *Murphy*?

A. Molly Keane
B. James Joyce
C. Samuel Beckett
D. Liam O'Flaherty

Answer 1: A—crown palace.

Answer 2: D—New Hampshire.

Answer 3: A—Palace of Versailles (the treaty ending World War I was signed here in 1919).

Answer 4: C—Railway.

Answer 5: C—Malaysia.

MAINE LINE

1. What is the two-letter postal abbreviation for the state of Maine?

A. MA
B. ME
C. MI
D. MN

2. Born in Paris Hill, Maine, what gentleman held the offices of representative, senator, and governor for the state before becoming vice president under Abraham Lincoln?

A. Andrew Johnson
B. James Blaine
C. Hannibal Hamlin
D. George McClellan

3. Which of these Stephen King books was NOT set in his home state of Maine?

A. *It*
B. *Misery*
C. *Cujo*
D. *Insomnia*

4. Which of these superlatives about Maine is NOT true?

A. has the highest percentage of forested area of any state
B. it is the only state that borders only one other state
C. was home to America's first chartered town
D. it contains the northernmost point in the lower 48

5. The Appalachian Trail runs over 2,000 miles from Maine to what southern state?

A. Georgia
B. North Carolina
C. Alabama
D. Florida

Answer 1: D—foldaway bed (the type that disappears into a wall or closet).

Answer 2: C—San Diego.

Answer 3: B—*RoboCop*.

Answer 4: D—baseball.

Answer 5: C—Samuel Beckett.

A LOT IN COMMON

1. Who wrote the 1776 pamphlet *Common Sense*, calling for American independence from Great Britain?

A. Alexander Hamilton
B. Benjamin Franklin
C. John Jay
D. Thomas Paine

2. What legendary jurist wrote the 1881 book *The Common Law*?

A. Salmon P. Chase
B. Oliver Wendell Holmes
C. Charles Evan Hughes
D. Lyman Trumbull

3. Boston Common is all of these, EXCEPT:

A. a near-extinct variety of apple
B. a sitcom of the 1990s
C. one of America's oldest public parks
D. a style of Rockport shoes

4. The popularity of which of these computer innovations—all known by acronyms—led directly to the Y2K scare?

A. COBOL (Common Business-Oriented Language)
B. CMIP (Common Management Information Protocol)
C. CIFS (Common Internet File System)
D. CGI (Common Gateway Interface)

5. *The Book of Common Prayer* is the official prayer book of which of the following religious groups?

A. Jehovah's Witnesses
B. Orthodox Christians
C. Church of England
D. Latter-day Saints

Answer 1: B—ME.

Answer 2: C—Hannibal Hamlin.

Answer 3: B—*Misery* (which was set in Colorado, like *The Shining*).

Answer 4: D—it contains the northernmost point in the lower 48 (that honor goes to Minnesota).

Answer 5: A—Georgia.

SCARLET FEVER

1. What was the name of the lead character in Nathaniel Hawthorne's novel *The Scarlet Letter*?

A. Elizabeth Barton
B. Hester Prynne
C. Jo March
D. Katherine Ormand

2. Cochineal, a scarlet-colored dye, was originally made from:

A. lamb's blood
B. ground seashells
C. crushed insects
D. maple leaves

3. Which of these universities' male sports teams are known as the Scarlet Knights?

A. Temple
B. William & Mary
C. Oral Roberts
D. Rutgers

4. A "scarlet runner" is a type of:

A. plant
B. rug
C. mixed drink
D. bird

5. The story "A Study in Scarlet" marked the first appearance of which literary character?

A. Ellery Queen
B. Hercule Poirot
C. Sherlock Holmes
D. Perry Mason

Answer 1: D—Thomas Paine.

Answer 2: B—Oliver Wendell Holmes.

Answer 3: A—a near-extinct variety of apple.

Answer 4: A—COBOL (which, until 1974, used only two-digit indicators for years).

Answer 5: C—Church of England.

FAMOUS LASTS

1. In 1869, what U.S. state was site of the final (or golden) spike being driven, linking the Central and Union Pacific into a transcontinental railroad?

A. Colorado
B. Kansas
C. Nevada
D. Utah

2. "Hello, Clara?" is the last line from what Oscar-winning film?

A. *The African Queen*
B. *Marty*
C. *Driving Miss Daisy*
D. *Come Back, Little Sheba*

3. Frank Wathernam was the last inmate to leave what infamous prison?

A. Alcatraz
B. Marshalsea
C. Devil's Island
D. San Lucas

4. As of 2012, who was the last U.S. soldier to be executed for desertion?

A. Louis Quigley
B. Benedict Arnold
C. Eddie Slovik
D. William Calley

5. On May 31, 2003, Air France's Concorde service made its very last Paris-to-U.S. flight when it landed safely in what city?

A. Washington
B. Boston
C. New York
D. Los Angeles

Answer 1: B—Hester Prynne.

Answer 2: C—crushed insects.

Answer 3: D—Rutgers.

Answer 4: A—plant.

Answer 5: C—Sherlock Holmes.

NUTS TO YOU

1. What poison is known for having the aroma of bitter almonds?

A. arsenic
B. cyanide
C. strychnine
D. thallium

2. For what purpose did George Washington Carver originally encourage farmers to grow peanuts?

A. peanut oil
B. cattle feed
C. crop rotation
D. peanut butter

3. Who was 19 years of age when he co-wrote "The Christmas Song (Chestnuts Roasting on an Open Fire)"?

A. Paul Anka
B. Burt Bacharach
C. Paul Williams
D. Mel Tormé

4. Which tree is the only nut-bearer native to North America?

A. pecan
B. Brazil nut
C. macadamia
D. cashew

5. "It May Look Like a Walnut" placed at #15 on *TV Guide*'s list of all-time best television sitcom episodes. On what show did this episode appear?

A. *Mr. Ed*
B. *The Twilight Zone*
C. *The Odd Couple*
D. *The Dick Van Dyke Show*

Answer 1: D—Utah.

Answer 2: B—*Marty*.

Answer 3: A—Alcatraz.

Answer 4: C—Eddie Slovik (near the end of World War II).

Answer 5: C—New York (British Airways' Concorde line also ceased operations later that year).

WITH A LITTLE FLASH

1. On what part of a house would you find "flashing"?

A. the flooring
B. the basement
C. the walls
D. the roof

2. In 1976, a severe flash flood in the Big Thompson Canyon proved to be the costliest in what state's history?

A. Colorado
B. Arkansas
C. New Mexico
D. South Dakota

3. Someone who is called a "flash in the pan" could also be described as:

A. a show-off
B. indecisive
C. a one-hit wonder
D. ill-tempered

4. In what year were three American astronauts (Gus Grissom, Edward White, and Roger Chaffee) tragically killed by a flash fire during an Apollo training simulation?

A. 1965
B. 1967
C. 1969
D. 1971

5. Alan Arkin and son Adam appeared in which of these "flashy" motion pictures?

A. *Flash Gordon*
B. *Chu Chu and the Philly Flash*
C. *Jumpin' Jack Flash*
D. *Royal Flash*

Answer 1: B—cyanide.

Answer 2: C—crop rotation.

Answer 3: D—Mel Tormé.

Answer 4: A—pecan.

Answer 5: D—*The Dick Van Dyke Show.*

BUILDING A NEST

1. Where do bumblebees normally nest?

A. in hives
B. underground
C. in trees
D. alongside buildings

2. Where on a ship would you find the crow's nest?

A. on the tallest mast
B. in the galley
C. on the bridge
D. in the engine room

3. The '80s–'90s sitcom *Empty Nest* was a spin-off from what show?

A. *The Hogan Family*
B. *Family Matters*
C. *The Golden Girls*
D. *Wings*

4. During the American Revolution, British General Charles Cornwallis called what city "a hornet's nest of rebellion" because of the fierce fighting of its residents?

A. Boston, Massachusetts
B. Dover, Delaware
C. Annapolis, Maryland
D. Charlotte, North Carolina

5. What actor, who later appeared on TV's *Taxi*, made his big-screen debut in the Oscar-winning 1975 motion picture *One Flew Over the Cuckoo's Nest*?

A. Danny DeVito
B. Tony Danza
C. Christopher Lloyd
D. Randall Carver

Answer 1: D—the roof (it's often used to help waterproof jointed parts of a roof).

Answer 2: A—Colorado.

Answer 3: C—a one-hit wonder.

Answer 4: B—1967.

Answer 5: B—*Chu Chu and the Philly Flash*.

BUG OFF

Questions and answers about bugs, insects & spiders.

1. The poisonous brown recluse spider is identifiable by a silhouette of what shape on its body?

A. crescent
B. hourglass
C. violin
D. teardrop

2. What classic 1960s sitcom once received a visit from Bingo, Bango, Bongo, and Irving, a musical quartet collectively known as the Mosquitoes?

A. *Green Acres*
B. *I Dream of Jeannie*
C. *The Monkees*
D. *Gilligan's Island*

3. What insect's name is a derivation of the sound it makes?

A. katydid
B. cricket
C. bumblebee
D. hornet

4. The 1954 sci-fi film *Them!* told of attacks by what giant insects?

A. grasshoppers
B. ants
C. flies
D. praying mantises

5. What record company, once home to such acts as the Doors, Queen, and the Cars, alternated between featuring a butterfly and a caterpillar on its record labels?

A. Warner Bros.
B. Chrysalis
C. Elektra
D. Sire

Answer 1: B—underground.

Answer 2: A—on the tallest mast (it's where lookouts are often posted).

Answer 3: C—*The Golden Girls*.

Answer 4: D—Charlotte, North Carolina (this was a key reason the city's former NBA team was named the Hornets).

Answer 5: C—Christopher Lloyd (Danny DeVito appeared in the film as well, but it was not his movie debut).

ROMAN IF YOU WANT TO

1. A bar that appears over a Roman numeral indicates:

A. a repetitive number
B. a fraction of 10
C. a negative number
D. to multiply it by 1000

2. Audrey Hepburn won an Oscar for her performance as what princess in the 1953 motion picture *Roman Holiday*?

A. Agnes
B. Ann
C. Amanda
D. Alice

3. A roman à clef book is:

A. based on reality
B. a personal diary
C. not divided into chapters
D. written in an archaic language

4. Lulu Roman was an original cast member of what long-running television series?

A. *Adam-12*
B. *Sesame Street*
C. *Gunsmoke*
D. *Hee Haw*

5. A Roman nose is notable for its prominent:

A. tip
B. bridge
C. nostrils
D. width

Answer 1: C—violin.

Answer 2: D—*Gilligan's Island* (they were portrayed by the Wellingtons, who also sang the show's theme song).

Answer 3: A—katydid.

Answer 4: B—ants.

Answer 5: C—Elektra.

JUST US AUGUSTUSES

1. Augustus Saint-Gaudens was a well-known turn-of-the-century:

A. tennis great
B. physicist
C. sculptor
D. barrister

2. Which of these well-known people did NOT have the middle name Augustus?

A. Charles A. Lindbergh (first solo transatlantic flyer)
B. Thomas A. Watson (assistant to Alexander Graham Bell)
C. Lee A. Iacocca (long-time automotive executive)
D. Samuel A. Maverick (great American cattleman)

3. In the 1971 motion picture *Willy Wonka and the Chocolate Factory*, how did Augustus Gloop lose out on the grand prize?

A. miniaturized by a TV camera
B. blew up like a blueberry
C. fell into a chocolate stream
D. drank a Fizzy Lifting Drink

4. Augustus Caesar was the _____ emperor of Rome.

A. first
B. second
C. third
D. fourth

5. What Scottish landmark borders on Fort Augustus?

A. Edinburgh Castle
B. Loch Ness
C. St. Andrews
D. Hadrian's Wall

Answer 1: D—to multiply it by 1000.

Answer 2: B—Ann.

Answer 3: A—based on reality (it is a French term meaning "novel with key").

Answer 4: D—*Hee Haw* (her real first name was Bertha).

Answer 5: B—bridge.

AN EGG-SAMINATION

1. What Beatles tune was originally known as "Scrambled Eggs" before Paul McCartney penned some proper lyrics?

A. "Come Together"
B. "Yesterday"
C. "Ticket to Ride"
D. "Hey Jude"

2. In what country did doctors first implant a fertilized egg into a woman's womb in 1977, after which she gave birth to the world's first test tube baby?

A. Great Britain
B. Japan
C. the United States
D. Germany

3. The 1947 motion picture *The Egg and I* spawned what film series?

A. Blondie
B. Andy Hardy
C. Ma & Pa Kettle
D. Charlie Chan

4. Ostriches lay the largest eggs and hummingbirds lay the smallest eggs, but what birds lay the largest eggs in relation to their own body size?

A. penguins
B. owls
C. pelicans
D. kiwis

5. In 1878, what U.S. president conducted the very first Easter egg hunt on the White House lawn, a tradition performed annually ever since?

A. Rutherford Hayes
B. Ulysses Grant
C. Grover Cleveland
D. Chester Arthur

Answer 1: C—sculptor.

Answer 2: C—Lee Iacocca (his middle name is Anthony).

Answer 3: C—fell into a chocolate stream.

Answer 4: A—first.

Answer 5: B—Loch Ness.

PLASTIC WRAP

1. "I just want to say one word to you—plastics," revealed Walter Brooke to Dustin Hoffman in which motion picture?

A. *Midnight Cowboy*
B. *Lenny*
C. *The Graduate*
D. *Papillon*

2. The first consumer products made from plastic (celluloid, to be specific) were what?

A. hair combs
B. billiard balls
C. drinking cups
D. film slides

3. In 1827, Dr. Peter Mettauer became the first so-called "plastic surgeon" in the U.S. when he repaired ... what?

A. a cauliflower ear
B. a cleft palate
C. webbed fingers
D. a club foot

4. Which former member of the Beatles recorded albums with the Plastic Ono Band?

A. John Lennon
B. Ringo Starr
C. Paul McCartney
D. George Harrison

5. DuPont chemist Wallace Carothers developed what new plastic material in 1930?

A. lucite
B. plexiglas
C. polypropylene
D. nylon

Answer 1: B—"Yesterday."

Answer 2: A—Great Britain (her name is Louise Brown).

Answer 3: C—Ma & Pa Kettle.

Answer 4: D—kiwis.

Answer 5: A—Rutherford Hayes.

GET THE POINT?

1. In archery, how many points are awarded for a bull's eye?

A. 10
B. 25
C. 50
D. 100

2. What president delivered his "Fourteen Points" speech to Congress in 1918?

A. Warren Harding
B. William Taft
C. Woodrow Wilson
D. Teddy Roosevelt

3. What singer-songwriter composed the children's fable *The Point!*, released in 1971 as both an album and an animated television special?

A. Paul Williams
B. Harry Nilsson
C. Van Dyke Parks
D. Paul Simon

4. Which former NFL star was the author of a book about needlepoint for men?

A. Rosey Grier
B. O.J. Simpson
C. Alex Karras
D. Deacon Jones

5. What William Faulkner novel presented its plot from four different points of view?

A. *Sanctuary*
B. *As I Lay Dying*
C. *Sartoris*
D. *The Sound and the Fury*

Answer 1: C—*The Graduate.*

Answer 2: A—hair combs.

Answer 3: B—a cleft palate.

Answer 4: A—John Lennon.

Answer 5: D—nylon.

YOU'RE THE TOPS

1. The structure of the Earth is comprised of several layers; the top layer is called the:

A. outer core
B. crust
C. upper mantle
D. asthenosphere

2. James Cagney proclaimed: "Made it, ma! Top of the world!" in what classic film?

A. *White Heat*
B. *Yankee Doodle Dandy*
C. *Public Enemy*
D. *Mister Roberts*

3. A "top-sider" is a type of:

A. sailboat
B. tent
C. raincoat
D. shoe

4. Which of the following was a hit single for the Four Tops?

A. "Papa Was a Rollin' Stone"
B. "Ain't Too Proud to Beg"
C. "It's the Same Old Song"
D. "My Girl"

5. Which cast member of NBC's hit *Friends* previously starred in a short-lived Fox sitcom titled *Top of the Heap*?

A. David Schwimmer
B. Jennifer Aniston
C. Matt LeBlanc
D. Lisa Kudrow

Answer 1: A—10.

Answer 2: C—Woodrow Wilson.

Answer 3: B—Harry Nilsson.

Answer 4: A—Rosey Grier.

Answer 5: D—*The Sound and the Fury*.

LEATHER

1. Which of these titles was NOT part of James Fenimore Cooper's collection of books known as *The Leatherstocking Tales*?

A. *The Prairie*
B. *The Pioneers*
C. *The Passenger*
D. *The Pathfinder*

2. What singer portrayed the role of Leather Tuscadero, Pinky's younger sister, on the TV sitcom *Happy Days*?

A. Lita Ford
B. Wendy O. Williams
C. Joan Jett
D. Suzi Quatro

3. Leather is the traditional gift for which wedding anniversary?

A. first
B. third
C. fifth
D. seventh

4. What gentleman's vocals accompanied Stevie Nicks on the hit single "Leather and Lace"?

A. Don Henley
B. Tom Petty
C. Lindsay Buckingham
D. Kenny Loggins

5. In 1709, with his addition of leather, Bartolommeo Cristofori revolutionized ... what?

A. the game of golf
B. the umbrella
C. the piano
D. the shoe

Answer 1: B—crust.

Answer 2: A—*White Heat.*

Answer 3: D—shoe (top-siders are soft leather or canvas shoes with rubber soles).

Answer 4: C—"It's the Same Old Song" (the other three were hits for the Temptations).

Answer 5: C—Matt LeBlanc.

LION EYES

1. What ethologist told the story of Elsa the lioness in her book *Born Free*?

A. Joy Adamson
B. Dian Fossey
C. Anna Merz
D. Jane Goodall

2. What was the name of the aging yet "sensuous" lion at California's Lion Country Safari, who sired 35 cubs in the 16 months prior to his death?

A. Henry
B. Delbert
C. Frasier
D. Clarence

3. A group of lions is called a:

A. herd
B. pride
C. exaltation
D. den

4. What area of London, England, is home to two large lion statues?

A. Oxford Circus
B. Leicester Square
C. Piccadilly Circus
D. Trafalgar Square

5. Despite its changes over the years, what has always appeared directly below Leo the lion's head in the Metro-Goldwyn-Mayer logo?

A. a mask
B. a star
C. the word "trademark"
D. a crown

Answer 1: C—*The Passenger.*

Answer 2: D—Suzi Quatro.

Answer 3: B—third.

Answer 4: A—Don Henley (of the Eagles).

Answer 5: C—the piano (he covered the hammers with leather, allowing the player to alter the tone by the force used on the keys).

HALO THERE

1. What illegal drug is commonly referred to as "angel dust"?

A. heroin
B. cocaine
C. PCP
D. mescaline

2. The "Blue Angels," the U.S. Navy's precision flight team, started out using what type of aircraft?

A. the Grumman Hellcat
B. the Grumman Cougar
C. the McDonnell-Douglas Phantom
D. the McDonnell-Douglas Skyhawk

3. Angel Falls, the world's tallest waterfall, is located in what national park?

A. Galápagos
B. Los Katios
C. Canaima
D. Yosemite

4. The pastry confection known as an "angel wing" is also referred to by what Polish name?

A. paczki
B. chiacchiere
C. csoroge
D. chrusciki

5. Which of the following stadiums was NOT once home to the American League baseball team known as the Angels?

A. Dodger Stadium
B. Anaheim Stadium
C. Wrigley Field
D. Miller Park

Answer 1: A—Joy Adamson.

Answer 2: C—Frasier.

Answer 3: B—pride.

Answer 4: D—Trafalgar Square.

Answer 5: A—mask.

OLYMPIC MOMENTS

1. After a French judge admitted her vote had been influenced, members of which country's mixed pairs ice skating team were awarded belated gold medals for the 2002 Olympics?

A. Austria
B. U.S.
C. Canada
D. Norway

2. What American gold medalist was stripped of his award after raising a gloved fist during the national anthem at the 1968 games?

A. Tommie Smith
B. Ben Johnson
C. Carl Lewis
D. Mike Marsh

3. Who was the only female competitor that was excused from taking a sex test at the 1976 Summer Olympics?

A. Olga Korbut
B. Anne Windsor
C. Nadia Comaneci
D. Kornelia Ender

4. 1996 marked the first time that what nation participated in an Olympics held on American soil?

A. Vietnam
B. Cuba
C. Ethiopia
D. China

5. Name the terrorist group that invaded the Munich Olympic Village in 1972.

A. Sol Rojo
B. 17 November
C. Red Brigade
D. Black September

Answer 1: C—PCP.

Answer 2: A—the Grumman Hellcat.

Answer 3: C—Canaima.

Answer 4: D—chrusciki (pronounced kroosh-CHEE-kee).

Answer 5: D—Miller Park (there was an L.A. stadium known as Wrigley Field where the Angels once played, named after the same chewing gum king as Chicago's more famous Wrigley Field).

BEAN THERE, DONE THAT

1. In what U.S. state did Leon Leonwood (L.L.) Bean open his first retail store?

A. Maine
B. New York
C. Texas
D. Nevada

2. Judge Roy Bean loved to refer to himself as "the law west of ..." what river?

A. the Mississippi
B. the Pecos
C. the Rio Grande
D. the Colorado

3. Who portrayed the role of a San Francisco police detective named Bean in the 1974 motion picture *Freebie and the Bean*?

A. Alan Thicke
B. Alan Alda
C. Alan Arkin
D. Alan Ladd

4. Actor/game show panelist Orson Bean was christened with what name at birth?

A. James Egbert
B. Dallas Burrows
C. Saffron Burrows
D. Dallas Egbert

5. Alan L. Bean was famous as:

A. an astronaut who landed on the moon
B. a character portrayed by comedian Rowan Atkinson
C. a Grand Ole Opry star nicknamed String Bean
D. the first man ever taken in the MLB amateur draft

Answer 1: C—Canada.

Answer 2: A—Tommie Smith.

Answer 3: B—Anne Windsor (better known as Britain's Prince Anne, she participated in the three-day equestrian event).

Answer 4: A—Vietnam.

Answer 5: D—Black September.

COURTING LAWYERS

1. Marvin Mitchelson made "palimony" a household word when he represented the spurned lover of what celebrity?

A. Anthony Quinn
B. Phil Spector
C. Rod Stewart
D. Lee Marvin

2. High-profile attorney Melvin Belli played "Friendly Angel" Gorgan in an episode of what television series?

A. *Star Trek*
B. *The X-Files*
C. *Lost in Space*
D. *Space: 1999*

3. Clarence Darrow was coaxed out of retirement to defend what infamous duo?

A. Charles Starkweather & Caril Fugate
B. Sacco & Vanzetti
C. Julius & Ethel Rosenberg
D. Leopold & Loeb

4. Flamboyant barrister and Jack "Dr. Death" Kevorkian mouthpiece Geoffrey Fieger has a brother (Doug) who served as the lead singer for which rock band?

A. the Replacements
B. the Knack
C. the Romantics
D. the Kingsmen

5. For what does the "F." stand in the name F. Lee Bailey?

A. Florian
B. Frederic
C. Francis
D. Ferdinand

Answer 1: A—Maine.

Answer 2: B—the Pecos.

Answer 3: C—Alan Arkin.

Answer 4: B—Dallas Burrows.

Answer 5: A—an astronaut who landed on the moon (he did so as a member of the Apollo XII mission).

COUNTIN' FOUNTAINS

1. According to tradition, if you throw a coin over your left shoulder into this fountain, you will return to Rome one day. Name it.

A. Tritone
B. Trevi
C. Bellagio
D. Tivoli

2. What long-running sitcom's opening credits included a shot of Chicago's Buckingham Fountain?

A. *Family Matters*
B. *Who's the Boss?*
C. *Full House*
D. *Married ... With Children*

3. On what island did Juan Ponce de León believe he would find the fabled Fountain of Youth?

A. Bimini
B. Antigua
C. Aruba
D. Cuba

4. Legend has it that which actress was discovered sitting at the soda fountain in Schwab's Drug Store in Hollywood?

A. Jayne Mansfield
B. Marilyn Monroe
C. Lana Turner
D. Ava Gardner

5. Who patented the first practical fountain pen back in 1884?

A. Lewis Waterman
B. Peter Schaefer
C. Alonzo Cross
D. George Parker

Answer 1: D—Lee Marvin.

Answer 2: A—*Star Trek.*

Answer 3: D—Leopold & Loeb.

Answer 4: B—the Knack (whose biggest hit was "My Sharona").

Answer 5: C—Francis.

K9s WITH IQs

Movie dogs with intelligent names.

1. Einstein was the name of what character's dog in the film *Back to the Future*?

A. Marty McFly
B. Emmett Brown
C. Biff Tannen
D. Lorraine Baines

2. What type of dog was Beethoven, star of two feature films, several straight-to-video sequels, and his own television show?

A. beagle
B. Great Dane
C. cocker spaniel
D. St. Bernard

3. Edison was the name of the Potts family dog in which family movie?

A. *Chitty Chitty Bang Bang*
B. *The Secret Garden*
C. *The Sound of Music*
D. *Mary Poppins*

4. A schnauzer named Chaucer was the pet of the character played by what comedic star of the 1978 motion picture *Foul Play*?

A. Steve Martin
B. Robin Williams
C. Chevy Chase
D. Dan Aykroyd

5. In what 1986 motion picture did Nick Nolte try to drown himself in a swimming pool after he lost his dog, Kerouac?

A. *Under Fire*
B. *Down and Out in Beverly Hills*
C. *Heart Beat*
D. *Three Fugitives*

Answer 1: B—Trevi.

Answer 2: D—*Married ... With Children.*

Answer 3: A—Bimini.

Answer 4: C—Lana Turner.

Answer 5: A—Lewis Waterman.

EVERYDAY "PEOPLE"

1. Who was the first American president to appear on the cover of *People* magazine?

A. John F. Kennedy
B. Jimmy Carter
C. Richard Nixon
D. Gerald Ford

2. The 2008 Summer Olympic Games were held in what city in the People's Republic of China?

A. Beijing
B. Tianjin
C. Shanghai
D. Guangzhou

3. The organization PETA stands for "People for ..." what?

A. Environmental Terrestrial Alternatives
B. Eradication of Taxation in America
C. Ethical Treatment of Animals
D. Ecological Trade in Asia

4. Which airline absorbed the no-frills carrier known as People Express in 1987?

A. U.S. Air
B. Continental
C. Delta
D. TWA

5. Which of these actresses spent two years (before Hollywood came calling) as a member of the "feel good" entertainment group known as Up With People?

A. Julia Roberts
B. Meg Ryan
C. Sally Field
D. Glenn Close

Answer 1: B—Emmett Brown (back in 1955, his dog's name was Copernicus).

Answer 2: D—St. Bernard.

Answer 3: A—*Chitty Chitty Bang Bang.*

Answer 4: C—Chevy Chase.

Answer 5: B—*Down and Out in Beverly Hills.*

READY, AIM ...

Famous job firings.

1. What variety show host fired crooner Julius LaRosa live, on the air?

A. Ed Sullivan
B. Arthur Godfrey
C. Jack Paar
D. Art Linkletter

2. Which member of the Beatles received a black eye (from a fan) during a scuffle outside of Liverpool's Cavern Club after the firing of drummer Pete Best became public?

A. George Harrison
B. John Lennon
C. Paul McCartney
D. Ringo Starr

3. How many times was Billy Martin fired (or "forced to resign") as manager of the New York Yankees?

A. twice
B. three times
C. four times
D. five times

4. Richard Nixon's presidency was doomed after he tried to force the hand of what attorney general to fire Watergate special prosecutor Archibald Cox?

A. Richard Kleindienst
B. John Mitchell
C. Elliot Richardson
D. William Saxbe

5. What U.S. President fired the country's air traffic controllers after he determined that they were violating the law when they went on strike?

A. George H.W. Bush
B. Jimmy Carter
C. Ronald Reagan
D. Gerald Ford

Answer 1: D—Gerald Ford.

Answer 2: A—Beijing.

Answer 3: C—Ethical Treatment of Animals.

Answer 4: B—Continental.

Answer 5: D—Glenn Close.

THE MIGHTY MISSISSIPPI

1. Heading from Cincinnati to New Orleans, what was the name of the riverboat that Mark Twain booked passage on for $16 in *Life on the Mississippi*?

A. *Anna Augusta*
B. *Paul Jones*
C. *River Master*
D. *Delta Queen*

2. What is the only waterfall on the entire length of the Mississippi River?

A. St. Anthony Falls
B. Niagara Falls
C. Tahquamenon Falls
D. Sable Falls

3. What famous weapon was developed as a result of an 1827 duel fought on a sandbar in the Mississippi River?

A. Derringer pistol
B. Marine sword
C. Elgin Cutlass pistol
D. Bowie knife

4. Which of these European explorers is popularly credited with "discovering" the Mississippi River?

A. Zebulon Pike
B. John Cabot
C. Hernando de Soto
D. Sir Francis Drake

5. What entertainer performed the classic Mississippi River song "Ol' Man River" on Broadway in the musical *Show Boat*, and ultimately made it his signature tune?

A. Paul Robeson
B. Harry Belafonte
C. Josh White
D. Cab Calloway

Answer 1: B—Arthur Godfrey.

Answer 2: A—George Harrison.

Answer 3: D—five times (in 1978, 1979, 1983, 1985, and 1988).

Answer 4: C—Elliot Richardson.

Answer 5: C—Ronald Reagan.

GREETING CARDS

1. Which of the following is true about Joyce Hall, the founder of Hallmark Cards?

A. was blind
B. was an atheist
C. was illiterate
D. was a man

2. Which of these films told the story of a character who tried to make a living as a writer of greeting cards?

A. *Mr. Magoo*
B. *Mr. Deeds*
C. *Mr. Saturday Night*
D. *Mr. Destiny*

3. Second only to Christmas, on which of these holidays are the most greeting cards sent annually in the U.S.?

A. Valentine's Day
B. Mother's Day
C. Easter
D. Father's Day

4. Which of these legendary comic book artists started out by designing greeting cards?

A. Kevin Eastman
B. Stan Lee
C. Bob Kane
D. Robert Crumb

5. What TV spy often tried to pass himself off as a salesman for the Pontiac Greeting Card Company?

A. John Steed
B. Napoleon Solo
C. Maxwell Smart
D. Alexander Scott

Answer 1: B—*Paul Jones.*

Answer 2: A—St. Anthony Falls (in Minnesota).

Answer 3: D—Bowie knife.

Answer 4: C—Hernando de Soto.

Answer 5: A—Paul Robeson.

WE HAVE THE POWER!

1. What author penned the successful book *The Power of Positive Thinking*?

A. Robert Ringer
B. Horatio Alger
C. George Santanaya
D. Norman Vincent Peale

2. Which of these was NOT a color of one of the Mighty Morphin' Power Rangers?

A. Yellow
B. Purple
C. Black
D. Pink

3. Three raised to the fourth power is equal to:

A. 12
B. 27
C. 81
D. 243

4. "Fight the Power" was a 1990 hit for which rap group?

A. Run-D.M.C.
B. Boogie Down Productions
C. Public Enemy
D. EPMD

5. In what year was the "Power Mac" (a version of the Apple Macintosh computer based on the Power PC processor) first offered to the public?

A. 1984
B. 1989
C. 1994
D. 1999

Answer 1: D—was a man (full name Joyce Clyde Hall).

Answer 2: B—*Mr. Deeds.*

Answer 3: A—Valentine's Day.

Answer 4: D—Robert Crumb.

Answer 5: C—Maxwell Smart.

EDDIE, EDIE, IDI ...
Let's call the whole thing off.

1. In 1934, Seattle native Eddie Bauer patented a
regulation-sized shuttlecock which popularized what
sport in the U.S.?

A. archery
B. badminton
C. skeet shooting
D. tennis

2. Model/'60s cult icon Edie Sedgwick was a protégé of
what quirky artist?

A. Roy Lichtenstein
B. Salvador Dalí
C. Peter Max
D. Andy Warhol

3. In oceanography, an "eddy" is defined as:

A. a water current that runs contrary to the main current
B. water that falls back from the flood stage
C. a broad, deep undulation of the ocean
D. a narrow surface current that flows away from shore

4. Who was the president of Uganda immediately before and after Idi Amin's reign?

A. Milton Obote
B. Robert Mugabe
C. Jean-Bidel Bokassa
D. Jomo Kenyatta

5. Husband and wife Steve Lawrence and Eydie Gorme first met while each was appearing on what television show?

A. *The Perry Como Show*
B. *The Tonight Show*
C. *Texaco Star Theatre*
D. *Your Hit Parade*

Answer 1: D—Norman Vincent Peale.

Answer 2: B—Purple.

Answer 3: C—81 (3 × 3 × 3 × 3 = 81).

Answer 4: C—Public Enemy.

Answer 5: C—1994.

EIGHT ARMS TO HOLD YOU

1. What British singer once played with a semi-fictional backing band known as the Spiders from Mars?

A. Ian Hunter
B. Cliff Richard
C. David Bowie
D. Al Stewart

2. A spider ordinarily has eight legs and also eight:

A. teeth
B. poison glands
C. spinnerets
D. eyes

3. Who was convicted of negligent homicide in the 1976 shooting death of skiing champion Spider Sabich?

A. Catherine Deneuve
B. Liv Ullmann
C. Claudine Longet
D. Jacqueline Bisset

4. What dancer's first performance with Fred Astaire (who was to become her regular dance partner) was seen in the motion picture *Daddy Long Legs?*

A. Barrie Chase
B. Leslie Caron
C. Ginger Rogers
D. Cyd Charisse

5. The novel *Kiss of the Spider Woman* is set in what country?

A. Colombia
B. Argentina
C. Brazil
D. Mexico

Answer 1: B—badminton.

Answer 2: D—Andy Warhol.

Answer 3: A—a water current that runs contrary to the main current.

Answer 4: A—Milton Obote.

Answer 5: B—*The Tonight Show.*

INITIAL OFFERING

Identify the correct initials for these well-known companies and brands.

1. __. __. Kraft (food)

A. J.L.
B. F.A.
C. B.F.
D. J.Q.

2. __. __. Woolworth (retail stores)

A. R.M.
B. W.H.
C. A.B.
D. F.W.

3. __. __. Heinz (food)

A. P.D.
B. V.O.
C. H.J.
D. C.A.

4. __. __. Smucker (jams & jellies)

A. A.S.
B. J.M.
C. T.L.
D. J.D.

5. __. __. Reese (candy)

A. E.A.
B. Y.A.
C. M.W.
D. H.B.

Answer 1: C—David Bowie (in the Ziggy Stardust era).

Answer 2: D—eyes.

Answer 3: C—Claudine Longet.

Answer 4: A—Barrie Chase.

Answer 5: B—Argentina.

ACCENTS

Identify these five accents, used in various foreign languages.

1. ^

A. acute
B. circumflex
C. grave
D. tilde
E. umlaut

2. ¨

A. acute
B. circumflex
C. grave
D. tilde
E. umlaut

3. `

A. acute
B. circumflex
C. grave
D. tilde
E. umlaut

4. ´

A. acute
B. circumflex
C. grave
D. tilde
E. umlaut

5. ~

A. acute
B. circumflex
C. grave
D. tilde
E. umlaut

Answer 1: A—J.L. (James Lewis Kraft).

Answer 2: D—F.W. (Frank Winfield Woolworth).

Answer 3: C—H.J. (Henry John Heinz).

Answer 4: B—J.M. (Jerome Monroe Smucker).

Answer 5: D—H.B. (Harry Burnett Reese).

NICK OF TIME

1. Nick Carraway was the narrating lead character in which classic novel?

A. *The Great Gatsby*
B. *A Farewell to Arms*
C. *The Catcher in the Rye*
D. *Of Mice and Men*

2. Nick Faldo and Nick Price are both known for their prowess in what sport?

A. billiards
B. auto racing
C. golf
D. tennis

3. What is the parent company of the Nickelodeon and Nick at Nite television network?

A. Paramount
B. Turner
C. Fox
D. Viacom

4. Nick and Nora Charles were a detective couple developed by what author?

A. Raymond Chandler
B. Dashiell Hammett
C. Erle Stanley Gardner
D. Rex Stout

5. Nick Carter was a member of which of these boy bands?

A. 98°
B. 'N Sync
C. Backstreet Boys
D. New Edition

Answer 1: B—circumflex.

Answer 2: E—umlaut.

Answer 3: C—grave.

Answer 4: A—acute.

Answer 5: D—tilde.

TRADE & LABOR UNIONS

1. What Nobel Peace Prize recipient was instrumental in the foundation of Solidarity, Poland's first independent trade union?

A. Leonid Brezhnev
B. Alexander Dubcek
C. Lech Walesa
D. Vaclav Havel

2. What union was behind the "Look for the Union Label" advertising campaign?

A. ILGWU (International Ladies' Garment Workers' Union)
B. AFL-CIO (American Federation of Labor/Congress of Industrial Organizations)
C. UAW (United Auto Workers)
D. AFSCME (American Federation of State, County & Municipal Employees)

3. Dr. Martin Luther King Jr. made that fateful trip to Memphis in 1968 to support striking workers of what profession?

A. teachers
B. garbage collectors
C. firemen
D. bricklayers

4. The original Teamsters union was formed to protect:

A. coal miners
B. stevedores
C. railroad porters
D. horse carriage drivers

5. When she joined the American Newspapers Guild, who became the very first U.S. First Lady to become a union member?

A. Jackie Kennedy
B. Pat Nixon
C. Eleanor Roosevelt
D. Lou Hoover

Answer 1: A—*The Great Gatsby*.

Answer 2: C—golf.

Answer 3: D—Viacom.

Answer 4: B—Dashiell Hammett.

Answer 5: C—Backstreet Boys.

THE WRONG SONG?

1. "Entry of the Gladiators" is best known as the song that
is heard:

A. during "Final Jeopardy"
B. at the circus
C. during military funerals
D. before Warner Bros. cartoons

2. What's the title of the bugle tune sounded as the
introduction to a horse race?

A. "Hunting Fanfare"
B. "First Call"
C. "Horse and Horn"
D. "The King's Saddle"

3. What song was used as the theme for the Three Stooges?

A. "Mary Had a Little Lamb"
B. "The Alphabet Song"
C. "Merrily We Roll Along"
D. "Three Blind Mice"

4. Which of these Christmas carols is sung to the tune of "Greensleeves"?

A. "What Child Is This?"
B. "Jingle Bells"
C. "Good King Wenceslas"
D. "We Three Kings"

5. Which song was adopted as the national anthem of the Confederate States of America by its Congress in 1861?

A. "Bonnie Blue Flag"
B. "Heart of Oak"
C. "Dixie"
D. "Swanee River"

Answer 1: C—Lech Walesa.

Answer 2: A—ILGWU (International Ladies' Garment Workers' Union).

Answer 3: B—garbage collectors.

Answer 4: D—horse carriage drivers.

Answer 5: C—Eleanor Roosevelt.

ONE ELVIS, TWO ELVII

1. Elvis Stojko won two Olympic silver medals in figure skating for his home country of:

A. the United States
B. Hungary
C. Poland
D. Canada

2. What singer broke Elvis Presley's long-standing record of 22 consecutive years with at least one Top 40 hit single on the pop charts?

A. Elton John
B. Michael Jackson
C. Stevie Wonder
D. Aretha Franklin

3. Elvis Buzzard (and his "Pappy") appeared in a series of cartoons for:

A. Hanna-Barbera
B. Walt Disney
C. Walter Lantz
D. Warner Bros.

4. Quarterback Elvis Grbac retired from pro football after signing with what team in 2001 and failing to take them back to the Super Bowl?

A. New York Giants
B. Pittsburgh Steelers
C. Baltimore Ravens
D. San Francisco 49ers

5. Which of these is NOT an alias that musician Elvis Costello has used during his recording career?

A. Roscoe DeVille
B. Howard Coward
C. Dagwood Pimple
D. Napoleon Dynamite

Answer 1: B—at the circus.

Answer 2: B—"First Call."

Answer 3: D—"Three Blind Mice."

Answer 4: A—"What Child Is This?"

Answer 5: A—"Bonnie Blue Flag."

DREAM A LITTLE DREAM

1. "A Dream Is a Wish Your Heart Makes" was originally featured in what Disney film?

A. *Cinderella*
B. *Snow White*
C. *Pinocchio*
D. *Lady and the Tramp*

2. Martin Luther King Jr. made his "I have a dream" speech in front of what Washington, D.C., landmark?

A. Washington Monument
B. U.S. Capitol
C. Lincoln Memorial
D. Supreme Court

3. Who coached the U.S. basketball "Dream Team" to a gold medal at the 1992 Barcelona Olympic Games?

A. George Karl
B. Chuck Daly
C. Larry Brown
D. Pat Riley

4. Which of the following was NOT a fairy in William Shakespeare's *A Midsummer Night's Dream*?

A. Titania
B. Puck
C. Merriweather
D. Oberon

5. What TV sitcom's final episode revealed that the previous seasons had all been a dream?

A. *Taxi*
B. *Newhart*
C. *Cheers*
D. *Who's the Boss?*

Answer 1: D—Canada.

Answer 2: A—Elton John (he still holds the record at 30 years, ending in 2000).

Answer 3: D—Warner Bros.

Answer 4: C—Baltimore Ravens.

Answer 5: C—Dagwood Pimple.

THE AREA FORMERLY KNOWN AS ...

We provide the former name of a region/country; you identify its modern-day equivalent.

1. Asia Minor

A. Bahrain
B. Syria
C. Iraq
D. Turkey

2. Formosa

A. Taiwan
B. Singapore
C. Hong Kong
D. Korea

3. Dacia

A. Bulgaria
B. Romania
C. Greece
D. Hungary

4. Ceylon

A. Curaçao
B. Fiji
C. Sri Lanka
D. Bangladesh

5. Dutch Guiana

A. Suriname
B. Colombia
C. Venezuela
D. Panama

Answer 1: A—*Cinderella.*

Answer 2: C—Lincoln Memorial

Answer 3: B—Chuck Daly.

Answer 4: C—Merriweather.

Answer 5: B—*Newhart.*

GONE TO SEED

1. What was the real last name of American folk hero Johnny Appleseed?

A. Billings
B. Ward
C. Alden
D. Chapman

2. Who wrote the novel *Dragon Seed*?

A. Thomas Merton
B. Pearl S. Buck
C. William March
D. Sir Laurens Van Der Post

3. The "Seed Dry Plate" was a revolutionary:

A. political party
B. dental prosthetic
C. photographic device
D. gold-mining aid

4. Hartz Mountain, the leading purveyor of birdseed, is named after a peak in what country?

A. Germany
B. Canada
C. New Zealand
D. Kenya

5. In 1701, who invented the seed-planting drill?

A. Thomas Coke
B. Eli Whitney
C. Jethro Tull
D. Robert Bakewell

Answer 1: D—Turkey.

Answer 2: A—Taiwan.

Answer 3: B—Romania.

Answer 4: C—Sri Lanka.

Answer 5: A—Suriname.

JAWS CAUSE

1. Which of the following saltwater creatures is NOT a type of shark?

A. porbeagle
B. mako
C. dogfish
D. remora

2. Shark Island was an infamous Civil War–era prison in what U.S. state?

A. Pennsylvania
B. North Carolina
C. Florida
D. Maryland

3. What author published a compilation of works titled *The Great Shark Hunt*?

A. Thomas Wolfe
B. Aldous Huxley
C. Ken Kesey
D. Hunter S. Thompson

4. A young shark is known as a:

A. cub
B. sprag
C. pup
D. spike

5. Which of these motion pictures revolved around a fictional professional football team known as the Miami Sharks?

A. *The Longest Yard*
B. *Any Given Sunday*
C. *Semi-Tough*
D. *The Replacements*

Answer 1: D—Chapman.

Answer 2: B—Pearl S. Buck.

Answer 3: C—photographic device.

Answer 4: A—Germany.

Answer 5: C—Jethro Tull.

DOIN' THE LAUNDRY

1. What company introduced the first automatic washing machine at the Louisiana State Fair back in 1937?

A. Kenmore
B. Bendix
C. Whirlpool
D. Seeburg

2. Which of these children's literary characters created havoc at a laundromat by adding too much "Sudso" to the wash?

A. the Cat in the Hat
B. Homer Price
C. Madeline
D. Curious George

3. The 1986 film *My Beautiful Laundrette* was the star-making vehicle for which actor?

A. Daniel Day-Lewis
B. Hugh Grant
C. Gary Sinise
D. Liam Neeson

4. What color liquid mixture has long been sold as a laundry wash water additive in order to make whites come out whiter?

A. blue
B. green
C. red
D. yellow

5. The ghost of what former First Lady can allegedly still be seen heading toward the East Room of the White House, her outstretched arms filled with laundry?

A. Sarah Polk
B. Dolley Madison
C. Martha Washington
D. Abigail Adams

Answer 1: D—remora (the remora, or suckerfish, attaches itself to larger creatures such as sharks in order to feed).

Answer 2: C—Florida.

Answer 3: D—Hunter S. Thompson.

Answer 4: A—cub.

Answer 5: B—*Any Given Sunday*.

WORTH YOUR SALT?

1. What is the active ingredient in smelling salts?

A. vinegar
B. capsaicin
C. sulfur
D. ammonia

2. The "Old Salt Route," a major medieval trade passage, is located in the northern part of what country?

A. Germany
B. China
C. Spain
D. Egypt

3. The superstition of spilled salt equaling bad luck is thought to be linked to the overturned salt cellar in what famous painting?

A. *American Gothic*
B. *The Spirit of '76*
C. *The Last Supper*
D. *The Birth of Venus*

4. The SALT II treaty was signed by Jimmy Carter and:

A. Mikhail Gorbachev
B. Konstantin Chernenko
C. Yuri Andropov
D. Leonid Brezhnev

5. What Biblical figure's wife was turned into a pillar of salt?

A. Moses
B. Lot
C. Noah
D. Abraham

Answer 1: B—Bendix.

Answer 2: D—Curious George.

Answer 3: A—Daniel Day-Lewis.

Answer 4: A—blue.

Answer 5: D—Abigail Adams.

CLAY IS OKAY

1. The first cable car in the world began service in 1873 on Clay Street in what city?

A. Omaha
B. Montreal
C. San Francisco
D. Vienna

2. In 1850, Senator (and former presidential candidate) Henry Clay introduced what would become known as "Clay's Compromise," which:

A. made campaign contributions legal
B. fixed the terms of U.S. Senators
C. made California a new non-slave state
D. gave Native Americans the right to vote

3. In what year did Cassius Clay win an Olympic gold medal for boxing in the light heavyweight division?

A. 1956
B. 1960
C. 1964
D. 1968

4. What Texas city's name is Spanish for "yellow," referencing the color of the clay on the banks of a stream that ran near the town?

A. Pecos
B. Nacogdoches
C. Laredo
D. Amarillo

5. What is mixed with clay, baked in a kiln, and then pulverized in order to make Portland cement?

A. limestone
B. shale
C. quartz
D. soapstone

Answer 1: D—ammonia.

Answer 2: A—Germany.

Answer 3: C—The Last Supper.

Answer 4: D—Leonid Brezhnev (SALT stood for Strategic Arms Limitation Treaty).

Answer 5: B—Lot.

SPECTACLES OF GLORY

1. "Lorgnette" is the proper term for a pair of glasses with ... what?

A. a handle
B. jeweled frames
C. progressive tint
D. square lenses

2. What service organization began the practice of collecting used eyeglasses in the U.S. for distribution in developing nations (for their underprivileged citizens)?

A. Rotary Club
B. Benevolent and Protective Order of Elks
C. Lions Club
D. Optimists Club

3. Paintings of which Roman emperor suggest that he may have been nearsighted, as he sometimes wore a monocle?

A. Augustus
B. Tiberius
C. Claudius
D. Nero

4. Which of the following women could be identified by her red-framed eyeglasses?

A. Janet Reno
B. Carrie Donovan
C. Sally Jessy Raphael
D. Anne Slater

5. Who was the first major league baseball pitcher to throw a no-hitter while wearing eyeglasses?

A. Cy Young
B. Bill "Bullfrog" Dietrich
C. Grover Cleveland Alexander
D. Robert "Lefty" Grove

Answer 1: C—San Francisco.

Answer 2: C—made California a non-slave state (this followed his similar "Missouri Compromise").

Answer 3: B—1960.

Answer 4: D—Amarillo.

Answer 5: A—limestone.

OH, DEER

1. Name the U.S. president known for having a sign on his desk that read "The Buck Stops Here."

A. Dwight Eisenhower
B. Woodrow Wilson
C. Franklin Roosevelt
D. Harry Truman

2. Former Washington secretary Fawn Hall made newspaper headlines in 1986 for her expertise with what piece of office equipment?

A. paper shredder
B. typewriter
C. fax machine
D. photocopier

3. Who was inspired to establish a Vietnam memorial while consulting on the film *The Deer Hunter*?

A. John Wheeler
B. Jan Scruggs
C. Ron Kovic
D. John Warner

4. What automaker's luxury model, produced from 1970 to 1977, was known as the Stag?

A. Triumph
B. Audi
C. Renault
D. Volkswagen

5. Samuel Doe, captured and killed by rebel forces during a revolution in 1990, was the president of what African nation?

A. Kenya
B. Angola
C. Liberia
D. South Africa

Answer 1: A—a handle.

Answer 2: C—Lions Club.

Answer 3: D—Nero.

Answer 4: C—Sally Jessy Raphael.

Answer 5: B—Bill "Bullfrog" Dietrich.

PICTURE THIS

1. Who was the first president of the Academy of Motion Picture Arts and Sciences?

A. Harold Lloyd
B. Mary Pickford
C. Douglas Fairbanks Sr.
D. Frank Capra

2. Who penned the classic novel about vanity and superfluous desire titled *The Picture of Dorian Gray*?

A. Oscar Wilde
B. Thomas Hardy
C. F. Scott Fitzgerald
D. Nathaniel Hawthorne

3. The sand dunes, cliffs, and beaches of Pictured Rocks National Lakeshore are located in Munising in what U.S. state?

A. Maine
B. Oregon
C. Nevada
D. Michigan

4. Rod Stewart's album *Every Picture Tells a Story* spawned what #1 hit single?

A. "Downtown Train"
B. "Maggie May"
C. "Tonight's the Night"
D. "Young Turks"

5. Which comedian hosted a segment on the *Captain Kangaroo* show known as "Picture Pages"?

A. Steve Martin
B. Buddy Hackett
C. Robin Williams
D. Bill Cosby

Answer 1: D—Harry Truman.

Answer 2: A—paper shredder (she claimed to have assisted Oliver North in the shredding of documents relating to the Iran-Contra affair).

Answer 3: B—Jan Scruggs.

Answer 4: A—Triumph.

Answer 5: C—Liberia.

MATH IN THE MOVIES

1. High school math teacher Edward James Olmos gets a group of inner city kids to learn calculus in what 1988 film?

A. *Lean on Me*
B. *The Principal*
C. *Stand and Deliver*
D. *It's My Turn*

2. Who directed the 1971 film *Straw Dogs*, in which the bored wife of mathematician Dustin Hoffman mischievously changes a plus sign to a minus sign in a set of his gravitational equations?

A. Sam Peckinpah
B. Francis Ford Coppola
C. Martin Scorsese
D. Stanley Kubrick

3. Two men are given a five-gallon and a three-gallon jug and must put exactly four gallons of water on a scale (to keep a bomb from exploding) in the third film in what series?

A. *Lethal Weapon*
B. *Dirty Harry*
C. *Die Hard*
D. *RoboCop*

4. In the 1996 film *The Mirror Has Two Faces*, hunky math professor Jeff Bridges explains the twin prime conjecture to what actress?

A. Mercedes Ruehl
B. Isabella Rossellini
C. Andie MacDowell
D. Barbra Streisand

5. Former teacher Mel Gibson shows a boy how to find the center of any circle by constructing the perpendicular bisectors of the two chords (whew!) in *The Man Without a Face*. In what country was Mel born?

A. the United States
B. Scotland
C. Australia
D. South Africa

Answer 1: C—Douglas Fairbanks Sr.

Answer 2: A—Oscar Wilde.

Answer 3: D—Michigan.

Answer 4: B—"Maggie May."

Answer 5: D—Bill Cosby.

RAH RAH RAH
All about NFL cheerleaders.

1. What pro football team's cheerleaders first took the field on September 30, 1962, making them the oldest active cheerleading organization in the NFL?

A. Cowboys
B. Steelers
C. Redskins
D. Rams

2. Since 2004, the Baltimore Ravens have been the only cheerleading squad in the NFL to have:

A. their own plane
B. pompons
C. a live animal mascot
D. male yell-leaders

3. The "Top Cats" are cheerleaders for which of these NFL teams?

A. Panthers
B. Bengals
C. Jaguars
D. Lions

4. The cheerleaders for which of these NFL cities share the same name as the team for which they cheer (with the addition of a well-placed hyphen)?

A. Miami
B. Houston
C. San Diego
D. Cincinnati

5. What beautiful former Dallas Cowboys cheerleader of the early 1980s decided to go the actress route and went on to star on TV's *Dark Justice* and *Silk Stalkings*?

A. Sandra Bullock
B. Kim Basinger
C. Janet Gunn
D. Halle Berry

Answer 1: C—*Stand and Deliver.*

Answer 2: A—Sam Peckinpah.

Answer 3: C—*Die Hard.*

Answer 4: D—Barbra Streisand.

Answer 5: A—the United States (Gibson was born in New York State, although he grew up in Australia).

DRESS FOR SUCCESS
All about men's formal wear.

1. The tuxedo got its name from:

A. a breed of penguin
B. a town in New York
C. the inventor's last name
D. a church in Wales

2. Pratt, Windsor, and four-in-hand all make reference to what piece of men's attire?

A. pocket squares
B. shoes
C. neckties
D. gloves

3. The wide, patterned cravat known as an ascot is properly made of what material?

A. silk
B. wool
C. linen
D. satin

4. You would be correct in wearing a swallowtail coat if the invitation specifies:

A. black tie
B. semi-formal evening
C. white tie
D. formal daytime

5. Notch, peak, and shank are different types of what?

A. cuffs
B. vests
C. socks
D. lapels

Answer 1: C—Redskins.

Answer 2: D—male yell-leaders (and a male stunt team).

Answer 3: A—Panthers.

Answer 4: D—Cincinnati (the team is the Bengals, the cheerleaders are the Ben-Gals).

Answer 5: C—Janet Gunn.

HONK IF YOU'RE HORN-Y

1. In the U.S., the horn of plenty is a common symbol of which holiday?

A. Easter
B. Independence Day
C. Thanksgiving
D. Christmas

2. What was the name of the Green Hornet's car?

A. Stingray
B. Black Beauty
C. Honeybee
D. Mean Machine

3. Klaxon horns, typically found on Model T cars, were used on what vehicle during World War II?

A. jeeps
B. fighter planes
C. submarines
D. tanks

4. What explorer was the first to sail around the southern tip of South America, and name it Cape Horn?

A. Willem Schouten
B. Vasco de Gama
C. John Cabot
D. Ferdinand Magellan

5. Mezzo-soprano Marilyn Horne is considered the world's greatest interpreter of what opera composer?

A. Bellini
B. Rossini
C. Puccini
D. Wagner

Answer 1: B—a town in New York.

Answer 2: C—neckties (they are types of knot).

Answer 3: A—silk.

Answer 4: C—white tie.

Answer 5: D—lapels.

GOIN' TO THE CHAPEL

1. Which of these structures was originally a chapel?

A. Carnegie Hall
B. the Alamo
C. the Tower of London
D. the Washington Monument

2. Which state-chartered university is located in a town called Chapel Hill?

A. Massachusetts
B. California
C. North Carolina
D. Wisconsin

3. Which of the following is true about Majel Barrett, who portrayed Nurse Christine Chapel in the original *Star Trek* television series?

A. she married *Star Trek* creator Gene Roddenberry
B. she was second in command in the show's original pilot
C. she provided the female voice of the ship's computer
D. all of the above

4. Which of these chapels is part of the Vatican?

A. Sistine Chapel
B. Julian Chapel
C. Valois Chapel
D. Brancicci Chapel

5. Name the group that had #1 hit single with "Chapel of Love."

A. Dixie Chicks
B. the Dixiebelles
C. the Dixie Cups
D. the Dixie Hummingbirds

Answer 1: C—Thanksgiving.

Answer 2: B—Black Beauty

Answer 3: C—submarines.

Answer 4: A—William Schouten.

Answer 5: B—Rossini.

SCRABBLE

1. Until 2008, what color was the center square on a standard Scrabble board?

A. pink
B. red
C. light blue
D. dark blue

2. Of the four following Scrabble letters, which is worth the most points?

A. the letter "B"
B. the letter "C"
C. the letter "L"
D. the letter "W"

3. According to the original Scrabble rules, how many extra points does a player receive for using all seven tiles on a rack in a single play?

A. 25
B. 40
C. 50
D. 100

4. The numbers of tiles of each letter in the game were based on their frequency of appearance in English words, with the exception of one letter (which was changed to make the game more playable). Which letter was this?

A. the letter "E"
B. the letter "Q"
C. the letter "S"
D. the letter "T"

5. Selchow & Richter, long-time owner of the Scrabble board game, was bought by Coleco, who went bankrupt and was bought by Milton-Bradley, who was sold to the company that now owns the game. Name this company.

A. Pressman
B. Hasbro
C. Parker Brothers
D. Ideal

Answer 1: B—the Alamo.

Answer 2: C—North Carolina.

Answer 3: D—all of the above.

Answer 4: A—Sistine Chapel.

Answer 5: C—the Dixie Cups.

PIZZA PIZZA

1. What has long been the perennial favorite pizza topping (appearing on more than one-third of pizzas ordered in America)?

A. sausage
B. mushrooms
C. olives
D. pepperoni

2. What Spike Lee motion picture was centered in and around Sal's Pizzeria, located in the Bedford-Stuyvesant area of Brooklyn?

A. *Jungle Fever*
B. *Do the Right Thing*
C. *School Daze*
D. *Crooklyn*

3. Pizzerias began to flourish in the United States after servicemen were exposed to the tasty pies during which war?

A. Korean War
B. World War I
C. World War II
D. Spanish-American War

4. Two of the largest pizza delivery chains, Domino's and Little Caesars, started out in what midwestern state?

A. Illinois
B. Missouri
C. Nebraska
D. Michigan

5. The most common pizza cheese, authentic mozzarella (as has been produced since at least the 7th century) is made from the milk of what type of animal?

A. goat
B. buffalo
C. sheep
D. cow

Answer 1: A—pink (double word score).

Answer 2: D—the letter "W" (4 points).

Answer 3: C—50.

Answer 4: C—the letter "S" (the number of "S" tiles was reduced to limit the number of possible plurals).

Answer 5: B—Hasbro.

THE EPONYMOUS TEST

1. When something is described as being Rube Goldberg–like, it means that it is:

A. artistically abstract
B. kosher
C. unnecessarily complex
D. expensive, but tacky

2. A "Shirley Temple" is a beverage comprised of ginger ale and what?

A. grenadine
B. rum
C. orange juice
D. vermouth

3. In World War II military parlance, a "Mae West" was a:

A. double-barreled cannon
B. flotation device
C. blonde nurse
D. pompous officer

4. The original recipe for chicken Tetrazzini (named in honor of opera soprano Louisa Tetrazzini) called for chicken, mushrooms, spaghetti noodles, and what type of cheese?

A. mozzarella
B. provolone
C. gorgonzola
D. parmesan

5. Massachusetts governor Elbridge Gerry lent his name to the political term "gerrymander," which is a verb meaning to:

A. apply local influence to a national situation
B. organize a meeting of party members
C. rearrange voting districts
D. obstruct passage of a Senate bill

Answer 1: D—pepperoni.

Answer 2: B—*Do the Right Thing*.

Answer 3: C—World War II.

Answer 4: D—Michigan.

Answer 5: B—buffalo.

COPPER

1. Which of these brands of consumer batteries is known for its copper top?

A. Eveready
B. Duracell
C. Ultralife
D. Energizer

2. Which of these landmarks does NOT contain copper?

A. the Gateway Arch
B. the Eiffel Tower
C. the Liberty Bell
D. the Statue of Liberty

3. *Throwing Copper* was a hit album of the 1990s for which band?

A. Everclear
B. Matchbox 20
C. Collective Soul
D. Live

4. What gave the snake known as the copperhead its name?

A. the distinct taste of copper present after being bitten
B. the image of the snake on early copper pennies
C. the copper-alloy tools used to kill the snakes
D. the color of the snake's head

5. Originally known as the Copper Bowl, the college football game now known as the Insight Bowl is held in which southwestern state?

A. Arizona
B. Nevada
C. Utah
D. New Mexico

Answer 1: C—unnecessarily complex.

Answer 2: A—grenadine.

Answer 3: B—flotation device.

Answer 4: D—parmesan.

Answer 5: C—rearrange voting districts.

NOSTALGIC "TROUBLE"

1. What was unique about the dice in the classic board game known as Trouble?

A. they were 12-sided
B. encased in plastic
C. digits instead of pips
D. made of marble

2. What pulp author penned a trio of Western books titled *Trouble Kid*, *Trouble Trail*, and *Trouble in Timberline*?

A. Max Brand
B. Johnston McCulley
C. Frank Gruber
D. Jack Schaefer

3. "The Trouble With Tribbles" was the title of a well-known episode of which of these 1960s television shows?

A. *Bewitched*
B. *Gilligan's Island*
C. *Star Trek*
D. *The Munsters*

4. What member of Fleetwood Mac released a 1981 solo hit single titled "Trouble"?

A. Lindsay Buckingham
B. Christine McVie
C. Mick Fleetwood
D. Stevie Nicks

5. What star of the motion picture *9 to 5* was once quoted as saying: "The trouble with the rat race is that even if you win, you're still a rat"?

A. Dolly Parton
B. Elizabeth Wilson
C. Jane Fonda
D. Lily Tomlin

Answer 1: B—Duracell.

Answer 2: B—the Eiffel Tower (it's made of wrought iron; the Gateway Arch is made of stainless steel containing copper).

Answer 3: D—Live.

Answer 4: D—the color of the snake's head.

Answer 5: A—Arizona.

CIAO, ITALIA

Stories set in Italy.

1. Carol Gino completed *The Family*, a novel about a Renaissance-era family in Rome, after what initial author's death?

A. G.K. Chesterton
B. Dashiell Hammett
C. Raymond Chandler
D. Mario Puzo

2. What actress fell for an American reporter in the 1953 film *Roman Holiday*?

A. Audrey Hepburn
B. Leslie Caron
C. Judy Garland
D. Katharine Hepburn

3. In a 2003 film, Diane Lane portrays a writer who buys a villa in what region of Italy?

A. Campania
B. Umbria
C. Tuscany
D. Sardinia

4. On what sitcom did the title character brawl in a wine vat while studying for a part in the Italian film *Bitter Grapes*?

A. *Roseanne*
B. *I Love Lucy*
C. *That Girl*
D. *Grace Under Fire*

5. What *Dynasty* alum was the star of the 1969–71 sitcom *To Rome With Love*?

A. Joan Collins
B. James Farentino
C. John Forsythe
D. Pamela Sue Martin

Answer 1: B—encased in plastic (specifically, in a bubble with a feature known as Pop-o-matic).

Answer 2: A—Max Brand.

Answer 3: C—*Star Trek*.

Answer 4: A—Lindsay Buckingham.

Answer 5: D—Lily Tomlin.

AMERICA ON PAPER

All about important documents from U.S. history.

1. The Treaty of Ghent, effectively ending the War of 1812, was signed in what country?

A. Switzerland
B. Luxembourg
C. France
D. Belgium

2. Name the last surviving signer of the Declaration of Independence, who passed away at 95 years of age in 1832.

A. Charles Carroll
B. Benjamin Franklin
C. Samuel Chase
D. Elbridge Gerry

3. Originally referred to by critics as "Seward's Folly," the U.S. signed an agreement purchasing what territory for less than two cents per acre?

A. Cuba
B. Alaska
C. Manhattan
D. Louisiana

4. At 9:04 in the morning on September 2, 1945, General Douglas MacArthur affixed his signature to Japan's "Instrument of Surrender" aboard what U.S. ship?

A. USS *Missouri*
B. USS *Indianapolis*
C. USS *Enterprise*
D. USS *Lexington*

5. The obverse (front) of Great Seal of the United States is used on official documents to authenticate the signature of the president. The reverse (back) is not used as a seal, but can be seen:

A. on the Delaware state flag
B. on an obelisk on the moon
C. on the one-dollar bill
D. at the base of the Statue of Liberty

Answer 1: D—Mario Puzo.

Answer 2: A—Audrey Hepburn.

Answer 3: C—Tuscany (the film was titled *Under a Tuscan Sun*).

Answer 4: B—*I Love Lucy*.

Answer 5: C—John Forsythe.

I WANT CANDY

1. A "candy striper" is a volunteer helper in a:

A. library
B. polling place
C. hospital
D. prison

2. John Candy's 1991 film *Only the Lonely* was essentially an update of what Paddy Chayefsky story?

A. *Marty*
B. *The Bachelor Party*
C. *Holiday Song*
D. *Hospital*

3. What brand of boxed candy was the first to include an "index" that indicated the filling of each piece?

A. Whitman
B. Cadbury
C. Fanny Farmer
D. Godiva

4. What poet coined the phrase "candy is dandy, but liquor is quicker"?

A. T.S. Eliot
B. Ogden Nash
C. Robert Frost
D. Carl Sandburg

5. Candy Lightner was the founder of what organization?

A. Parents Music Resource Center
B. Travelers Aid
C. Young Women's Christian Organization
D. Mothers Against Drunk Driving

Answer 1: D—Belgium.

Answer 2: A—Charles Carroll.

Answer 3: B—Alaska.

Answer 4: A—USS *Missouri*.

Answer 5: C—on the one-dollar bill (it's the circle with the pyramid on the bill's back side).

UP A TREE

1. What movie featured grumpy apple trees that pitched their fruit at some unsuspecting, hungry (albeit singing and dancing) wanderers?

A. *Willy Wonka and the Chocolate Factory*
B. *Yellow Submarine*
C. *Spice World*
D. *The Wizard of Oz*

2. Joshua Tree National Park is located in what U.S. state?

A. California
B. Utah
C. Nevada
D. Arizona

3. What legendary vocal group requested that you "don't sit under the apple tree with anyone else but me"?

A. the Lennon Sisters
B. the Ames Brothers
C. the McGuire Sisters
D. the Andrews Sisters

4. Commercials for which brand of cold cereal featured kids in a tree house "hideout"?

A. Trix
B. Cocoa Puffs
C. Honeycomb
D. Kix

5. What was the name of Francie's younger brother in Betty Smith's classic novel *A Tree Grows in Brooklyn*?

A. Ned
B. Neely
C. Newton
D. Nelson

Answer 1: C—hospital (so named after their red and white striped uniforms, which resembled a candy cane).

Answer 2: A—*Marty*.

Answer 3: A—Whitman.

Answer 4: B—Ogden Nash.

Answer 5: D—Mothers Against Drunk Driving.

NEW ZEALAND

1. Name the capital city of New Zealand.

A. Dunedin
B. Wellington
C. Auckland
D. Christchurch

2. Which of these explorers was born in New Zealand?

A. Henry Hudson
B. James Cook
C. Robert Peary
D. Sir Edmund Hillary

3. Back in 1893, New Zealand became the first country to:

A. legalize abortion
B. enact automobile traffic laws
C. allow women to vote
D. be granted dominion status by Great Britain

4. In 1995, what was the name of the New Zealand yacht that became the first from that country (and only the second non-U.S. entry) to win the America's Cup race?

A. *Black Magic*
B. *Kookaburra III*
C. *Southern Cross*
D. *New Zealand*

5. Which of these motion pictures was written and directed by one Oscar-winning New Zealander and won an acting Oscar for another New Zealander?

A. *The Cider House Rules*
B. *The Hours*
C. *The Piano*
D. *The Red Shoes*

Answer 1: D—*The Wizard of Oz.*

Answer 2: A—California.

Answer 3: D—the Andrews Sisters.

Answer 4: C—Honeycomb.

Answer 5: B—Neely.

A GIRL'S BEST FRIEND

1. What color is the legendary Hope Diamond?

A. white
B. pink
C. yellow
D. blue

2. Who played Neil Diamond's love interest in the 1980 remake of the motion picture *The Jazz Singer*?

A. Valerie Perrine
B. Lucie Arnaz
C. Bo Derek
D. Jamie Lee Curtis

3. The Hawaiian landmark known as Diamond Head was formed from:

A. clay
B. magma
C. sand
D. coal

4. What appears with the king of diamonds on a standard English deck of cards?

A. an ax
B. a rose
C. an orb
D. a sword

5. American financier "Diamond Jim" Brady founded a urological institute at which of these medical facilities?

A. Bellevue Hospital
B. Johns Hopkins
C. St. Eligius Hospital
D. Mayo Clinic

Answer 1: B—Wellington.

Answer 2: D—Sir Edmund Hillary (first to reach the summit of Mt. Everest).

Answer 3: C—allow women to vote.

Answer 4: A—*Black Magic*.

Answer 5: C—*The Piano* (the writer/director was Jane Campion; the actor was Anna Paquin).

IN A MAJOR KEY

1. What is a "major-domo"?

A. a primary shareholder
B. a restaurant kitchen
C. a Japanese meeting
D. a chief steward

2. Who wrote the play *Major Barbara*, the story of a disillusioned Salvation Army worker?

A. Harold Pinter
B. George Bernard Shaw
C. Oscar Wilde
D. Arthur Miller

3. Which is true of the 1969 Major League Baseball All-Star Game, but not a single All-Star Game since?

A. played during the day
B. went into extra innings
C. called due to rain
D. ended in a tie

4. TV's *Major Dad* was in what branch of the armed forces?

A. Army
B. Navy
C. Air Force
D. Marines

5. Which of the following is NOT true of former British prime minister John Major?

A. quit school at age 16
B. youngest British prime minister of the 20th century
C. member of the Conservative Party
D. replaced Margaret Thatcher

Answer 1: D—blue.

Answer 2: B—Lucie Arnaz (daughter of Desi Arnaz and Lucille Ball).

Answer 3: B—magma.

Answer 4: A—an ax.

Answer 5: B—Johns Hopkins.

POLITICS IN 1968

1. In March of 1968, Cesar Chavez announced a worldwide boycott of what California food product?

A. grapes
B. lettuce
C. avocados
D. oranges

2. Who was nominated as the Democratic Party's presidential candidate for the 1968 election?

A. George McGovern
B. Hubert Humphrey
C. Lyndon Johnson
D. Walter Mondale

3. What U.S. Navy intelligence vessel was attacked by North Korea on January 23, 1968?

A. USS *Vincennes*
B. USS *Cole*
C. USS *Hazard*
D. USS *Pueblo*

4. What *Smothers Brothers Comedy Hour* regular ran for president in 1968 and garnered 200,000 write-in votes?

A. Don Novello
B. Mason Reese
C. Pat Paulsen
D. Lorenzo Music

5. Harold Holt drowned on December 17, 1967, and was replaced by John Gorton as the prime minister of what country?

A. Canada
B. Jamaica
C. Australia
D. South Africa

Answer 1: D—a chief steward.

Answer 2: B—George Bernard Shaw.

Answer 3: A—played during the day (prior to 1969, most All-Star games were played in daylight; this was changed because TV ratings were better in the evening).

Answer 4: D—Marines.

Answer 5: B—youngest British prime minister of the 20th century (in fact, he did hold this superlative until he was replaced by the even younger Tony Blair in 1997).

IT'S MURDER

1. A group of which of these animals is called a "murder"?

A. squirrels
B. crows
C. porcupines
D. bats

2. What author penned the mystery *The Murders in the Rue Morgue*?

A. Arthur Conan Doyle
B. P.D. James
C. Edgar Allan Poe
D. Agatha Christie

3. What was the name of the character portrayed by Angela Lansbury on TV's *Murder, She Wrote*?

A. Margaret Rutherford
B. Nora Charles
C. Minette Walters
D. Jessica Fletcher

4. Murder, Inc. was an arm of the American Crime Syndicate founded by Bugsy Siegel and:

A. Meyer Lansky
B. Dutch Schulz
C. Abe "Kid Twist" Reles
D. George Rudnick

5. Which of these factors is most important in distinguishing a murder charge from a manslaughter charge?

A. premeditation
B. voluntary status
C. provocation
D. intent

Answer 1: A—grapes.

Answer 2: B—Hubert Humphrey.

Answer 3: D—USS *Pueblo*.

Answer 4: C—Pat Paulsen.

Answer 5: C—Australia.

VIRGINIA

1. Virginia Dare, the first child to be born (in 1587) to English parents in the "New World," was born in (what is now) which U.S. state?

A. Massachusetts
B. Virginia
C. North Carolina
D. Delaware

2. Who made his directorial debut with the 1966 film *Who's Afraid of Virginia Woolf?*

A. Sydney Pollack
B. Mike Nichols
C. Steven Soderbergh
D. Milos Forman

3. Which of these feel-good TV series was set in the Blue Ridge Mountains of Virginia?

A. *The Life and Times of Grizzly Adams*
B. *I'll Fly Away*
C. *Picket Fences*
D. *The Waltons*

4. From 1972 until 1994, Virginia Slims cigarettes were the chief sponsor of what women's professional sport?

A. golf
B. gymnastics
C. tennis
D. bowling

5. What newspaper received a now-famous letter from Virginia O'Hanlon in 1897 inquiring as to the existence of Santa Claus?

A. *Philadelphia Inquirer*
B. *Boston Herald*
C. *New York Sun*
D. *Washington Post*

Answer 1: B—crows.

Answer 2: C—Edgar Allan Poe.

Answer 3: D—Jessica Fletcher.

Answer 4: A—Meyer Lansky.

Answer 5: D—intent (murder may occur with or without premeditation, voluntary status, or provocation, but intent is always a factor—without intent, murder becomes manslaughter).

ROCKIN' ROBIN

1. Name the William Shakespeare work in which Robin Goodfellow remarked: "Lord, what fools these mortals be!"

A. *As You Like It*
B. *Othello*
C. *The Tempest*
D. *A Midsummer Night's Dream*

2. In the original *Batman* comic book series (and the 1960s TV show), the young superhero Robin, the Boy Wonder, was known in civilian life as:

A. Jack Napier
B. Dick Grayson
C. Britt Reid
D. Bruce Wayne

3. Which of the following statements about the American robin is NOT true?

A. female sings during courtship
B. chiefly eats fruit
C. will not nest in marshes
D. migrates south in cold weather

4. Comedian Robin Williams made his Hollywood leading-role debut in which of these motion pictures?

A. *Popeye*
B. *Moscow on the Hudson*
C. *The World According to Garp*
D. *Good Morning, Vietnam*

5. According to legend, Robin Hood was born in what area of Nottinghamshire?

A. Southwell
B. Retford
C. Locksley
D. Mansfield

Answer 1: C—North Carolina (on Roanoke Island).

Answer 2: B—Mike Nichols.

Answer 3: D—*The Waltons*.

Answer 4: C—tennis.

Answer 5: C—*New York Sun*.

COMEDY ALBUMS

Name the comedian who recorded each listed trio of albums.

1. *It's True! It's True! ... 200 MPH ... Why Is There Air?*

A. Bill Murray
B. Bill Cosby
C. Bill Maher
D. Bill Hicks

2. *Indecent Exposure ... On the Road ... What Am I Doing in New Jersey?*

A. Robin Williams
B. Steve Martin
C. Lenny Bruce
D. George Carlin

3. *Have You Seen Me Lately ... Leader of the Banned ... Louder Than Hell*

A. Chris Rock
B. Andrew "Dice" Clay
C. Sam Kinison
D. Eddie Murphy

4. *This Is It ... The Windmills Are Weakening ... Behind the Button-Down Mind*

A. Bob Newhart
B. Carl Reiner
C. Emo Phillips
D. Dick Gregory

5. *Is It Something I Said? ... Wanted ... Who, Me? I'm Not Him*

A. Redd Foxx
B. Lily Tomlin
C. Howie Mandel
D. Richard Pryor

Answer 1: D—*A Midsummer Night's Dream* (Robin Goodfellow is also known as Puck).

Answer 2: B—Dick Grayson.

Answer 3: A—female sings during courtship.

Answer 4: A—*Popeye*.

Answer 5: C—Locksley.

THE PLAIN TRUTH

1. What U.S. president was born and raised in a town known as Plains?

A. Bill Clinton
B. Franklin D. Roosevelt
C. Jimmy Carter
D. Woodrow Wilson

2. *The Plain Dealer* is the best-selling newspaper in which U.S. state?

A. Louisiana
B. Minnesota
C. Arizona
D. Ohio

3. Who directed and starred in the 1973 motion picture Western titled *High Plains Drifter*?

A. Clint Eastwood
B. John Wayne
C. Maureen O'Hara
D. Paul Newman

4. In the Revolutionary War, what leader won the Battle of White Plains in New York state?

A. Henry Knox
B. William Howe
C. George Washington
D. Charles Cornwallis

5. The "Boss of the Plains" was a type of:

A. hat
B. pistol
C. tractor
D. locomotive

Answer 1: B—Bill Cosby.

Answer 2: D—George Carlin.

Answer 3: C—Sam Kinison.

Answer 4: A—Bob Newhart.

Answer 5: D—Richard Pryor.

DESERT TRANSPORTATION
Camel questions & answers

1. A camel's hump contains mostly:

A. water
B. fat
C. bone
D. air

2. Camel brand cigarettes were introduced in 1913 using a logo based on a Barnum & Bailey circus animal named:

A. Quasimodo
B. King
C. Jamel
D. Old Joe

3. In what sport did the "Hamill camel" become a signature move in the 1970s?

A. figure skating
B. roller derby
C. soccer
D. gymnastics

4. What British engine-builder designed the BR1 rotary engine that powered many Sopwith Camel planes during World War I?

A. Healey
B. Bentley
C. Royce
D. Morgan

5. What computer programming language is often referred to by coders as Camel?

A. Visual Basic
B. Java
C. Perl
D. LISP

Answer 1: C—Jimmy Carter

Answer 2: D—Ohio (it is the main newspaper in the city of Cleveland).

Answer 3: A—Clint Eastwood.

Answer 4: B—William Howe (he defeated Washington).

Answer 5: A—hat (it was the name of John Stetson's first version of what became known as the "ten-gallon hat").

IT'S OTTO-MATIC

1. The name "Otto" is German and means:

A. wealth
B. scent
C. eight
D. poet

2. Which comic strip character is the owner of a dog named Otto?

A. Daddy Warbucks ("Annie")
B. Jon Arbuckle ("Garfield")
C. Zonker Harris ("Doonesbury")
D. Sgt. Snorkel ("Beetle Bailey")

3. In the late 19th century, what U.S. state's capital was renamed after a gentleman whose first name was Otto?

A. California
B. North Dakota
C. West Virginia
D. Missouri

4. In what madcap motion picture comedy is an inflatable actor known as Otto credited as playing himself?

A. *Weekend at Bernie's*
B. *The Blues Brothers*
C. *Airplane!*
D. *Caddyshack*

5. Who was the first person named Otto to win a Nobel Prize?

A. Otto Hahn
B. Otto Stern
C. Otto Loewi
D. Otto Wallach

Answer 1: B—fat

Answer 2: D—Old Joe.

Answer 3: A—figure skating (it was a spin developed by American skater Dorothy Hamill).

Answer 4: B—Bentley.

Answer 5: C—Perl (due to Reilly & Associates' use of a camel on the cover of the first Perl programming book).

HAMMER TIME

All about home run king Henry "Hank" Aaron.

1. Hank Aaron began his major league baseball career in Milwaukee. For what city's team did he end his playing days?

A. Milwaukee
B. Cleveland
C. San Diego
D. Atlanta

2. On April 8, 1974, Aaron broke Babe Ruth's long-standing record when he hit his 715th home run. Hank ended his career with how many homers?

A. 785
B. 855
C. 825
D. 755

3. What jersey number did Aaron wear, inspiring many others (such as Reggie Jackson) to wear it as well?

A. 1
B. 13
C. 25
D. 44

4. While his home run record has (arguably) been broken by Barry Bonds, Hank Aaron still leads all major league players in which other career statistic?

A. walks
B. RBIs
C. doubles
D. strikeouts

5. What was the name of Hank's younger brother who played with him on the Braves from 1962 to 1966 and again in 1971?

A. Jimmie
B. Lonnie
C. Tommie
D. Morrie

Answer 1: A—wealth

Answer 2: D—Sgt. Snorkel ("Beetle Bailey"), whose look-alike bulldog is named Otto.

Answer 3: B—North Dakota (the capital is Bismarck, after the German chancellor of the same name).

Answer 4: C—*Airplane!*

Answer 5: D—Otto Wallach (in 1910 for Chemistry; later Nobel winners named Otto included Diels, Hahn, Loewi, Meyerhof, Stern, and Warburg).

THAT'S WHAT I MINT

1. What is the type of alcohol used in the vast majority of versions of the drink known as the mint julep?

A. gin
B. schnapps
C. rum
D. bourbon

2. Clorets brand breath mints and chewing gum have long been advertised as containing ... what?

A. retsyn
B. liquid centers
C. no sugar
D. chlorophyll

3. Where was the first U.S. Mint constructed in 1792?

A. New York
B. Philadelphia
C. Washington
D. Boston

4. "Incense and Peppermints" was a hit for what flavorful group of the late 1960s?

A. the Lemon Pipers
B. Vanilla Fudge
C. Strawberry Alarm Clock
D. the Chocolate Watch Band

5. Which of these herbs is NOT a member of the mint family?

A. parsley
B. sage
C. rosemary
D. thyme

Answer 1: A—Milwaukee (he went with the Braves when they moved from Milwaukee to Atlanta in 1966, then was traded to the Milwaukee Brewers in 1975, retiring after the next year)

Answer 2: D—755.

Answer 3: D—44.

Answer 4: B—RBIs (his 2,297 is still the all-time record).

Answer 5: C—Tommie.

BERRY BERRY GOOD

1. Early American colonists boiled blueberries in milk to make:

A. hair dye
B. gray paint
C. cake frosting
D. alcohol

2. Chuck Berry's only U.S. #1 single on the pop charts was:

A. "Maybellene"
B. "No Particular Place to Go"
C. "My Ding-A-Ling"
D. "Johnny B. Goode"

3. Since 1940, what U.S. state has been home to Knott's Berry Farm amusement park?

A. California
B. Virginia
C. Texas
D. Kentucky

4. What type of berry was once believed to cause birthmarks when eaten by pregnant women?

A. blackberry
B. raspberry
C. blueberry
D. strawberry

5. Hanna-Barbera cartoon character Huckleberry Hound had an obvious fondness for which song?

A. "Camptown Races"
B. "My Darling Clementine"
C. "Carolina in the Morning"
D. "Oh! Susannah"

Answer 1: D—bourbon.

Answer 2: D—chlorophyll.

Answer 3: B—Philadelphia.

Answer 4: C—Strawberry Alarm Clock.

Answer 5: A—parsley.

SECOND CHANCE

Actors who turned down roles in hit films & television series.

1. Predicting it would be the "biggest flop in Hollywood history," Gary Cooper turned down a lead role in what 1939 film blockbuster?

A. *Goodbye, Mr. Chips*
B. *Gone With the Wind*
C. *The Wizard of Oz*
D. *Mr. Smith Goes to Washington*

2. Producer Gary David Goldberg originally had Matthew Broderick in mind for a starring role in which of his TV series?

A. *Lou Grant*
B. *Spin City*
C. *Brooklyn Bridge*
D. *Family Ties*

3. Jerry Van Dyke turned down the title role on the TV sitcom *Gilligan's Island* in favor of what series?

A. *Holmes and Yo-Yo*
B. *Rango*
C. *My Mother the Car*
D. *Me and the Chimp*

4. Although it's said that Ian Fleming modeled James Bond after him, he wasn't interested in playing him on film. Name this actor.

A. Tony Curtis
B. Rock Hudson
C. Cary Grant
D. Anthony Quinn

5. What laid-back crooner was the original choice for TV's Columbo (but turned it down for fear it would interfere with his golf game)?

A. Perry Como
B. Bing Crosby
C. Pat Boone
D. Dean Martin

Answer 1: B—gray paint.

Answer 2: C—"My Ding-A-Ling" (a live version from 1972).

Answer 3: A—California (located in Buena Park).

Answer 4: D—strawberry.

Answer 5: B—"My Darling Clementine."

THE -EX QUIZ

All about companies and brand names ending with the letters "ex."

1. Before it became part of a huge 1996 merger, the company known as NYNEX was in the business of providing:

A. petroleum products
B. stock information
C. telephone service
D. paper goods

2. Which of these brand names was first known as Celucotton?

A. Kotex
B. Purex
C. Playtex
D. Kleenex

3. Which of the following is NOT a trademarked name?

A. Spandex
B. Pyrex
C. Windex
D. Rolodex

4. In 1956, what company introduced the first successful videotape recording unit?

A. Graflex
B. Ampex
C. Timex
D. Asahiflex

5. What product is marketed in England under the name Perspex?

A. Gatorade
B. Febreze
C. Liquid Paper
D. Plexiglas

Answer 1: B—*Gone With the Wind.*

Answer 2: D—*Family Ties.*

Answer 3: C—*My Mother the Car.*

Answer 4: C—Cary Grant.

Answer 5: B—Bing Crosby.

NUMBER NINE ... NUMBER NINE ...

1. A cat-o'-nine tails is a type of:

A. sea anemone
B. whip
C. marshy plant
D. grooming brush

2. According to the nursery rhyme, what was "in the pot, nine days old"?

A. curds and whey
B. pease porridge
C. shortnin' bread
D. cockle shells

3. Which of the nine Muses was the goddess of dancing?

A. Terpsichore
B. Clio
C. Thalia
D. Calliope

4. The 9 Lives spokescat, Morris, is known for being:

A. ambitious
B. lazy
C. destructive
D. finicky

5. Which of these is NOT one of the nine largest objects in our solar system?

A. Mars
B. Ganymede
C. Mercury
D. Earth

Answer 1: C—telephone service (it merged with Bell Atlantic).

Answer 2: A—Kotex.

Answer 3: A—Spandex.

Answer 4: B—Ampex.

Answer 5: D—Plexiglas (and, yes, the brand name is properly spelled with only one "s").

THE SWORD IS THE WORD

1. An imminent menace or threat is often described as the "sword of ..." whom?

A. Daedalus
B. Dionysus
C. Demeter
D. Damocles

2. What brand of razor features crossed swords in its logo?

A. Gillette
B. Wilkinson
C. Schick
D. Remington

3. The town of Swords is located just north of what European city?

A. Rome
B. Madrid
C. Brussels
D. Dublin

4. Which of the following statements is NOT true about the swordfish?

A. females are larger than males
B. one of the slowest fish
C. often migrates over 1,000 miles
D. prefers to feed on squid

5. The legendary King Arthur, who was said to have pulled the sword Excalibur from a stone, was the son of what British king?

A. Gawain
B. Percival
C. Uther
D. Mordred

Answer 1: B—whip.

Answer 2: B—pease porridge.

Answer 3: A—Terpsichore.

Answer 4: D—finicky.

Answer 5: C—Mercury (Ganymede is a moon of Jupiter and is larger than Mercury).

OPERATIC

1. To computer users, "Opera" is a type of:

A. DVD format
B. mouse
C. video card
D. Web browser

2. In 1975, what became the first television soap opera to regularly broadcast hour-long shows?

A. *As the World Turns*
B. *General Hospital*
C. *Another World*
D. *One Life to Live*

3. What rock band recorded the albums *A Night at the Opera* and *A Day at the Races*?

A. Foreigner
B. Queen
C. the Kinks
D. Dream Theater

4. Describe the money that changes hands when someone draws the "Grand Opera Opening" Chance card in a Monopoly game.

A. $150 paid by recipient
B. $50 collected from every player
C. $100 given to recipient
D. $50 paid to every player

5. Portrayed by Lon Chaney, what was the first name of the Phantom of the Opera in the 1925 silent film of the same name?

A. Erik
B. Gerald
C. Sandor
D. Raul

Answer 1: D—Damocles.

Answer 2: B—Wilkinson.

Answer 3: D—Dublin.

Answer 4: B—one of the slowest fish.

Answer 5: C—Uther.

THREE SIDES

1. What road sign is typically shaped like a triangle?

A. speed limit
B. yield
C. merge
D. stop

2. Which Teletubby has a triangle on its head?

A. Dipsy
B. Laa-Laa
C. Po
D. Tinky Winky

3. Tribeca, short for "triangle below Canal," is an area in which U.S. city?

A. New York
B. Chicago
C. New Orleans
D. San Francisco

4. A "tetrahedron" is composed of how many triangles?

A. two
B. three
C. four
D. six

5. In 1911, the Triangle Shirtwaist Factory was the site of a famous:

A. strike
B. fire
C. speech
D. robbery

Answer 1: D—Web browser.

Answer 2: C—*Another World.*

Answer 3: B—Queen.

Answer 4: B—$50 collected from every player.

Answer 5: A—Erik.

PUNCH BOWL

1. A rabbit punch is a blow to what part of the body?

A. kidney
B. groin
C. stomach
D. neck

2. Brought over from Italy, "Punch & Judy" puppet shows have been held in England since:

A. the 1600s
B. the 1700s
C. the 1800s
D. the 1900s

3. Herman Hollerith was known for what contribution to society?

A. the punching bag
B. punch card accounting
C. planter's punch
D. the film *Punchline*

4. In which country was the long-running humor magazine *Punch* based?

A. the U.S.
B. France
C. the Netherlands
D. England

5. Punch Imlach coached what NHL team to four Stanley Cup championships over a six-year span in the 1960s?

A. Toronto Maple Leafs
B. Boston Bruins
C. New York Rangers
D. Montreal Canadiens

Answer 1: B—yield.

Answer 2: D—Tinky Winky.

Answer 3: A—New York.

Answer 4: C—four (it is a four-sided pyramid with triangular sides).

Answer 5: B—fire.

IN THE POUCH

1. Besides Australia, kangaroos are also native to which of these countries?

A. Philippines
B. New Guinea
C. Japan
D. Singapore

2. What company, featuring a kangaroo as its logo, was the first publisher to distribute mass market paperbacks in the United States?

A. Bantam Books
B. Fawcett Crest
C. Pocket Books
D. Ballantine Books

3. What is the proper term for a baby kangaroo?

A. a kit
B. a puggle
C. a cub
D. a joey

4. Which classic TV sitcom set a Nielsen ratings record with an episode where a kangaroo was mistaken for a giant jackrabbit?

A. *Leave It to Beaver*
B. *The Beverly Hillbillies*
C. *Green Acres*
D. *The Andy Griffith Show*

5. What English author wrote the 1923 book *Kangaroo*?

A. D.H. Lawrence
B. Graham Greene
C. Evelyn Waugh
D. L.H. Myers

Answer 1: D—neck (the back of the neck, to be specific).

Answer 2: A—the 1600s.

Answer 3: B—punch card accounting.

Answer 4: D—England (the magazine temporarily ceased publication in 1992, followed by a short revival in 1996, ending publication again in 2002).

Answer 5: A—Toronto Maple Leafs.

ALL TRICKS, NO TREATS

1. Who both wrote and starred in the 1980 motion picture *One Trick Pony*?

A. Paul Newman
B. Paul Simon
C. Paul Lynde
D. Paul Anka

2. Which of the following sometimes uses an "honor trick" scoring method?

A. a steeplechase
B. a joust
C. a bridge game
D. a rodeo

3. In hockey, a player earns a "hat trick" when he scores three goals. Which of these factors makes it the even rarer "natural hat trick"?

A. three goals scored in succession
B. four goals instead of three
C. all against the same goalie
D. all three occurred in one period

4. Which of these popular songs of the '50s and '60s was NOT later covered and released as a single by the rock band Cheap Trick?

A. "Ain't That a Shame"
B. "Magical Mystery Tour"
C. "(I Can't Get No) Satisfaction"
D. "Don't Be Cruel"

5. What 17th-century British playwright's works included *A Trick to Catch the Old One*?

A. John Donne
B. Thomas Middleton
C. Samuel Butler
D. James Shirley

Answer 1: B—New Guinea.

Answer 2: C—Pocket Books (the kangaroo's name is Gertrude).

Answer 3: D—a joey.

Answer 4: B—*The Beverly Hillbillies.*

Answer 5: A—D.H. Lawrence.

CALL OUT

1. What was the name of the dog stolen and sold to be a sled dog in Jack London's *Call of the Wild*?

A. Buddy
B. Bingo
C. Buck
D. Babe

2. Although there are exceptions, what is the de facto dividing line in the U.S. for radio station call letters (from "W" to "K")?

A. the 38th parallel
B. the Mississippi River
C. the Rocky Mountains
D. the Mason-Dixon Line

3. What paper doll made her first appearance in *McCall's* magazine in 1951?

A. Betsy
B. Patsy
C. Susie
D. Maggie

4. Blondie's number one hit "Call Me" was the theme song for which Richard Gere film?

A. *Runaway Bride*
B. *American Gigolo*
C. *An Officer and a Gentleman*
D. *Breathless*

5. In his first successful telephone transmission, Alexander Graham Bell spoke to his assistant, Watson; where was Watson when this happened?

A. on the roof
B. underneath the table
C. across the street
D. in the next room

Answer 1: B—Paul Simon.

Answer 2: C—a bridge game.

Answer 3: A—goals scored in succession.

Answer 4: C—"(I Can't Get No) Satisfaction."

Answer 5: B—Thomas Middleton.

GEM DANDY

1. Which of these once-common household devices had a component usually made out of a tiny diamond?

A. can opener
B. phonograph
C. sewing machine
D. trash compactor

2. What actor in *The Wizard of Oz* did extra duty in the 1939 film by playing five different roles, four of them in the Emerald City?

A. Frank Morgan
B. Bert Lahr
C. Jack Haley
D. Charley Grapewin

3. Dallas nightclub owner Jack Ruby gained fame for murdering whom?

A. Mark David Chapman
B. James Earl Ray
C. Sirhan Sirhan
D. Lee Harvey Oswald

4. What type of gemstone was historically worn with the mistaken belief that it would prevent the wearer from becoming drunk?

A. garnet
B. amethyst
C. topaz
D. opal

5. Sapphire was the wife of Kingfish on what long-running radio program?

A. *Baby Snooks*
B. *Fibber McGee & Molly*
C. *Amos 'n' Andy*
D. *Life of Riley*

Answer 1: C—Buck.

Answer 2: B—the Mississippi River.

Answer 3: A—Betsy.

Answer 4: B—*American Gigolo.*

Answer 5: D—in the next room.

ANIMAL NICKNAMES

1. Golf great Tiger Woods was christened at birth with what first name?

A. Elmer
B. Eldrick
C. Eldridge
D. Elroy

2. Soprano Jenny Lind was known as the Swedish:

A. Sparrow
B. Canary
C. Nightingale
D. Swan

3. Which of these U.S. presidents was known as the Red Fox of Kinderhook?

A. Warren G. Harding
B. Calvin Coolidge
C. Andrew Johnson
D. Martin Van Buren

4. Former French prime minister Georges Clemenceau was called:

A. the Cobra
B. the Tiger
C. the Bear
D. the Panther

5. What country singer is affectionately known as the Possum?

A. George Jones
B. Clint Black
C. Hank Williams Jr.
D. Alan Jackson

Answer 1: B—phonograph (the stylus is often made of diamond).

Answer 2: A—Frank Morgan (he portrayed Professor Marvel, the Wizard, a doorman, a guard, and a carriage driver).

Answer 3: D—Lee Harvey Oswald.

Answer 4: B—amethyst.

Answer 5: C—*Amos 'n' Andy*.

ARE YOU A POST-GRADUATE?

1. What computer software company introduced the PostScript language for graphics and text?

A. Apple
B. IBM
C. Adobe
D. Lotus

2. Which of these celebrities died in an Alaska accident while riding in a plane piloted by aviator-adventurer Wiley Post?

A. Glenn Miller
B. Patsy Cline
C. Carole Lombard
D. Will Rogers

3. Long before he became a household name, what future American president anonymously wrote a series of Western stories for publication in *The Washington Post*?

A. Teddy Roosevelt
B. Harry Truman
C. Lyndon Johnson
D. Ronald Reagan

4. Which of these cereals is NOT made by Post?

A. Alpha-Bits
B. Cap'n Crunch
C. Grape Nuts
D. Honeycomb

5. The first post office in the American colonies opened in the 17th century. In what year did the first U.S. postage stamps go on sale?

A. 1787
B. 1817
C. 1847
D. 1877

Answer 1: B—Eldrick.

Answer 2: C—Nightingale.

Answer 3: D—Martin Van Buren.

Answer 4: B—the Tiger.

Answer 5: A—George Jones.

NAPOLEON FILL-IN-THE-BLANK

1. Napoleon Bonaparte was born on the island of
_____.

A. Corsica
B. St. Helena
C. Elba
D. Sardinia

2. Napoleon borrowed from one of Adam Smith's writings
when he uttered the quote: "England is a nation of
_____."

A. haircuts
B. cattle
C. shopkeepers
D. numbers

3. Napoleon fought the Battle of Waterloo against a
coalition of enemies in a location that is now part of
present-day _____.

A. Germany
B. the Netherlands
C. Belgium
D. Luxembourg

4. For only $15 million, Napoleon offered to sell the Louisiana Territory to representatives to U.S. president _____.

A. Jefferson
B. Adams
C. Madison
D. Washington

5. Upon his coronation as emperor of France, Napoleon said: "I am the successor, not of Louis XVI, but of _____."

A. Hugh Capet
B. Julius Caesar
C. the spirit of France
D. Charlemagne

Answer 1: C—Adobe.

Answer 2: D—Will Rogers.

Answer 3: A—Teddy Roosevelt.

Answer 4: B—Cap'n Crunch.

Answer 5: C—1847.

CALL ME
Identify the rock musician behind the nickname.

1. "The Lizard King"

A. Jimi Hendrix
B. Joe Cocker
C. Eric Burdon
D. Jim Morrison

2. "The Thin White Duke"

A. Iggy Pop
B. David Bowie
C. Gary Numan
D. Ric Ocasek

3. "The Ox"

A. John Popper
B. John Entwistle
C. John Lennon
D. John Cafferty

4. "The Brown-Eyed Handsome Man"

A. Chuck Berry
B. Harry Belafonte
C. Nat King Cole
D. Little Richard

5. "The Jesus of Cool"

A. Tom Jones
B. Bono
C. Nick Lowe
D. Lou Reed

Answer 1: A—Corsica.

Answer 2: C—shopkeepers.

Answer 3: C—Belgium.

Answer 4: A—Jefferson.

Answer 5: D—Charlemagne.

HEY, MACK!

1. Producer/director Mack Sennett is perhaps best known for his slapstick films featuring:

A. the Keystone Kops
B. the Three Stooges
C. Laurel & Hardy
D. the Bowery Boys

2. Which of the following is an alternate title of the song popularly known as "Mack the Knife"?

A. "Santa Catalina"
B. "Moritat"
C. "Nel Blu Dipinto Di Blu"
D. "Jean's Song"

3. Detroit's Mack Avenue was the location of the home of:

A. Motown Records headquarters
B. the original Tiger Stadium
C. rapper Eminem
D. Henry Ford's first plant

4. The logo for Mack Trucks features what animal?

A. bighorn sheep
B. jackrabbit
C. bulldog
D. grizzly bear

5. What was Philadelphia Athletics manager and baseball Hall of Famer Connie Mack's real first name?

A. Constantine
B. Cameron
C. Cornelius
D. Conrad

Answer 1: D—Jim Morrison.

Answer 2: B—David Bowie.

Answer 3: B—John Entwistle.

Answer 4: A—Chuck Berry.

Answer 5: C—Nick Lowe.

MAKE IT A QUIZ LIGHT

1. The phrase "a thousand points of light" was written by Peggy Noonan for what U.S. president?

A. Ronald Reagan
B. Bill Clinton
C. John F. Kennedy
D. George H.W. Bush

2. Where would you usually find a klieg light?

A. on a street corner
B. on a film set
C. in a traffic signal
D. at a baseball stadium

3. *The Guiding Light*, the longest-running radio and TV daytime drama until its cancellation in 2009, was set in what fictional town?

A. Springfield
B. Port Charles
C. Salem
D. Pine Valley

4. According to the FDA, in order for a consumer food or drink product to be advertised as "light," it has to be reduced in fat by what degree?

A. one-quarter (25%)
B. one-third (33.3%)
C. one-half (50%)
D. two-thirds (66.6%)

5. "The Northern Lights have seen queer sights" is a line from which of the following poems?

A. "The Wanderings of Oisin"
B. "The Shooting of Dan McGrew"
C. "John Anderson, My Jo"
D. "The Cremation of Sam McGee"

Answer 1: A—the Keystone Kops.

Answer 2: B—"Moritat" (the song is also known as "Theme from *The Threepenny Opera*").

Answer 3: D—Henry Ford's first plant.

Answer 4: C—bulldog.

Answer 5: C—Cornelius.

CIVIL WAR FILMS

1. What John Wayne film, set during the Civil War, was based on a true story?

A. *The Searchers*
B. *The Fighting Kentuckian*
C. *The Horse Soldiers*
D. *Reap the Wild Wind*

2. The motion picture *The Birth of a Nation* made its premiere under what alternate title?

A. *The Bishop of the Ozarks*
B. *The Clansman*
C. *An Outcast Among Outcasts*
D. *The Bandit's Son*

3. Which of the following directors did NOT work on the blockbuster film *Gone With the Wind*?

A. King Vidor
B. Victor Fleming
C. Sam Wood
D. George Cukor

4. In the 1989 Civil War film *Glory*, Matthew Broderick portrayed Colonel Robert Shaw, the leader of the first Union company that:

A. was captured and held at Andersonville
B. saw action in the first battle at Fort Sumter
C. guarded the border of the new state of West Virginia
D. was comprised of African-American volunteers

5. In what 1993 film did the role of General Robert E. Lee pass through the hands of William Hurt, Tommy Lee Jones, and Robert Duvall before it was finally awarded to Martin Sheen?

A. *Gettysburg*
B. *The Lincoln Conspiracy*
C. *The Killing Box*
D. *Ride With the Devil*

Answer 1: D—George H.W. Bush.

Answer 2: B—a film set (a klieg light is an incredibly bright carbon-arc light).

Answer 3: A—Springfield.

Answer 4: C—one-half (50%).

Answer 5: D—"The Cremation of Sam McGee."

CARB-LOADING

Identify these terms that each begin with the letters "carb."

1. Carbine

A. a coal derivative
B. a type of rifle
C. part of the brain
D. a two-horse carriage

2. Carbonara

A. a percussion instrument
B. a flower-topped hat
C. a pasta sauce
D. tea made from bark

3. Carbuncle

A. a skin infection
B. part of a vehicle's axle
C. a rain-filled cave
D. a stack of cut wood

4. Carboy

A. a deep shade of green
B. a porter
C. a large jug
D. a type of collar

5. Carbondale

A. an elastic resin
B. an orchard
C. an indigestion remedy
D. an Illinois city

Answer 1: C — *The Horse Soldiers.*

Answer 2: B — *The Clansman.*

Answer 3: A — King Vidor.

Answer 4: D — was comprised of African-American
        volunteers.

Answer 5: A — *Gettysburg.*

GRAB THE WHEEL

1. What type of pasta is usually shaped like little wagon wheels?

A. cavatelli
B. fusilli
C. penne
D. rotelle

2. On a standard color wheel, what color is opposite blue?

A. orange
B. green
C. yellow
D. red

3. How many wheels are on the trailer of an "18-wheeler" truck?

A. six
B. eight
C. ten
D. twelve

4. Which of these gymnastics moves is closest to a cartwheel?

A. kip
B. salto
C. aerial
D. roundoff

5. The lyric "big wheel a-keep on turning" appears in which hit single by Creedence Clearwater Revival?

A. "Bad Moon Rising"
B. "Up Around the Bend"
C. "Proud Mary"
D. "Green River"

Answer 1: B—a type of rifle.

Answer 2: C—a pasta sauce.

Answer 3: A—a skin infection.

Answer 4: C—a large jug.

Answer 5: D—an Illinois city.

O-TOWN
Towns and cities that begin with the letter "O."

1. What Ottawa-born star of TV's long-running hit
Bonanza was known as the "Voice of Canada"?

A. Michael Landon
B. Dan Blocker
C. Pernell Roberts
D. Lorne Greene

2. Annually for over half a century, the city of Oslo,
Norway, has sent a Christmas tree to London, England,
to be displayed where?

A. Trafalgar Square
B. St. James Palace
C. Hyde Park
D. Houses of Parliament

3. What was the name of the Oklahoma City Federal
Building that was destroyed by an act of terrorism on
April 19, 1995?

A. Mealer
B. McNamara
C. Murrah
D. Montgomery

4. Which of the following attractions in the area of Orlando, Florida, opened first?

A. SeaWorld
B. Cypress Gardens
C. Walt Disney World
D. Gatorland

5. The Bavarian village of Oberammergau is famous for its:

A. Black Forest cakes
B. Lipizzaner stallions
C. cuckoo clocks
D. passion plays

Answer 1: D—rotelle.

Answer 2: A—orange.

Answer 3: B—eight (the other ten are on the cab).

Answer 4: D—roundoff.

Answer 5: C—"Proud Mary."

PAN ACROSS JAPAN

1. In the 2000s, Japan's current leader proposed a change in the rules of succession to place which of the following in line to become the country's first modern female emperor?

A. Princess Kako
B. Princess Aiko
C. Princess Kikuko
D. Princess Mako

2. Japan's most populous city is also the world's most populous—Tokyo. What is the second-largest city in Japan?

A. Osaka
B. Yokohama
C. Kyoto
D. Nagoya

3. Which of the following is NOT the name of a team in the Japanese NPB professional baseball league?

A. Swallows
B. Sharks
C. Buffaloes
D. Carp

4. Members of Japan's famous organized crime unit, the Yakuza, reputedly use what rather radical method to apologize for their own transgressions?

A. cutting off part of a finger
B. branding themselves
C. piercing their stomachs
D. shaving their heads

5. In 1943, the One Thousand Mile War began when Japan invaded what set of islands?

A. Philippines
B. Marshall
C. Galápagos
D. Aleutian

Answer 1: D—Lorne Greene.

Answer 2: A—Trafalgar Square.

Answer 3: C—Murrah.

Answer 4: B—Cypress Gardens (sadly, the park closed in 2009 after nearly three-quarters of a century of operation; its botanic gardens are now part of Legoland Florida).

Answer 5: D—passion plays.

FASTER, FASTER!

1. Which of these characters was called "Prontito" in Spanish-speaking countries?

A. Speedy Gonzales
B. Speed Racer
C. Speedy Alka-Seltzer
D. Speed Buggy

2. Which of the following was NOT a speed used for phonograph records?

A. 16
B. 45
C. 56
D. 78

3. Which of the following names is synonymous with speed reading?

A. Mavis Bacon
B. Evelyn Wood
C. Evelyn Keyes
D. Carlton Sheets

4. Which Amendment to the Constitution of the United States guarantees the right to a speedy trial?

A. Sixth
B. Sixteenth
C. Twenty-second
D. Twenty-sixth

5. Which songstress made her Broadway debut in David Mamet's *Speed-the-Plow*?

A. Debbie Harry
B. Cher
C. Stevie Nicks
D. Madonna

Answer 1: B—Princess Aiko (she is the only child of Crown Prince Naruhito and Princess Masako).

Answer 2: A—Osaka.

Answer 3: B—Sharks.

Answer 4: A—cutting off part of a finger.

Answer 5: D—Aleutian.

GUI-TARNATION!

1. Which of these rock legends was well-known for his "duck walk" move while playing guitar?

A. Jimi Hendrix
B. B.B. King
C. Chuck Berry
D. Buddy Holly

2. What actress starred as Vienna in the 1954 motion picture *Johnny Guitar*?

A. Bette Davis
B. Eve Arden
C. Marilyn Monroe
D. Joan Crawford

3. According to legend, blues guitarist Robert Johnson did what in order to learn to play his instrument so well?

A. sold his soul to the devil
B. slept with his guitar each night
C. kept his eyes closed while playing
D. drank nothing but apple juice

4. What guitarist still plays his trademark homemade guitar not using a plectrum, but a British sixpence coin?

A. Eric Clapton
B. Jeff Beck
C. Brian May
D. Keith Richards

5. From 1948 to 1950, the Fender Telecaster was known by what alternate name?

A. Lancaster
B. Broadcaster
C. Forecaster
D. Sportscaster

Answer 1: C—Speedy Alka-Seltzer.

Answer 2: C—56 (though uncommon, the 16 speed was used for long-running spoken-language records).

Answer 3: B—Evelyn Wood.

Answer 4: A—Sixth.

Answer 5: D—Madonna.

ATHLETIC SUPPORTERS
All about famous athletes promoting consumer brands.

1. What beverage did "Dandy" Don Meredith promote in several TV commercials and print ads?

A. Postum
B. Sanka
C. Nestle's Quik
D. Lipton tea

2. What baseball pitcher achieved his greatest "exposure" in 1977 when he posed in his Jockey shorts?

A. Jim Palmer
B. Phil Niekro
C. Tom Seaver
D. Catfish Hunter

3. What brand of pantyhose did Joe Namath model in a 1974 TV commercial?

A. Beautymist
B. L'eggs
C. London Aire
D. No Nonsense

4. Who was the first figure skater to appear on a Wheaties box?

A. Nancy Kerrigan
B. Sonja Henie
C. Kristi Yamaguchi
D. Peggy Fleming

5. Which of the following products has NOT been publicly endorsed by Michael Jordan?

A. Ball Park franks
B. Hanes T-shirts
C. Rayovac batteries
D. Ore-Ida fries

Answer 1: C—Chuck Berry.

Answer 2: D—Joan Crawford.

Answer 3: A—sold his soul to the devil.

Answer 4: C—Brian May.

Answer 5: B—Broadcaster.

HOTSCAKES!

Notoriously bad sitcom cooks

1. Which of the *Gilligan's Island* castaways once tried to cook a meal, and ended up with a rather grotesque "Fish Pie"?

A. Gilligan
B. the Professor
C. Mrs. Howell
D. Ginger

2. Name the Greenwich Village 12th Precinct detective (as seen on *Barney Miller*) who was known for the horrible coffee he made.

A. Phil Fish
B. Nick Yemana
C. Stan Wojciehowicz
D. Arthur Dietrich

3. Which of *The Golden Girls* created mouth-watering dishes like herring and caramel, which had to be eaten while holding one's nose closed?

A. Dorothy Zbornak
B. Rose Nylund
C. Sophia Petrillo
D. Blanche Devereaux

4. What TV mom's inability (or unwillingness) to cook made her family scrounge for food, surviving on toaster scrapings and the occasional toothpaste sandwich?

A. Jill Taylor
B. Edith Bunker
C. Peg Bundy
D. Kate Bradley

5. After tasting his own concoction, dubbed "goop melange," what sitcom character treated it like most other dishes by saying: "Mmm, needs ketchup"?

A. Paul Buchman
B. Oscar Madison
C. Richie Cunningham
D. George Jefferson

Answer 1: D—Lipton tea.

Answer 2: A—Jim Palmer.

Answer 3: A—Beautymist.

Answer 4: C—Kristi Yamaguchi.

Answer 5: D—Ore-Ida fries.

LIGHTNING NOISE

1. What type of mythological creature was tasked with forging thunderbolts for mighty Zeus?

A. Cyclops
B. Harpy
C. Gorgon
D. satyr

2. Who portrayed James Bond, Agent 007, in the 1965 film *Thunderball*?

A. Roger Moore
B. George Lazenby
C. Sean Connery
D. Timothy Dalton

3. Marshall University's athletic teams are known as the Thundering Herd, also the title of a book by what American author?

A. Rex Stout
B. Lloyd Alexander
C. Stephen Crane
D. Zane Grey

4. What professional wrestler portrayed a character known as Thunderlips in the 1982 film sequel *Rocky III*?

A. Jerry Lawler
B. Andre the Giant
C. Hulk Hogan
D. Ric Flair

5. After a relatively unsuccessful period in the late 1980s, which band came storming back in 1990 with the song "Thunderstruck"?

A. Rush
B. AC/DC
C. Duran Duran
D. Kiss

Answer 1: D—Ginger.

Answer 2: B—Nick Yemana.

Answer 3: B—Rose Nylund.

Answer 4: C—Peg Bundy.

Answer 5: B—Oscar Madison.

MUSCLE CARS

1. When the Corvette was first introduced in 1953 (before it became a muscle car), it was only available in what color?

A. red
B. white
C. gray
D. black

2. First sold in 1970, what short-lived Dodge model was the brand's answer to the "pony" cars made by Ford and GM?

A. Charger
B. Demon
C. Super Bee
D. Challenger

3. The Chevy model that ended up becoming known as the Camaro was originally intended to be called what?

A. Panther
B. Cordata
C. Wildcat
D. Puma

4. AMC entered the muscle car race in 1968 when it brought what model to market?

A. Matador
B. Gremlin
C. Javelin
D. Hornet

5. The Malibu was first introduced in 1964 as a muscle-car version of which of Chevrolet's models?

A. Corvair
B. Chevy II
C. Impala
D. Chevelle

Answer 1: A—Cyclops (the winged horse Pegasus transported the bolts to Zeus).

Answer 2: C—Sean Connery.

Answer 3: D—Zane Grey.

Answer 4: C—Hulk Hogan.

Answer 5: B—AC/DC (the sequence of the first four answers was a slight clue!).

IN A PICKLE

1. Elizabeth Daily provides the voice for which of the Pickles family members on the Nickelodeon kids' show *Rugrats*?

A. Stu
B. Didi
C. Tommy
D. Drew

2. The word "gherkin," a small pickle, is based on the Dutch word "gurken," meaning:

A. cucumbers
B. infant
C. rowboat
D. sour

3. What company's century-old logo consists of its name in block letters inside a pickle?

A. Kroger
B. Franco-American
C. Vlasic
D. Heinz

4. What American folk singer's "Motorcycle Song" lamented about how he didn't want a pickle (with a live version going further into what he termed "the significance of the pickle")?

A. Bob Dylan
B. John Prine
C. Arlo Guthrie
D. Pete Seeger

5. What Scottish novelist introduced the world to *The Adventures of Peregrine Pickle*?

A. Sir Walter Scott
B. Tobias Smollett
C. Sir J.M. Barrie
D. Robert Louis Stevenson

Answer 1: B—white.

Answer 2: D—Challenger.

Answer 3: A—Panther.

Answer 4: C—Javelin.

Answer 5: D—Chevelle.

THIS LITTLE QUIZ WENT TO MARKET

1. Which of the following is the largest stock market In the United States?

A. NYSE
B. DJIA
C. AMEX
D. NASDAQ

2. The term "black market" was first used during what war?

A. U.S. Civil War
B. World War I
C. Thirty Years' War
D. French Revolution

3. Later bought by McDonald's, the restaurant chain now known as Boston Market was originally:

A. The Minuteman
B. Boston Homestyle
C. New England Market
D. Boston Chicken

4. The "Common Market" was established in 1957 to promote trade in countries from what area of the world?

A. Africa
B. South America
C. Europe
D. Southeast Asia

5. Gilmore Island is the name of the area that is home to what city's landmark Farmer's Market?

A. Baltimore
B. Los Angeles
C. Chicago
D. New Orleans

Answer 1: C—Tommy.

Answer 2: A—cucumbers.

Answer 3: D—Heinz.

Answer 4: C—Arlo Guthrie.

Answer 5: B—Tobias Smollett.

SILKY SMOOTH

1. The path known as the "Silk Road" stretched for some 4,000 miles from China to:

A. Paris
B. Rome
C. London
D. Cairo

2. The TV show *Silk Stalkings* found a home on the USA Network cable station after spending its first two seasons on what broadcast network?

A. ABC
B. CBS
C. Fox
D. NBC

3. Which of the following would wear clothing known as silks?

A. ballerinas
B. painters
C. jockeys
D. farmers

4. French Silk Pie is most commonly flavored with:

A. chocolate
B. bananas
C. absinthe
D. grapes

5. A silk-screened print is also known as a:

A. glyptograph
B. pyrograph
C. nomograph
D. serigraph

Answer 1: A—NYSE.

Answer 2: B—World War I.

Answer 3: D—Boston Chicken.

Answer 4: C—Europe.

Answer 5: B—Los Angeles.

IT'S A THREE-FOR-ALL

How well do you know your trios?

1. Three gold balls are a universal symbol for what type of business?

A. pharmacy
B. barber shop
C. pawn shop
D. travel agent

2. Which of the following songs was a hit for the pop-folk musical trio known as Peter, Paul & Mary?

A. "Jet"
B. "Leaving on a Jet Plane"
C. "Bennie and the Jets"
D. "Jet Airliner"

3. Emanuel Rosenfeld, Maurice Strauss, and Graham Jackson are better known as whom?

A. the Three Stooges
B. Three Dog Night
C. the Dead End Kids
D. the Pep Boys

4. Which of these groups from classical mythology was NOT typically depicted as a trio?

A. the Fates
B. the Titans
C. the Furies
D. the Graces

5. In what city did d'Artagnan meet *The Three Musketeers* in the Alexandre Dumas story?

A. Avignon
B. Brussels
C. Paris
D. Marseilles

Answer 1: B—Rome.

Answer 2: B—CBS.

Answer 3: C—jockeys.

Answer 4: A—chocolate.

Answer 5: D—serigraph.

LASER BEAMS

1. The word "laser" stands for "Light Amplification by ..." what?

A. Serial Electrical Resistance
B. Stimulated Emission of Radiation
C. Synchronized Elevated Routings
D. Standard Electronic Resources

2. The Laser, a Plymouth car model discontinued in the mid-1990s, was originally sold under what nameplate?

A. Dodge
B. Mitsubishi
C. Eagle
D. Chrysler

3. What company developed the first laser printer in the 1970s?

A. Xerox
B. Canon
C. Hewlett-Packard
D. IBM

4. What was the first arcade video game controlled by laser disc technology?

A. NFL Blitz
B. Tempest
C. Dragon's Lair
D. Pole Position

5. Laser, Star, Europe, Finn, Tornado, Mistral, and Soling are all:

A. book binding techniques
B. types of Olympic yachting events
C. Yamaha motorcycles
D. names of Beanie Babies

Answer 1: C—pawn shop.

Answer 2: B—"Leaving on a Jet Plane."

Answer 3: D—the Pep Boys (Manny, Moe & Jack).

Answer 4: B—the Titans (at first, there were an indeterminate number of Furies, but eventually they settled into their more common form of a group of three).

Answer 5: C—Paris.

WHAT'S IN STORE

1. Which of the following established the first mail-order catalog in the United States?

A. Montgomery Ward
B. Spiegel
C. Sears & Roebuck
D. J.C. Penney

2. According to a 2008 issue of *Time* magazine, Walmart's computer database is second in capacity only to the one owned by:

A. Microsoft
B. the IRS
C. General Motors
D. the Pentagon

3. Which of the following signature lines has not been carried by Kmart?

A. Kathy Ireland
B. Cheryl Tiegs
C. Martha Stewart
D. Jaclyn Smith

4. Marshall Field III, who ran the department store chain started by his grandfather, bought and merged two newspapers in 1948 to create what paper?

A. *San Diego Union-Tribune*
B. *Chicago Sun-Times*
C. *Atlanta Journal-Constitution*
D. *Pittsburgh Post-Gazette*

5. Isidor Strauss, co-owner of Macy's with his brother Nathan, was tragically killed in what well-known disaster?

A. the Great Chicago Fire
B. the crash of the *Hindenburg*
C. the sinking of the *Titanic*
D. the San Francisco Earthquake

Answer 1: B—Stimulated Emission of Radiation.

Answer 2: D—Chrysler.

Answer 3: A—Xerox.

Answer 4: C—Dragon's Lair.

Answer 5: B—types of Olympic yachting events.

TEN-DAY WAR

1. In what century did Pope Gregory XIII add ten days to the old Julian calendar to compensate for time lost over the centuries?

A. 15th century
B. 16th century
C. 17th century
D. 18th century

2. What Canadian city has been home to the world's largest Winter Carnival, which officially began in 1955 as a ten-day event?

A. Quebec City
B. Toronto
C. Vancouver
D. Montreal

3. What pioneering female journalist spent ten days in an insane asylum on Blackwell's Island, New York, to find out first-hand about conditions there?

A. Victoria Woodhull
B. Edna Furber
C. Nellie Bly
D. Anne McCormick

4. According to Article I of the U.S. Constitution, if the president fails to sign or veto a bill within ten days, what happens to it?

A. it becomes law
B. it is automatically vetoed
C. it is given to the vice president for action
D. it returns to the Congress for a special vote

5. John Reed's 1919 book *Ten Days That Shook the World* was an eyewitness account of:

A. the Paris Peace Conference
B. the first Transatlantic flight
C. the effects of Prohibition
D. the Russian Revolution

Answer 1: A—Montgomery Ward.

Answer 2: D—the Pentagon.

Answer 3: B—Cheryl Tiegs.

Answer 4: B—*Chicago Sun-Times*.

Answer 5: C—the sinking of the *Titanic*.

NO FIGS HERE

All about the name "Newton."

1. In science, a "newton" is a unit of:

A. force
B. heat
C. mass
D. time

2. The Apple Newton was one of the very first:

A. laptop computers
B. video-editing software programs
C. personal data assistants
D. mouse-driven operating systems

3. In 1779, Reverend John Newton published the *Olney Hymns*, which included his song "Faith's Review and Expectation," now known by what title?

A. "Onward, Christian Soldiers"
B. "Amazing Grace"
C. "What a Friend We Have in Jesus"
D. "Ave Maria"

4. Which of the following political organizations was cofounded by Huey P. Newton and Bobby Seale?

A. the Christian Coalition
B. the NAACP
C. the Black Panthers
D. the American Civil Liberties Union

5. Newton was the real first name of which of these American authors?

A. Ezra Pound
B. Herman Melville
C. William Faulkner
D. Booth Tarkington

Answer 1: B—16th century (1582, to be specific).

Answer 2: A—Quebec City.

Answer 3: C—Nellie Bly.

Answer 4: A—it becomes law (a "pocket veto" occurs if the president does not sign a bill given to him less than ten days before Congress adjourns).

Answer 5: D—the Russian Revolution.

YOU CAN CALL ME ...

Celebrities with unusual first names.

1. Which of the following is NOT a sibling of Dweezil Zappa?

A. Diva
B. Moon
C. Phaedra
D. Ahmet

2. Olympic medal–winning skier Picabo Street was named after a town in what U.S. state?

A. Iowa
B. Indiana
C. Illinois
D. Idaho

3. Comic actor Doodles Weaver was the real-life uncle of:

A. Sigourney Weaver
B. Fritz Weaver
C. Dennis Weaver
D. Charley Weaver

4. Oscar-winning actress Whoopi Goldberg was not christened with that name at birth; her real name is Caryn:

A. Jurgenson
B. Jackson
C. Jameson
D. Johnson

5. Actress Swoosie Kurtz was named after:

A. an airplane
B. her grandfather
C. a book character
D. a family pet

Answer 1: A—force.

Answer 2: C—personal data assistants.

Answer 3: B—"Amazing Grace."

Answer 4: C—the Black Panthers.

Answer 5: D—Booth Tarkington.

NON-CANDY CANES

1. Charlie Chaplin's trademark cane was made from what material?

A. ivory
B. bamboo
C. ebony
D. hickory

2. Which "service club" introduced the widespread use of white canes for people who are visually impaired?

A. Lions Club
B. Kiwanis Club
C. Optimists Club
D. Rotary Club

3. What anthropologist wore a distinctive cape and carried a tall, forked walking stick?

A. Ruth Benedict
B. Louis Leakey
C. Edward Sapir
D. Margaret Mead

4. Which of these advertising icons is NOT usually depicted carrying a cane?

A. Colonel Sanders
B. Johnny Walker
C. Cap'n Crunch
D. Mr. Peanut

5. What gunfighter of the Old West was known for being equally effective using his cane as a weapon?

A. John Wesley Hardin
B. William Masterson
C. James Hickok
D. Wyatt Earp

Answer 1: C—Phaedra.

Answer 2: D—Idaho (her home state).

Answer 3: A—Sigourney Weaver.

Answer 4: D—Johnson.

Answer 5: A—an airplane (during World War II, her father was in the Air Force and flew a B-17 named Swoose, a word for a combination of a swan and a goose that appeared in an old song).

WRAP IT UP

1. Bubble Wrap was invented accidentally by researchers who were trying to develop a new type of:

A. wallpaper
B. synthetic cloth
C. insulation
D. carpet padding

2. British chanteuse Marianne Faithfull was wrapped in a rug (and nothing else) when she was arrested in 1967 with members of what band?

A. the Beach Boys
B. the Kinks
C. the Rolling Stones
D. the Beatles

3. What new wave band's song "Christmas Wrapping" remains a holiday favorite?

A. the Shirts
B. Blondie
C. Devo
D. the Waitresses

4. Despite a rumor that's been circulating for at least half a century, a "Chief Shooting Star" wrapper is not redeemable for free samples of what brand of candy?

A. Dum-Dums
B. Charms Blow Pops
C. Tootsie Pops
D. Chupa Chups

5. What avant-garde artist staged 1967's *Wrapping Event*, in which London's Trafalgar Square lions were covered in white cloth?

A. Andy Warhol
B. Christo
C. John Cage
D. Yoko Ono

Answer 1: B—bamboo.

Answer 2: A—Lions Club.

Answer 3: D—Margaret Mead.

Answer 4: C—Cap'n Crunch.

Answer 5: B—William Masterson (his skilled cane-wielding led to his nickname, Bat).

BABY, IT'S COLD OUTSIDE
All about the North Pole.

1. Who was the first person to reach the geographic North Pole?

A. Richard Byrd
B. Roald Amundsen
C. Pavel Senko
D. Robert Peary

2. The starting point of the Alaska Highway is a Canadian town with a name that's similar to the title of a TV show. Name the town.

A. Dawson Creek
B. Northwest Wing
C. Apple Way
D. Falconer Crest

3. What superhero built a "Fortress of Solitude" at the North Pole?

A. Wonder Woman
B. Superman
C. Captain America
D. Batman

4. Which of these does NOT border the Arctic Ocean?

A. Russia
B. Greenland
C. Finland
D. Canada

5. What award is presented to the last musher to cross the finish line in the Iditarod?

A. Gold Coast
B. Battered Boot
C. Red Lantern
D. Salty Dog

Answer 1: A—wallpaper.

Answer 2: C—the Rolling Stones.

Answer 3: D—the Waitresses (the song was more recently covered by the Spice Girls).

Answer 4: C—Tootsie Pops (an image of a Native American shooting an arrow at a star is the symbol used on Tootsie Pop wrappers to represent a "mystery" flavor).

Answer 5: D—Yoko Ono.

RED & GREEN

1. The White House is home to the Red Room, where the First Lady receives guests, and the Green Room, used for what purpose?

A. formal dinners
B. guest accommodations
C. informal receptions
D. private staff meetings

2. Red-green colorblindness is known by all of the following names, EXCEPT:

A. dichromatism
B. deuteranopia
C. daltonism
D. protanopia

3. "Red Book" and "Green Book" are two specifications for:

A. bridge scoring
B. automobile prices
C. insurance coverage
D. compact discs

4. One of many flags used by the Sons of Liberty was a 1775 version seen at Cambridge, Massachusetts, which was red with a green _____ on it.

A. tree
B. snake
C. cross
D. stripe

5. Which female British author wrote *The Red and the Green*?

A. Dorothy Sayers
B. Mary Wollstonecraft
C. Iris Murdoch
D. P.D. James

Answer 1: C—Pavel Senko (most scientists now agree that the spot Richard Byrd visited was actually about 20 miles from the North Pole).

Answer 2: A—Dawson Creek.

Answer 3: B—Superman.

Answer 4: C—Finland.

Answer 5: C—Red Lantern.

A SHORT QUIZ

Actually, it's five questions like our other quizzes ... it's just about things that lasted only a short time.

1. Who reigned as Queen of England for only nine days?

A. Mary I
B. Empress Maud
C. Lady Jane Grey
D. Elizabeth I

2. Which of the following famous speeches lasted for only about two minutes?

A. Patrick Henry: "Give Me Liberty or Give Me Death"
B. Abraham Lincoln: Gettysburg Address
C. Dr. Martin Luther King Jr.: "I Have a Dream"
D. Ronald Reagan: Tearing Down of the Berlin Wall

3. Broadway star Ethel Merman was married to the original center square on TV's *Hollywood Squares* for just 32 days. Name him.

A. Ernest Borgnine
B. Don Rickles
C. Buddy Hackett
D. Paul Lynde

4. In what year did Pope John Paul I serve for only 33 days before dying?

A. 1968
B. 1973
C. 1978
D. 1983

5. What *Carol Burnett Show* regular hosted *Turn-On*, a clone of *Rowan & Martin's Laugh-In* that was canceled after only one episode?

A. Harvey Korman
B. Lyle Waggoner
C. Vicki Lawrence
D. Tim Conway

Answer 1: C—informal receptions.

Answer 2: B—deuteranopia (deuteranopia is a difficulty in distinguishing green only).

Answer 3: D—compact discs.

Answer 4: A—tree.

Answer 5: C—Iris Murdoch.

BACK IN THE USSR

1. Nicknamed "Muttnick" in the U.S., what was the name of the unfortunate pooch the Soviets launched into space in 1957?

A. Belka
B. Laika
C. Chernushka
D. Strelka

2. What beverage was the first American consumer product made widely available in the USSR?

A. Pepsi-Cola
B. Tang
C. Budweiser
D. Coca-Cola

3. The Soviets named a diamond, a flower, a ship, a mountain, and even a newly discovered planet after what American?

A. Neil Armstrong
B. John F. Kennedy
C. Samantha Smith
D. Martin Luther King Jr.

4. Which of these dance legends did NOT defect to the West from the USSR?

A. Vaslav Nijinsky
B. George Balanchine
C. Rudolf Nureyev
D. Mikhail Baryshnikov

5. In what part of the former Soviet Union did the Chernobyl nuclear disaster occur?

A. Belarus
B. Georgia
C. Ukraine
D. Kazakhstan

Answer 1: C—Lady Jane Grey.

Answer 2: B—Abraham Lincoln: Gettysburg Address.

Answer 3: A—Ernest Borgnine.

Answer 4: C—1978.

Answer 5: D—Tim Conway.

BEAN THERE, DONE THAT

1. What variety of beans is used to prepare Boston baked beans?

A. navy
B. lima
C. pinto
D. kidney

2. Which motion picture included a controversial scene in which Ann-Margret writhed around in a shower of beans?

A. *C.C. and Company*
B. *Middle Age Crazy*
C. *Tommy*
D. *Carnal Knowledge*

3. In addition to being Hannibal Lecter's favorite, fava beans have the distinction of being the only food that can cause:

A. thrush
B. arthritis
C. diabetes
D. anemia

4. What industrialist believed that "a good cook should be able to make a ten-course meal out of soybeans"?

A. Howard Hughes
B. Frederick Maytag
C. Andrew Carnegie
D. Henry Ford

5. "Stringbean," as portrayed by David Akeman, was a regular character on which of the following TV shows?

A. *Love, American Style*
B. *Hee Haw*
C. *Flip*
D. *Rowan & Martin's Laugh-In*

Answer 1: B—Laika.

Answer 2: A—Pepsi-Cola.

Answer 3: C—Samantha Smith (who wrote a well-publicized letter to Yuri Andropov).

Answer 4: A—Vaslav Nijinsky.

Answer 5: C—Ukraine.

TICK TOCK
Well-known clocks around the world.

1. A light shining atop the clockface of Big Ben's tower
Indicates:

A. changing of the guards
B. the Queen is in residence
C. Parliament is in session
D. the time is P.M.

2. What silent film star dangled from the hands of a giant
clock in a memorable scene from the 1923 motion
picture *Safety Last*?

A. Buster Keaton
B. Harold Lloyd
C. Charlie Chaplin
D. Stan Laurel

3. Munich's famous Glockenspiel features figures that
dance the Schafflertanz, which celebrates the end of:

A. the Plague
B. the First Reich
C. the Franco-Prussian War
D. the Latin Mass

4. What medical TV series' run included an acclaimed episode titled "Life Time," during which an onscreen clock kept time for a surgery that had to be completed in 20 minutes?

A. *Chicago Hope*
B. *ER*
C. *M*A*S*H*
D. *St. Elsewhere*

5. Swiss Timing, best known for providing timekeeping services for sporting events around the world, is a division of which of the following?

A. Timex
B. Seiko
C. Casio
D. Swatch

Answer 1: A—navy.

Answer 2: C—*Tommy.*

Answer 3: D—anemia.

Answer 4: D—Henry Ford.

Answer 5: B—*Hee Haw.*

HELP ME OUT

How well do you know your literary sidekicks?

1. What was the first name of Sherlock Holmes's faithful assistant Dr. Watson?

A. John
B. Clive
C. Ian
D. Herbert

2. What kiddie lit character is usually accompanied by his canine pal Ribsy?

A. Harry Potter
B. Homer Price
C. Henry Huggins
D. Herbie Jones

3. What author created the characters of cattle rustler Oldring and his mysterious sidekick, the Masked Rider?

A. Max Brand
B. Louis L'Amour
C. Bret Harte
D. Zane Grey

4. Who was the valet that followed Phileas Fogg when he traveled around the world in 80 days?

A. Henri Charpak
B. Giles French
C. Jean Passepartout
D. Lynn Belvedere

5. Which of the following was NOT a sidekick in a Robert Ludlum novel?

A. Tim Drake
B. Marie St. Jacques
C. Sam Devereaux
D. Anna Navarro

Answer 1: C—Parliament is in session.

Answer 2: B—Harold Lloyd.

Answer 3: A—the Plague.

Answer 4: C—M*A*S*H.

Answer 5: D—Swatch.

DELICIOUS DESSERTS

1. The Parker House Hotel is credited with inventing Boston cream pie, they also originated a variation of what food item?

A. cheesecake
B. green salad
C. dinner rolls
D. soup

2. Cherries jubilee was created (and named) in honor of what?

A. Victoria's 75th year as queen
B. America's centennial
C. the ancient Jewish "holy year"
D. George Washington's birthday

3. Bananas Foster originated in what city?

A. Barcelona
B. New Orleans
C. Venice
D. Honolulu

4. Spotted dick is a traditional British confection of boiled suet pudding with:

A. raisins
B. chocolate chips
C. walnuts
D. blueberries

5. Which of the following is NOT another name for baked Alaska?

A. Norwegian omelette
B. glace au four
C. omelette surprise
D. frozen folly

Answer 1: A—John.

Answer 2: C—Henry Huggins.

Answer 3: D—Zane Grey.

Answer 4: C—Jean Passepartout.

Answer 5: A—Tim Drake.

IT'S A GAS!

1. Which animated TV character makes a living selling what he likes to refer to as "propane and propane accessories"?

A. Homer Simpson
B. Peter Griffin
C. Stu Pickles
D. Hank Hill

2. What company was the source of a deadly gas leak in Bhopal, India, in 1984?

A. Union Carbide
B. Exxon
C. Monsanto
D. Dupont

3. What brand of gasoline introduced an additive called "Platformate" in 1968?

A. Texaco
B. Gulf
C. Shell
D. Mobil

4. There are four normal states of matter, of which "gas" is one. Which of the following is NOT one of the remaining three?

A. liquid
B. antimatter
C. plasma
D. solid

5. What death row inmate published a bestseller entitled *Cell 2455, Death Row* before his date with the gas chamber?

A. John Wayne Gacy
B. Caryl Chessman
C. Bruno Hauptmann
D. Ted Bundy

Answer 1: C—dinner rolls.

Answer 2: A—Victoria's 75th anniversary as queen.

Answer 3: B—New Orleans.

Answer 4: A—raisins.

Answer 5: D—frozen folly.

BEST OF THE BEST

Some motion picture "bests."

1. *Best in Show* was a 2000 film mockumentary that examined the events surrounding a fictional:

A. stage play
B. musical concert
C. auto race
D. dog show

2. Which of the following won his/her second Academy Award for a role in the 1946 film classic *The Best Years of Our Lives*?

A. Myrna Loy
B. Fredric March
C. Dana Andrews
D. Virginia Mayo

3. In order to avoid confusion, what 1986 basketball movie was known in certain overseas markets under the title *Best Shot*?

A. *Space Jam*
B. *The Fish That Saved Pittsburgh*
C. *Hoosiers*
D. *White Men Can't Jump*

4. The 2000 movie *The Next Best Thing* won what actress her fourth Razzie award as Worst Actress?

A. Madonna
B. Kim Basinger
C. Demi Moore
D. Bo Derek

5. In addition to appearing in *The Bodyguard*, the song "I Will Always Love You" was performed in which of these "Best" movies?

A. *The Best Man*
B. *My Best Friend's Wedding*
C. *The Best Little Whorehouse in Texas*
D. *Best Defense*

Answer 1: D—Hank Hill.

Answer 2: A—Union Carbide.

Answer 3: C—Shell.

Answer 4: B—antimatter.

Answer 5: B—Caryl Chessman.

FLOUR POWER

1. What flour brand has sponsored an annual "bake-off" since 1949?

A. Gold Medal
B. Swans Down
C. Pillsbury
D. King Midas

2. Lester Flatt and Earl Scruggs first gained national fame shilling for Martha White brand flour. What popular TV show's theme song did they later record?

A. *Bonanza*
B. *The Beverly Hillbillies*
C. *Petticoat Junction*
D. *The Dukes of Hazzard*

3. Self-rising flour contains what crucial ingredient?

A. baking powder
B. yeast
C. corn starch
D. baking soda

4. In what hippie-era film did the hero seek revenge after three Native American youngsters were doused with white flour?

A. *Walking Tall*
B. *Joe*
C. *Easy Rider*
D. *Billy Jack*

5. The original recipe for "pound cake" called for a pound of flour and a pound of each of the following, except:

A. butter
B. cream
C. sugar
D. eggs

Answer 1: D—dog show.

Answer 2: B—Fredric March.

Answer 3: C—*Hoosiers.*

Answer 4: A—Madonna (she added a fifth trophy for *Swept Away* in 2003).

Answer 5: C—*The Best Little Whorehouse in Texas* (in this film, the song was sung by its original composer, Dolly Parton).

SEEMS LIKE "OLD" TIMES

1. What World War II figure was known as "Old Blood and Guts"?

A. Douglas MacArthur
B. Charles DeGaulle
C. Winston Churchill
D. George Patton

2. The song "Old Folks at Home" is also known by what alternate title?

A. "Old Black Joe"
B. "Swanee River"
C. "Oh, Susannah"
D. "Camptown Races"

3. In what "teenage angst" movie did a character named Toad have difficulty buying a pint of Old Harper whiskey without ID?

A. *American Graffiti*
B. *Porky's*
C. *Fast Times at Ridgemont High*
D. *American Pie*

4. London's Old Bailey is a:

A. criminal court
B. subway station
C. wax museum
D. stage theater

5. Little Nell and her grandfather were on the run from what villainous dwarf in Charles Dickens's *The Old Curiosity Shop*?

A. Uriah Heep
B. Jerry Cruncher
C. Daniel Quilp
D. Martin Chuzzlewit

Answer 1: C—Pillsbury.

Answer 2: B—*The Beverly Hillbillies*.

Answer 3: A—baking powder.

Answer 4: D—*Billy Jack*.

Answer 5: B—cream.

SNUG AS A BUG

Carpets & rugs.

1. According to Islamic tradition, which of the following rode upon a magic carpet made of green silk?

A. Solomon
B. Aladdin
C. Ali Baba
D. Sinbad

2. So-called "carpetbaggers" played a dubious role in Reconstruction after what war?

A. Spanish-American War
B. World War I
C. U.S. Civil War
D. French & Indian War

3. What singer/songwriter's 1971 album *Tapestry* won four Grammy awards and set a record for most weeks on the Billboard album charts?

A. Barbra Streisand
B. Carole King
C. Linda Ronstadt
D. Etta James

4. Which of the following carpet textures consists of looped strands of yarn?

A. Plush
B. Frieze
C. Saxony
D. Berber

5. What actor sadly died of a head injury after tripping over a throw rug and cracking his cranium on a nightstand?

A. William Conrad
B. Robert Preston
C. Robert Young
D. William Holden

Answer 1: D—George Patton.

Answer 2: B—"Swanee River."

Answer 3: A—*American Graffiti.*

Answer 4: A—criminal court.

Answer 5: C—Daniel Quilp.

FIVE HUNDRED!

1. Although they haven't been printed since 1969, whose face appeared at that time on the $500 bill?

A. William McKinley
B. James Madison
C. Salmon P. Chase
D. Grover Cleveland

2. According to the Dewey Decimal System, library books numbered in the 500s are part of what category?

A. language
B. science
C. literature
D. the arts

3. Around what U.S. holiday is the Indianapolis 500 motorcar race scheduled each year?

A. Veterans Day
B. Independence Day
C. Labor Day
D. Memorial Day

4. Who was the only Major League Baseball pitcher to reach the 500-win plateau?

A. Walter Johnson
B. Christy Mathewson
C. Warren Spahn
D. Cy Young

5. After a second-place finish in 2001, what company topped the Fortune 500 rankings both in 2002 and 2003?

A. Coca-Cola
B. Walmart
C. General Motors
D. Time Warner

Answer 1: A—Solomon.

Answer 2: C—U.S. Civil War.

Answer 3: B—Carole King (her record for consecutive weeks on the album chart was later surpassed by Pink Floyd's album *The Dark Side of the Moon*).

Answer 4: D—Berber.

Answer 5: D—William Holden.

OCEAN DEPTHS

1. Decompression sickness, which can occur when a diver surfaces too quickly, is also called:

A. sea sickness
B. the bends
C. rickets
D. scurvy

2. What was the name of the world's first nuclear submarine?

A. *Tomahawk*
B. *Seawolf*
C. *Nautilus*
D. *Alexandria*

3. Which of the following oceans is the deepest?

A. Arctic
B. Pacific
C. Indian
D. Atlantic

4. What deep sea exploration device was invented by William Beebe?

A. diving bell
B. submarine
C. aquascope
D. bathysphere

5. Diatoms (the remains of algae with hard shells) are used in the manufacture of all of the following products, except:

A. rumble strips
B. catbox filler
C. swimming pool filters
D. automobile polish

Answer 1: A—William McKinley.

Answer 2: B—science.

Answer 3: D—Memorial Day.

Answer 4: D—Cy Young.

Answer 5: B—Walmart.

PUNCH OUT

Five questions related to the sport of boxing.

1. Which musician wrote and recorded a Top 40 song about controversial boxer Rubin "Hurricane" Carter?

A. Johnny Cash
B. Joan Baez
C. Bob Dylan
D. Joni Mitchell

2. Which of these boxers was stripped of his heavyweight championship after refusing induction into the U.S. Army?

A. Joe Louis
B. Muhammad Ali
C. George Foreman
D. Joe Frazier

3. What unlikely celebrity won the top prize on the TV game show *The $64,000 Question* by answering questions about boxing?

A. Shirley Temple
B. Carol Burnett
C. Patty Duke
D. Dr. Joyce Brothers

4. Who was the winner of the first heavyweight championship match in which both opponents wore boxing gloves?

A. James Jeffries
B. John L. Sullivan
C. Jim Corbett
D. Mike Donovan

5. What child star made his film debut in the 1979 tearjerking boxing flick *The Champ*?

A. Ricky Schroder
B. Neil Patrick Harris
C. Corey Feldman
D. Kirk Cameron

Answer 1: B—the bends.

Answer 2: C—*Nautilus*.

Answer 3: B—Pacific.

Answer 4: D—bathysphere.

Answer 5: A—rumble strips.

BY ANY OTHER NAME

We provide the last names of musical duos that were better known by their first names; you try to identify them. While it may not help much, the names in the clue are in the same order as the names in the correct answer.

1. Berry & Torrence

A. Elmo & Patsy
B. Peter & Gordon
C. Jan & Dean
D. Santo & Johnny

2. Melvoin & Coleman

A. Wendy & Lisa
B. Jon & Robin
C. Bob & Earl
D. Patience & Prudence

3. Moore & Prater

A. Mel & Tim
B. Ollie & Jerry
C. Dick & Dee Dee
D. Sam & Dave

4. Bramlett & Bramlett (née O'Farrell)

A. Paul & Paula
B. Delaney & Bonnie
C. Mickey & Sylvia
D. Dale & Grace

5. Stuart & Clyde

A. Chad & Jeremy
B. Homer & Jethro
C. David & David
D. Don & Juan

Answer 1: C—Bob Dylan.

Answer 2: B—Muhammad Ali.

Answer 3: D—Dr. Joyce Brothers.

Answer 4: C—Jim Corbett.

Answer 5: A—Ricky Schroder (who starred as a youngster
            on the sitcom *Silver Spoons* before dropping
            the Y from "Ricky" for his appearances on
            shows such as *NYPD Blue* … though he now
            goes by Ricky again).

TRIPLE-M

All questions have an MMM term or name.

1. The 3M Corporation was originally known as the
_____ Mining & Manufacturing Company.

A. Michigan
B. Missouri
C. Maryland
D. Minnesota

2. Margaret Munnerlyn Mitchell, author of *Gone With the Wind*, was born in what city?

A. Atlanta
B. Pittsburgh
C. Seattle
D. New York

3. For which sappy song of the 1970s is Michael Martin Murphey best known?

A. "Honey"
B. "Billy, Don't Be a Hero"
C. "Wildfire"
D. "Seasons in the Sun"

4. In what year did the African-American rally known as the Million Man March take place in Washington, D.C.?

A. 1980
B. 1985
C. 1990
D. 1995

5. Marion Michael Morrison (later known as John Wayne) was nicknamed "Duke" after:

A. the college he attended
B. a dog he owned
C. a song he often sang
D. his fighting prowess

Answer 1: C—Jan & Dean.

Answer 2: A—Wendy & Lisa.

Answer 3: D—Sam & Dave.

Answer 4: B—Delaney & Bonnie.

Answer 5: A—Chad & Jeremy.

SPIRO SPIRIT

1. Who succeeded Spiro Agnew as vice president of the United States?

A. Hubert Humphrey
B. Gerald Ford
C. Nelson Rockefeller
D. Richard Nixon

2. What toy company first produced the Spirograph drawing toy back in 1966?

A. Marx
B. Kenner
C. Hasbro
D. Ideal

3. Spirogyra is the genus for green algae; Spyro Gyra, on the other hand, is a band known for their musical mixture of pop and:

A. jazz
B. bluegrass
C. classical
D. rap

4. South Carolina's state motto is "Dum spiro spero," which literally means ... what?

A. "By valor and arms"
B. "The people rule"
C. "Labor conquers all things"
D. "While I breathe, I hope"

5. Spiro Mounds, an area that includes twelve Indian mounds, is the only archaeological park in what state?

A. Wisconsin
B. California
C. Oklahoma
D. Minnesota

Answer 1: D—Minnesota.

Answer 2: A—Atlanta (yes, she was a real Southerner).

Answer 3: C—"Wildfire."

Answer 4: D—1995.

Answer 5: B—a dog he owned (as a youngster, he had an Airedale named Duke).

WE'RE MOVIN' NOW!

Movin' questions about stage, screen, and music.

1. The Broadway show *Movin' Out* was based on songs written by what singing star?

A. Neil Sedaka
B. Billy Joel
C. George Michael
D. Elton John

2. Ja'net DuBois, who cowrote and sang vocals on "Movin' on Up" (the theme for TV's *The Jeffersons*), appeared in a regular role of her own in what sitcom?

A. *What's Happening!!*
B. *Sanford & Son*
C. *Good Times*
D. *Diff'rent Strokes*

3. The Emmy-winning 1967 special *Movin' With Nancy* includes the songs "Wait Till You See Him" and "See the Little Children," performed by:

A. Nancy Wilson
B. Nancy Harrow
C. Nancy Ames
D. Nancy Sinatra

4. The mid-1970s TV series *Movin' On* starred Claude Akins and Frank Converse as a pair of:

A. truck drivers
B. escaped convicts
C. moving men
D. struggling actors

5. What actor's first single, 1957's "Start Movin'," hit the top 10 and kicked off a short-lived singing career, though the song is not nearly as well-remembered as the movie he'd appeared in two years previously, *Rebel Without a Cause*?

A. Dennis Hopper
B. Jim Backus
C. Sal Mineo
D. Edward Platt

Answer 1: B—Gerald Ford.

Answer 2: B—Kenner.

Answer 3: A—jazz.

Answer 4: D—"While I breathe, I hope."

Answer 5: C—Oklahoma.

SUNNY DAY

1. "Beat the clear and sunny water, beat the shining Big-Sea-Water ..." is a line in what well-known poem?

A. "The Owl & the Pussy-Cat"
B. "Gunga Din"
C. "The Song of Hiawatha"
D. "The Raven"

2. What Japanese automobile company introduced a model known as the Sunny back in 1966?

A. Toyota
B. Isuzu
C. Datsun
D. Mitsubishi

3. What Biblical name literally means "the sunny one"?

A. Samson
B. Absalom
C. Jeremiah
D. Ezekiel

4. What 1990 motion picture was based on the twisted lives of socialite couple Claus and Martha "Sunny" von Bülow?

A. *Cookie's Fortune*
B. *Outrageous Fortune*
C. *Reversal of Fortune*
D. *Soldier of Fortune*

5. Who won both the Record and Song of the Year Grammy awards in 1998 with "Sunny Came Home"?

A. Paula Cole
B. Natalie Imbruglia
C. Tori Amos
D. Shawn Colvin

Answer 1: B—Billy Joel.

Answer 2: C—*Good Times* (she portrayed the role of neighbor Willona Woods).

Answer 3: D—Nancy Sinatra.

Answer 4: A—truck drivers.

Answer 5: C—Sal Mineo.

BONES ABOUT IT

1. How many bones are there in the human skull?

A. 3
B. 5
C. 8
D. 22

2. Studies show that bone fractures occur most often in what part of the human body?

A. foot
B. wrist
C. ribs
D. forearm

3. The femur (thighbone) is the largest bone in the human body. What bone is the second-largest?

A. tibia (lower leg)
B. scapula (shoulder blade)
C. humerus (upper arm)
D. sternum (breastbone)

4. The mastoid bone is located behind the:

A. voice box
B. breast
C. ear
D. kneecap

5. The hyoid is completely surrounded by tissue and is the only bone in the body not connected to another bone. It's located in the:

A. ear
B. ankle
C. backbone
D. throat

Answer 1: C—"The Song of Hiawatha" (by Henry Wadsworth Longfellow).

Answer 2: C—Datsun (now known as Nissan).

Answer 3: A—Samson.

Answer 4: C—*Reversal of Fortune*.

Answer 5: D—Shawn Colvin.

LIFT EV'RY VOICE

1. Back in 1955, in what city did Rosa Parks refuse to give up her seat for a white passenger?

A. Birmingham, Alabama
B. Jackson, Mississippi
C. Atlanta, Georgia
D. Montgomery, Alabama

2. Who was the first African-American to win an Academy Award for an acting role?

A. Louis Gossett Jr.
B. Butterfly McQueen
C. Hattie McDaniel
D. Sidney Poitier

3. On November 20, 1923, renowned black inventor Garrett Augustus Morgan received a U.S. patent for what roadway device?

A. the traffic light
B. the reflective road sign
C. the pylon
D. the speed bump

4. Which civil rights leader was appointed by Richard Nixon as the first African-American member of the Federal Communications Commission?

A. Benjamin Hooks
B. Jesse Jackson
C. Paul Robeson
D. Marcus Garvey

5. *The Block* is an artwork currently on display at the Metropolitan Museum of Art in New York City. What Harlem Renaissance artist created this work?

A. Jacob Lawrence
B. Romare Bearden
C. James Van Der Zee
D. Aaron Douglas

Answer 1: D—22.

Answer 2: B—wrist (the bone most commonly broken is a wrist bone called the navicular, or scaphoid, named because it's shaped like a boat).

Answer 3: A—tibia.

Answer 4: C—ear.

Answer 5: D—throat (it supports the muscles of the tongue).

KEEPING UP

Celebrity Joneses

1. Carolyn Jones was best known for her role as what 1960s sitcom character?

A. Kate Bradley
B. Lily Munster
C. Morticia Addams
D. Samantha Stephens

2. John Luther Jones is better known as:

A. folk hero Casey Jones
B. Led Zeppelin bassist John Paul Jones
C. comic book character Jughead Jones
D. baseball all-star Chipper Jones

3. Which of the following musicians was born Lindley Murray?

A. Davy Jones
B. Booker T. Jones
C. Jesus Jones
D. Spike Jones

4. Talk show host Jenny Jones got her start after appearing on TV's *Star Search* in which category?

A. dancing
B. singing
C. comedy
D. modeling

5. In his own film series of the 40s and 50s as well as an early TV series, what Western star was assisted by a sidekick named Fuzzy Q. Jones?

A. Roy Rogers
B. Lash LaRue
C. Hopalong Cassidy
D. Gene Autry

Answer 1: D—Montgomery, Alabama.

Answer 2: C—Hattie McDaniel (she won a Best Supporting Actress Oscar in 1940 for her role in *Gone With the Wind*).

Answer 3: A—the traffic light (he also invented a gas mask used by the U.S. Army during WWI).

Answer 4: A—Benjamin Hooks.

Answer 5: B—Romare Bearden.

PIC-A-NIC PLACES
U.S. National Parks

1. On March 1, 1872, what became the first National Park in the United States?

A. Yellowstone
B. Death Valley
C. Acadia
D. Yosemite

2. According to the National Park Service, which National Park is the most visited in the United States, with nearly 10 million visitors annually?

A. Great Smoky Mountains
B. Everglades
C. Carlsbad Caverns
D. Big Bend

3. In which U.S. state would you find Glacier National Park?

A. Oregon
B. Minnesota
C. Montana
D. North Dakota

4. Which of the following is NOT designated as a National Park?

A. Petrified Forest
B. Mount Rushmore
C. Kenai Fjords
D. Grand Canyon

5. What plants in Great Basin National Park are considered by many scientists to be the oldest living things on the planet?

A. maidenhair ferns
B. Joshua trees
C. giant sequoias
D. bristlecone pines

Answer 1: C—Morticia Addams.

Answer 2: A—folk hero Casey Jones (although the tale of the engineer was modified over many years, it is based on a true story).

Answer 3: D—Spike Jones (Jesus Jones, incidentally, is a band, not a musician)

Answer 4: C—comedy.

Answer 5: B—Lash LaRue (Lash had a horse named Rush).

I'M A LITTLE BIT COUNTRY

Try to name these countries, identified by their proper "local" names.

1. Bharat

A. Poland
B. India
C. Rwanda
D. Thailand

2. Elliniki Dhimokratia

A. Greece
B. Austria
C. Morocco
D. Bulgaria

3. Konungariket Sverige

A. Nepal
B. Congo
C. Sweden
D. Kuwait

4. Suomen Tasavalta

A. Finland
B. Zaire
C. Syria
D. Bangladesh

5. Taehan Min'guk

A. Turkey
B. Mongolia
C. Norway
D. South Korea

Answer 1: A—Yellowstone.

Answer 2: A—Great Smoky Mountains.

Answer 3: C—Montana.

Answer 4: B—Mount Rushmore (it is a National Memorial).

Answer 5: D—bristlecone pines (estimated to be more than 4,000 years old).

CORPS VALUES

1. The French phrase "esprit de corps" translates in English to:

A. alcohol
B. camaraderie
C. monetary worth
D. reincarnation

2. Which of these Marine Corps enlisted ranks is the highest?

A. Sergeant Major
B. Staff Sergeant
C. First Sergeant
D. Master Sergeant

3. Apple Corps, Ltd., is a British company that:

A. publishes tell-all paperback books
B. makes Macintosh computers
C. provides parts to Rolls-Royce
D. was owned by the Beatles

4. Before it became independent in 1981, the Peace Corps was originally headed up by what part of the U.S. government?

A. Department of Labor
B. Department of the Interior
C. Department of State
D. Department of Defense

5. Approximately how many military personnel are part of the U.S. Army Corps of Engineers?

A. 650
B. 6,500
C. 65,000
D. 650,000

Answer 1: B—India.

Answer 2: A—Greece.

Answer 3: C—Sweden.

Answer 4: A—Finland.

Answer 5: D—South Korea.

LIQUIDITY

1. What element's symbol, Hg, is based on the Latin hydrargyrum, meaning "liquid silver"?

A. Bismuth
B. Mercury
C. Hydrogen
D. Potassium

2. On what cable network could you have tuned in to a show called *Liquid Television* in the early 1990s?

A. Discovery
B. Nickelodeon
C. MTV
D. USA Network

3. Liquid Pred is the name of a what?

A. medication
B. industrial solvent
C. disinfectant
D. oil-based fuel

4. "LCD" stands for Liquid:

A. Current Duplication
B. Clock Diode
C. Crystal Display
D. Cable Design

5. Liquid Paper brand correction fluid was originally known by which of the following names?

A. Dab-a-Daub
B. Correkt
C. White Rub
D. Mistake Out

Answer 1: B—camaraderie.

Answer 2: A—Sergeant Major.

Answer 3: D—was owned by the Beatles.

Answer 4: C—Department of State.

Answer 5: A—650 (only three percent of the organization's employees are military personnel).

LOOK BEFORE YOU "LEAP"

1. What summer day marks the anniversary of Neil Armstrong's "giant leap for mankind"?

A. June 22
B. July 20
C. August 21
D. September 19

2. The Great Leap Forward was a mid-20th-century program that created widespread hardship in what country?

A. Ethiopia
B. China
C. Bolivia
D. USSR

3. What ballet move is executed when a dancer leaps from one foot, spreads the legs apart, then lands on the other foot?

A. jeté
B. entrechat
C. fouetté
D. pirouette

4. Singer Meat Loaf, who played a bus driver in the Steve Martin film *Leap of Faith*, also portrayed a bus driver in which of the following films?

A. *Bubble Boy*
B. *Dogma*
C. *Rat Race*
D. *Spice World*

5. The Jewish calendar doesn't add a "leap day" but rather a "leap month," known as Adar Sheni, which contains how many days?

A. 10
B. 20
C. 30
D. 40

Answer 1: B—Mercury.

Answer 2: C—MTV.

Answer 3: A—medication (it's a steroid-based treatment used for various ailments).

Answer 4: C—Crystal Display.

Answer 5: D—Mistake Out.

BEEP BEEP

1. Roadrunners are members of which family of birds?

A. loons
B. cuckoos
C. woodpeckers
D. pigeons

2. What company's high-speed cable Internet service is known by the name RoadRunner?

A. Cox
B. Charter
C. Time Warner
D. Comcast

3. In the Warner Bros. cartoon series, what color was the plume of feathers atop the Roadrunner's head?

A. yellow
B. red
C. green
D. blue

4. What automobile manufacturer produced a car known as the Roadrunner from 1968 until 1980?

A. Mercury
B. Renault
C. Plymouth
D. Buick

5. The roadrunner is the state bird of which U.S. state?

A. New Mexico
B. Arizona
C. Nevada
D. all of the above

Answer 1: B—July 20.

Answer 2: B—China.

Answer 3: A—jeté.

Answer 4: D—*Spice World* (Meat's character was named Dennis).

Answer 5: C—30.

MATH FLASHBACK

Okay, it may have been decades since you took a mathematics class, or you may be taking one now. Either way, try to calculate the answers to these questions:

1. American mathematician Edward Kasner asked his nephew, Milton Sirotta, to give him a name for the number 10^{100}. What name did the youngster come up with?

A. dekacent
B. googol
C. megaplex
D. zillion

2. By what name do we know the theorem stated as $a^2 + b^2 = c^2$, when dealing with right triangles?

A. Euclidean theorem
B. von Neumann's theorem
C. Pythagorean theorem
D. Rolle's theorem

3. Sir Isaac Newton and Gottfried Wilhelm von Leibniz are generally credited with independent development of which of the following branches of mathematics?

A. calculus
B. statistics
C. geometry
D. algebra

4. What is the name given to the sequence where each term is the sum of the previous two terms (0, 1, 1, 2, 3, 5, 8, 13 ...)?

A. Feynman sequence
B. Babbage's engine
C. Maxwell's equation
D. Fibonacci sequence

5. Which mathematician announced in 1993 that he had solved Fermat's Last Theorem?

A. Stephen Hawking
B. David Kendall
C. John Todd
D. Andrew Wiles

Answer 1: B—cuckoos.

Answer 2: C—Time Warner.

Answer 3: D—blue.

Answer 4: C—Plymouth.

Answer 5: A—New Mexico.

THE PENTAGON

1. In addition to its five sides, the Pentagon has how many stories?

A. two
B. five
C. nine
D. thirteen

2. Where is the Pentagon building physically located?

A. Washington, D.C.
B. Alexandria, Virginia
C. Bethesda, Maryland
D. Arlington, Virginia

3. During what war was construction on the Pentagon completed?

A. World War I
B. World War II
C. Korean War
D. Vietnam War

4. Name the president who said: "You know, even the Democrats go too far sometimes on downsizing government. One of them said we ought to turn the Pentagon into a triangle."

A. Bill Clinton
B. Lyndon Johnson
C. Jimmy Carter
D. John F. Kennedy

5. Beginning on June 13, 1971, what U.S. newspaper was the first to publish excerpts from the Pentagon Papers?

A. *The Miami Herald*
B. *The Chicago Tribune*
C. *The New York Times*
D. *The Washington Post*

Answer 1: B—googol.

Answer 2: C—Pythagorean theorem.

Answer 3: A—calculus (both men built their ideas for calculus on work of several previous mathematicians).

Answer 4: D—Fibonacci sequence.

Answer 5: D—Andrew Wiles.

A "COOL" QUIZ

1. Joe Cool is an alter ego of which of these comic strip characters?

A. Garfield
B. Zonker Harris
C. Snoopy
D. Beetle Bailey

2. Which of these movies featured the famous line: "What we've got here is failure to communicate"?

A. *Cool Runnings*
B. *Cool Hand Luke*
C. *Cool World*
D. *Cool as Ice*

3. "Keep cool" was a slogan successfully used by which of these U.S. presidential candidates?

A. Calvin Coolidge
B. John F. Kennedy
C. Bill Clinton
D. Jimmy Carter

4. What does the "J" stand for in the name of rapper LL Cool J?

A. John
B. Jams
C. Jock
D. James

5. What late musical legend is widely considered to be the father of the style that became known as cool jazz?

A. Duke Ellington
B. Miles Davis
C. Charlie Parker
D. Benny Goodman

Answer 1: B—five.

Answer 2: D—Arlington, Virginia.

Answer 3: B—World War II (the Pentagon opened in 1943).

Answer 4: A—Bill Clinton.

Answer 5: C—*The New York Times*.

COINS-IDENTAL

1. The two-cent piece was the first U.S. coin to feature:

A. "E pluribus unum"
B. a mint mark
C. the image of a U.S. president
D. "In God we trust"

2. What is the name of the baby depicted on the Sacagawea dollar coin?

A. Pomp
B. Cameahwait
C. Lizette
D. Antoine

3. Who was the first non-referee to toss the coin at the beginning of a Super Bowl game?

A. Vince Lombardi
B. Joe Namath
C. Red Grange
D. Bart Starr

4. Which Batman villain bases all his decisions on the flip of a special coin?

A. Cluemaster
B. Two-Face
C. Harley Quinn
D. The Mad Hatter

5. The purest gold coin of regular issue in the world is the:

A. American Eagle
B. Chinese Panda
C. Canadian Maple Leaf
D. French 20-franc "Rooster"

Answer 1: C—Snoopy.

Answer 2: B—*Cool Hand Luke.*

Answer 3: A—Calvin Coolidge.

Answer 4: D—James (the full name is "Ladies Love Cool James").

Answer 5: B—Miles Davis.

UNDERQUIZ

1. An insurance policy that is "underwritten" is one that has been:

A. taken on an individual
B. signed
C. changed
D. legally approved

2. What was the name of Underdog's girlfriend?

A. Penny
B. Poochy
C. Pamela
D. Polly

3. Mark Callaway is best known in his role as "the Undertaker" in:

A. Michael Jackson's video for "Thriller"
B. *Dark Shadows*
C. pro wrestling
D. *Buffy the Vampire Slayer*

4. *Understood Betsy* was a popular young adult book published in 1918 by what author?

A. Dorothy Canfield Fisher
B. Louise Fitzhugh
C. Kate Douglas Wiggin
D. Beatrix Potter

5. Who was Araminta Ross?

A. former Undersecretary of State
B. an award-winning underwater photographer
C. a rescuer on the Underground Railroad
D. a long-missing undercover FBI agent

Answer 1: D—"In God We Trust" (this motto became required on all U.S. coins and currency in 1955).

Answer 2: A—Pomp (his birth name was Jean Baptiste, but Captain Clark called him Pomp, a name that stuck with him his whole life).

Answer 3: C—Red Grange.

Answer 4: B—Two-Face.

Answer 5: C—Canadian Maple Leaf.

SPACING OUT

1. The star Polaris is more commonly known by what name?

A. the North Star
B. the morning star
C. the evening star
D. the Dog Star

2. The constellation Gemini contains two similar stars called "the Twins." What are the common names of these two stars?

A. Deneb and Altair
B. Archenar and Canopus
C. Rigel and Betelgeuse
D. Castor and Pollux

3. The asterism commonly called the "Big Dipper" can be seen in which constellation?

A. Hydra
B. Ursa Major
C. Ursa Minor
D. Orion

4. A renowned catalog by French astronomer Charles Messier describes many deep-sky astronomical objects, discovered when he was looking for:

A. comets
B. asteroids
C. supernovae
D. moons of other planets

5. At least 21 fragments of which comet smashed into Jupiter in July of 1994?

A. Kohoutek
B. Hale-Bopp
C. Shoemaker-Levy 9
D. Hyukatake

Answer 1: B—signed.

Answer 2: D—Polly (Polly Purebred, to be exact).

Answer 3: C—pro wrestling.

Answer 4: A—Dorothy Canfield Fisher.

Answer 5: C—a rescuer on the Underground Railroad (she was better known as Harriet Tubman).

GREEN AND FAB

Try to identify these Beatles songs from their lyrics, each of which contain the word "green."

1. "So we sailed up to the sun, till we found the sea of green ..."

A. "Helter Skelter"
B. "Day Tripper"
C. "Yellow Submarine"
D. "Magical Mystery Tour"

2. "Cellophane flowers of yellow and green, towering over your head ..."

A. "Strawberry Fields Forever"
B. "Lucy in the Sky With Diamonds"
C. "Nowhere Man"
D. "The Fool on the Hill"

3. "You say you've seen seven wonders and your bird is green ..."

A. "Free as a Bird"
B. "Mother Nature's Son"
C. "Blue Jay Way"
D. "And Your Bird Can Sing"

4. "Black, white, green, red, can I take my friend to bed?"

A. "Lovely Rita"
B. "Your Mother Should Know"
C. "All Together Now"
D. "Savoy Truffle"

5. "Everybody's green, 'cause I'm the one who won your love ..."

A. "I'll Follow the Sun"
B. "You Can't Do That"
C. "Good Day Sunshine"
D. "Twist and Shout"

Answer 1: A—the North Star.

Answer 2: D—Castor and Pollux.

Answer 3: B—Ursa Major (in Britain, the Big Dipper is known as the Plough).

Answer 4: A—comets.

Answer 5: C—Shoemaker-Levy 9.

PEPSI PEP

What made these earlier Pepsi incarnations unique?

1. Pepsi Twist

A. cherry flavor
B. unique bottle
C. red color
D. lemon flavor

2. Pepsi XL

A. clear color
B. extra caffeine
C. larger size
D. half the calories

3. Pepsi One

A. low cost
B. low carbonation
C. low calorie
D. low caffeine

4. Pepsi Blue

A. fruit juice added
B. berry flavoring
C. added guarana
D. half the caffeine

5. Pepsi Free

A. no sugar
B. no caffeine
C. clear (no coloring)
D. no artificial flavor

Answer 1: C—"Yellow Submarine."

Answer 2: B—"Lucy in the Sky With Diamonds."

Answer 3: D—"And Your Bird Can Sing."

Answer 4: C—"All Together Now."

Answer 5: B—"You Can't Do That."

FIVE ON TIN

1. What is usually added to tin to make solder?

A. carbon
B. lead
C. iron
D. aluminum

2. "One Tin Soldier" was the theme song for which motion picture of the 1970s?

A. *Magnum Force*
B. *Walking Tall*
C. *Billy Jack*
D. *Five Easy Pieces*

3. Which of these is made of 90 percent tin?

A. an Academy Award trophy
B. the Statue of Liberty
C. a Kennedy 50-cent piece
D. a Campbell's soup can

4. What actor who was cast as the Tin Man in *The Wizard of Oz* had a bad reaction to his metallic makeup, causing him to be replaced in the film by Jack Haley (wearing less toxic makeup)?

A. Edgar Bergen
B. Buster Keaton
C. W.C. Fields
D. Buddy Ebsen

5. Who reprised his Broadway role of "Big Daddy" in 1958 when Tennessee Williams's *Cat on a Hot Tin Roof* was made into a motion picture?

A. William Frawley
B. Burl Ives
C. Sid Caesar
D. Jackie Gleason

Answer 1: D—lemon flavor.

Answer 2: D—half the calories (this short-lived beverage was introduced nationally in 1995).

Answer 3: C—low calorie (this one-calorie beverage is still on the market, but sells very little compared to Diet Pepsi).

Answer 4: B—berry flavoring.

Answer 5: B—no caffeine.

1–4 PLANETS

A post-Pluto-demotion quiz.

1. How many planets in our solar system are smaller than Earth?

A. one
B. two
C. three
D. four

2. How many planets in our solar system do not have moons?

A. one
B. two
C. three
D. four

3. How many planets in our solar system are surrounded by rings?

A. one
B. two
C. three
D. four

4. How many planets in our solar system are not viewable from Earth at any time with the unaided eye?

A. one
B. two
C. three
D. four

5. How many planets in our solar system are closer to the Sun than the Earth is?

A. one
B. two
C. three
D. four

Answer 1: B—lead.

Answer 2: C—*Billy Jack*.

Answer 3: A—an Academy Award trophy.

Answer 4: D—Buddy Ebsen (W.C. Fields was originally selected for the role of the Wizard, but he and the studio couldn't agree on a contract).

Answer 5: B—Burl Ives.

JINKIES!
All about Scooby-Doo.

1. What breed of dog is Scooby-Doo?

A. German shepherd
B. Great Dane
C. English setter
D. Doberman pinscher

2. Which of these *Scooby-Doo* TV versions is the most recent?

A. *What's New, Scooby-Doo?*
B. *Scooby and Scrappy-Doo*
C. *The New Scooby-Doo Movies*
D. *The 13 Ghosts of Scooby-Doo*

3. What is the subtitle of the live-action movie sequel *Scooby-Doo 2*?

A. *Mystery Mix-Up*
B. *Night of Frights*
C. *Zombie Island*
D. *Monsters Unleashed*

4. Rogers is the last name of which *Scooby-Doo* character?

A. Velma
B. Shaggy
C. Fred
D. Daphne

5. What dispute with producers caused Casey Kasem to (temporarily) abandon his role of voicing Shaggy in 1995?

A. Shaggy's cowardly nature
B. Shaggy's slovenly clothes
C. Shaggy's eating habits
D. Shaggy's long hair

Answer 1: C—three (Mercury, Venus, and Mars are each smaller than Earth).

Answer 2: B—two (Mercury and Venus are the only two planets in our solar system without a natural satellite).

Answer 3: D—four (Jupiter, Saturn, Uranus, and Neptune are each surrounded by rings, with Saturn's being the most visible).

Answer 4: B—two (Uranus and Neptune are too dim and too distant to be seen from Earth without assistance).

Answer 5: B—two (Mercury and Venus are closer to the Sun than the Earth is).

THE TRIPLE QUIZ

1. Triple sec is a clear liqueur of what flavor?

A. mint
B. apple
C. coffee
D. orange

2. What was the name of the only Triple Crown winner to appear on the cover of *Time*, *Newsweek*, and *Sports Illustrated* in the same week?

A. Secretariat
B. Ruffian
C. Seabiscuit
D. Seattle Slew

3. Which of the following is NOT a standard ingredient in the traditional triple-decker club sandwich?

A. mustard
B. bacon
C. lettuce
D. turkey

4. The Triple Entente was an alliance formed in 1908 when England, France, and what other country entered a military pact?

A. Germany
B. Russia
C. Italy
D. Spain

5. In which holiday film does a character get his tongue stuck to a flagpole as a result of a "triple dog dare"?

A. *Home Alone 2*
B. *The Santa Clause*
C. *A Christmas Story*
D. *Scrooged*

Answer 1: B—Great Dane.

Answer 2: A—*What's New, Scooby Doo?* (which premiered in 2002).

Answer 3: D—*Monsters Unleashed.*

Answer 4: B—Shaggy (his "real" name was Norville Rogers).

Answer 5: C—Shaggy's eating habits (Kasem was a vegetarian, and demanded that Shaggy be one as well).

RHO, RHO, RHO YOUR BOAT

1. How many sides does a rhombus have?

A. three
B. four
C. five
D. six

2. As of 2012, who is the only U.S. president to have been a Rhodes Scholar?

A. Bill Clinton
B. Dwight Eisenhower
C. John Kennedy
D. Teddy Roosevelt

3. What was Rhoda Morgenstern's married name in the *Mary Tyler Moore Show* spin-off, *Rhoda*?

A. Levy
B. Venture
C. Molinari
D. Gerard

4. The flowers known as rhododendrons are most commonly shaped like:

A. bells
B. stars
C. spheres
D. tubes

5. What quality does a "rhopalic" sentence have?

A. contains each letter of the alphabet at least twice
B. each word has one more letter than the previous word
C. two or more words in the sentence are anagrams of each other
D. spells a different sentence when read backwards

Answer 1: D—orange.

Answer 2: A—Secretariat.

Answer 3: A—mustard.

Answer 4: B—Russia.

Answer 5: C—A Christmas Story.

IT ALL ENDS WITH THE "IRS"

Each answer ends with the letters "IRS."

1. Balsam, Fraser, and Douglas are all types of:

A. tapirs
B. chairs
C. eclairs
D. firs

2. Which of these words means "pirates"?

A. voussoirs
B. couloirs
C. corsairs
D. abattoirs

3. Which of these was a British television show that found stateside success on the PBS network in America?

A. *The State of Affairs*
B. *Upstairs, Downstairs*
C. *Ride the Windsor Chairs*
D. *Drawcansirs*

4. Which of the following is NOT an Arabic term describing a group of leaders?

A. Fakirs
B. Emirs
C. Pamirs
D. Vizirs

5. "Part of the Plan" became Dan Fogelberg's first Top 40 hit. It appeared on what 1974 album?

A. *Souvenirs*
B. *Crosshairs*
C. *Memoirs*
D. *Reservoirs*

Answer 1: B—four.

Answer 2: A—Bill Clinton.

Answer 3: D—Gerard (her husband's name was Joe Gerard).

Answer 4: A—bells.

Answer 5: B—each word has one more letter than the previous word (for instance, "I do not want spicy snacks without antacids available").

M'LADY

1. According to the British tradition of honorifics, the wife of which title would NOT be addressed as "Lady"?

A. Duke
B. Earl
C. Viscount
D. Baron

2. What singer/songwriter wrote "Lady," a song that became a number one hit for Kenny Rogers?

A. Smokey Robinson
B. Lionel Richie
C. Paul Anka
D. Neil Diamond

3. What is the real first name of the former First Lady known as Lady Bird Johnson?

A. Collette
B. Camilla
C. Claudia
D. Charlotte

4. Lady Godiva made her historic (and nude) ride through what British city?

A. Cambridge
B. Coventry
C. Canterbury
D. Chester

5. What was the name of the gamekeeper who became *Lady Chatterley's Lover* in the popular D.H. Lawrence novel?

A. Sharpe
B. Muir
C. Birkin
D. Mellors

Answer 1: D—firs.

Answer 2: C—corsairs (the name can be applied either to the pirates themselves or the ships they sailed).

Answer 3: B—*Upstairs, Downstairs.*

Answer 4: C—Pamirs (the Pamirs are mountains of south-central Asia).

Answer 5: A—*Souvenirs.*

BILLS, BILLS, BILLS
People with the last name "Williams."

1. Famed playwright Thomas Lanier "Tennessee" Williams was born in what U.S. state?

A. Mississippi
B. California
C. Vermont
D. Tennessee

2. Which of the following was the nickname often used for late baseball legend Ted Williams?

A. Big Train
B. Hoss
C. Splendid Splinter
D. Yankee Clipper

3. Composer John Williams won his first Academy Award for his work on the music for what motion picture?

A. *E.T., the Extra-Terrestrial*
B. *Fiddler on the Roof*
C. *Jaws*
D. *Schindler's List*

4. In 1636, Roger Williams founded Providence Plantations, the first permanent settlement in what future U.S. state?

A. Georgia
B. Virginia
C. Rhode Island
D. Maine

5. Before she resigned the position, Vanessa Williams won the Miss America pageant for what year?

A. 1980
B. 1984
C. 1988
D. 1992

Answer 1: A—Duke (a Duke's wife would be addressed as "Duchess" or "Your Grace" but not "Lady").

Answer 2: B—Lionel Richie.

Answer 3: C—Claudia.

Answer 4: B—Coventry.

Answer 5: D—Mellors.

SOCCER (OKAY, FÚTBOL)

1. How tall is a regulation adult soccer goal?

A. six feet
B. eight feet
C. ten feet
D. twelve feet

2. What country is scheduled to host the 2014 World Cup?

A. Brazil
B. Spain
C. Bolivia
D. China

3. How many "yellow card" infractions result in the ejection of a player from the game?

A. one
B. two
C. three
D. four

4. According to international rules, what's the only protective equipment that players are required to wear?

A. elbow pads
B. cleats
C. shin guards
D. athletic supporters

5. The word "soccer" is an abbreviated corruption of what term?

A. social ceremony
B. recommended sport
C. association football
D. sock color

Answer 1: A—Mississippi (he earned the nickname "Tennessee" while attending school in the north, due to his thick accent).

Answer 2: C—Splendid Splinter (in 2001, this was chosen by ESPN as the best baseball nickname of all time).

Answer 3: B—*Fiddler on the Roof.*

Answer 4: C—Rhode Island.

Answer 5: B—1984.

HIDE AND C.K.

This quiz centers around the initials "C.K."

1. Corbin, Kentucky is home to:

A. Churchill Downs racetrack
B. Jack Daniel's headquarters
C. Colonel Sanders's first Kentucky Fried Chicken restaurant
D. the Louisville Slugger factory

2. The Circle K organization is part of the:

A. Kiwanis Club
B. Knights of Columbus
C. Rotary Club
D. Kinsmen Club

3. How many Academy Awards were won by the legendary Orson Welles film *Citizen Kane*?

A. none
B. one
C. three
D. five

4. In what year was Florida's Cape Canaveral renamed Cape Kennedy to honor the late president?

A. 1963
B. 1968
C. 1973
D. 1978

5. Which of the following hosted a long-running television segment titled "On the Road"?

A. Christine Keeler
B. Calvin Klein
C. Carolyn Kilpatrick
D. Charles Kuralt

Answer 1: B—eight feet.

Answer 2: A—Brazil.

Answer 3: B—two (or one "red card").

Answer 4: C—shin guards.

Answer 5: C—association football.

WED ALERT!

1. Which quirky entertainer got married on TV's *The Tonight Show*?

A. Spike Jones
B. "Weird Al" Yankovic
C. Tiny Tim
D. Andy Kaufman

2. Which British royal bride's wedding dress included anchors in its elaborate design?

A. Sophie, Countess of Wessex
B. Diana, Princess of Wales
C. Sarah, Duchess of York
D. Anne, the Princess Royal

3. In 1982, who presided over a controversial mass wedding ceremony of 2,075 couples at Madison Square Garden?

A. L. Ron Hubbard
B. Jesse Jackson
C. Louis Farrakhan
D. Sun Myung Moon

4. What film actress made a cameo appearance during Luke and Laura's highly rated *General Hospital* wedding?

A. Sophia Loren
B. Elizabeth Taylor
C. Natalie Wood
D. Bette Davis

5. Which young actor starred in the 2003 motion picture *Just Married*?

A. Devon Sawa
B. Jesse Bradford
C. Matthew Lillard
D. Ashton Kutcher

Answer 1: C—Colonel Sanders' first KFC restaurant (the first KFC franchise was in Salt Lake City, Utah).

Answer 2: A—Kiwanis Club.

Answer 3: B—one (for Best Original Screenplay).

Answer 4: A—1963 (in 1973, the NASA site became Cape Canaveral once again).

Answer 5: D—Charles Kuralt.

ALOE THERE
All about the name "Vera."

1. Vera Lynn was an entertainer best known for singing patriotic songs to inspire the soldiers of what country during World War II?

A. France
B. Italy
C. the U.K.
D. Russia

2. 1882's *Vera, or the Nihilists* was the title of the first play by what playwright?

A. James M. Barrie
B. Oscar Wilde
C. Anton Chekhov
D. George Bernard Shaw

3. What actress portrayed a dimwitted waitress named Vera in the long-running sitcom *Alice*?

A. Polly Holliday
B. Linda Lavin
C. Diane Ladd
D. Beth Howland

4. A buxom lady named Vera Jayne Palmer gained quite an audience in films under what stage name?

A. Jayne Mansfield
B. Brigitte Bardot
C. Rita Hayworth
D. Jane Russell

5. In the early 20th century, Vera Menchik was widely known as the world's greatest female:

A. chess player
B. ballerina
C. golfer
D. sculptor

Answer 1: C—Tiny Tim.

Answer 2: C—Sarah, Duchess of York (the anchors were in honor of her Navy husband, Prince Andrew).

Answer 3: D—Sun Myung Moon.

Answer 4: B—Elizabeth Taylor.

Answer 5: D—Ashton Kutcher.

YOU GOTTA HAVE FRIENDS

Each question contains the first name of a character from TV's *Friends*.

1. What group had a #1 hit on the Modern Rock charts in 1990 with the song "Joey"?

A. Crowded House
B. The Cure
C. The Cult
D. Concrete Blonde

2. Two 19th-century British explorers with the last name Ross were known for their expeditions in what area of the world?

A. the Arctic
B. the South Pacific
C. the interior of Africa
D. Central America

3. The name Chandler literally means:

A. horse rider
B. lover of money
C. candlemaker
D. light from above

4. Rachel, the second wife of Jacob, appears in what book of the Bible?

A. Genesis
B. Ecclesiastes
C. Judges
D. Daniel

5. Which planet in our solar system has a moon named Phoebe?

A. Mars
B. Saturn
C. Neptune
D. Jupiter

Answer 1: C—the U.K.

Answer 2: B—Oscar Wilde.

Answer 3: D—Beth Howland.

Answer 4: A—Jayne Mansfield.

Answer 5: A—chess player.

GIVE 'EM ENOUGH ROPE

1. What board game features a rope as one of its playing pieces?

A. Mousetrap
B. Cootie
C. Monopoly
D. Clue

2. Alfred Hitchcock's 1948 film *Rope* was based on a real-life crime committed by:

A. Leopold & Loeb
B. Charles Starkweather
C. Charles Manson
D. Bonnie & Clyde

3. What boxer developed what he called the "rope-a-dope" technique?

A. Sugar Ray Leonard
B. Muhammad Ali
C. Joe Frazier
D. Marvin Hagler

4. Which of these TV sitcoms featured a pair of wacky neighbors called the Ropers?

A. *Full House*
B. *Who's the Boss?*
C. *Three's Company*
D. *Home Improvement*

5. What hit song from 1981 was based on a jump rope game?

A. "I Missed Again"
B. "Step by Step"
C. "The Stroke"
D. "Double Dutch Bus"

Answer 1: D—Concrete Blonde.

Answer 2: A—the Arctic.

Answer 3: C—candlemaker.

Answer 4: A—Genesis.

Answer 5: B—Saturn.

SOUNDS? ZOUNDS!

1. What actor recorded the 1968 album *Little Joe Sure Can Sing*?

A. Michael Landon
B. Joe Pesci
C. Joe E. Ross
D. Jack Webb

2. Sylvester Stallone croaked out the theme song to which of his films?

A. *Oscar*
B. *Cobra*
C. *Paradise Alley*
D. *Over the Top*

3. What *Back to the Future* star released a 1989 avant-garde album titled *The Big Problem*?

A. Crispin Glover
B. Michael J. Fox
C. Lea Thompson
D. Christopher Lloyd

4. What song was released as a single by Ted Cassidy, who portrayed Lurch on the 1960s TV version of *The Addams Family*?

A. "The Addams Family Theme"
B. "You Rang?"
C. "The Thing's Harpsichord"
D. "The Lurch"

5. Who admitted that he "couldn't stay within shootin' distance of a melody," but still hit #1 in the U.K. with the song "Wand'rin Star" from the *Paint Your Wagon* soundtrack?

A. Rod Steiger
B. Clint Eastwood
C. Eddie Albert
D. Lee Marvin

Answer 1: D—Clue.

Answer 2: A—Leopold & Loeb.

Answer 3: B—Muhammad Ali.

Answer 4: C—*Three's Company*.

Answer 5: D—"Double Dutch Bus."

HEY, MISTER!
Mister products and brand names.

1. What automaker takes pride in its Mr. Goodwrench mechanics?

A. Ford
B. Honda
C. GM
D. Chrysler

2. Coca-Cola introduced its Mr. Pibb soft drink to go up against which competing brand?

A. Mountain Dew
B. Dr Pepper
C. Sunkist
D. 7-Up

3. Mr. Clean not only wears a nifty earring, but a crisp T-shirt in what color?

A. white
B. yellow
C. orange
D. red

4. What New York Yankees great earned the nickname "Mr. Coffee" due to his many commercials for the coffeemakers in the 1970s?

A. Mickey Mantle
B. Reggie Jackson
C. Roger Maris
D. Joe DiMaggio

5. Which of the following was NOT once sold as a member of the Mr. Potato Head "Tooty-Frooty" gang?

A. Cooky the Cucumber
B. Oscar the Orange
C. Pete the Pepper
D. Benny the Banana

Answer 1: B—Joe Pesci.

Answer 2: C—*Paradise Alley.*

Answer 3: A—Crispin Glover.

Answer 4: D—"The Lurch."

Answer 5: D—Lee Marvin.

A STICKY SITUATION

1. On which of the following might you find a feature known as StickyKeys?

A. wireless remotes
B. electromagnetic locks
C. electric pianos
D. computer keyboards

2. The album *Sticky Fingers* was the first Rolling Stones release:

A. to hit number one
B. of the 1970s
C. on their own record label
D. without Brian Jones

3. "Sticky rice" is a key ingredient for which of the following?

A. sushi
B. rice cakes
C. lo mein
D. tapioca

4. The phrase "sticky wicket" (meaning a difficult situation) has its origins in what sport?

A. polo
B. cricket
C. croquet
D. lacrosse

5. What cartoon sitcom featured the voice of Orlando Brown as the cool and smooth character Sticky Webb?

A. *The Proud Family*
B. *Dave the Barbarian*
C. *SpongeBob SquarePants*
D. *Kim Possible*

Answer 1: C—GM.

Answer 2: B—Dr Pepper.

Answer 3: A—white.

Answer 4: D—Joe DiMaggio.

Answer 5: D—Benny the Banana.

EAST-WEST

1. What author's novel *East of Eden* was a symbolic recreation of the story of Cain and Abel?

A. Sinclair Lewis
B. Jack London
C. James Agee
D. John Steinbeck

2. Which of the following U.S. Army generals did NOT graduate from the United States Military Academy at West Point?

A. Colin Powell
B. Douglas MacArthur
C. George Patton
D. Norman Schwarzkopf

3. Adam West portrayed which superhero on television?

A. Spider-Man
B. Batman
C. Superman
D. The Green Hornet

4. The region of Asia formerly known as East Pakistan achieved independence in 1971 and is now known by what name?

A. East Timor
B. Kampuchea
C. Sri Lanka
D. Bangladesh

5. To what police officer do the Jets plead their case via song in the musical *West Side Story*?

A. Krupke
B. O'Malley
C. Greshler
D. Kowalski

Answer 1: D—computer keyboards (no, it's not spilling a soda pop into the keys; it's a feature that assists those with difficulty holding down more than one key at a time).

Answer 2: C—on their own label.

Answer 3: A—sushi.

Answer 4: B—cricket.

Answer 5: A—*The Proud Family*.

"CHIP" OFF THE OLD BLOCK

1. According to traditional rules, what color of poker chip has the highest value?

A. black
B. red
C. green
D. blue

2. "Munch a bunch!" was the long-time advertising slogan for what brand of snack chip?

A. Doritos
B. Fritos
C. Cheetos
D. Tostitos

3. What was the first name of the character known as "Ponch" on the TV series *CHiPs*?

A. Arthur
B. Jon
C. Francis
D. Joseph

4. Which U.S. president had a son named after him that went by the nickname Chip?

A. Jimmy Carter
B. Dwight Eisenhower
C. Ronald Reagan
D. Gerald Ford

5. What actor won an Academy Award for his portrayal of the former headmaster in the 1939 film *Goodbye, Mr. Chips*?

A. Sydney Greenstreet
B. Robert Donat
C. Clark Gable
D. Gary Cooper

Answer 1: D—John Steinbeck.

Answer 2: A—Colin Powell.

Answer 3: B—Batman.

Answer 4: D—Bangladesh.

Answer 5: A—Krupke.

TO "ERA" IS HUMAN

1. New Era is a company best known for what selling what specific sporting item?

A. running shoes
B. hockey sticks
C. baseball caps
D. tennis balls

2. Which of these geologic eras includes the present day?

A. Cenozoic Era
B. Paleozoic Era
C. Mesozoic Era
D. Proterozoic Era

3. In what year did the ERA (the Equal Rights Amendment) come within three states of ratification before the deadline passed?

A. 1965
B. 1974
C. 1982
D. 1990

4. Procter & Gamble introduced their Era brand to compete with the very first liquid laundry detergent in the U.S., which was:

A. Woolite
B. Dynamo
C. Biz
D. Wisk

5. A baseball pitcher who allowed one earned run in three innings pitched would have an ERA (earned run average) of:

A. 1.00
B. 3.00
C. 4.00
D. 9.00

Answer 1: A—black.

Answer 2: B—Fritos.

Answer 3: C—Francis (the character's full name was Francis Llewellyn Poncherello).

Answer 4: A—Jimmy Carter.

Answer 5: B—Robert Donat.

ALLEY TALLY

1. In 1903, music publisher Harry Von Tilzer coined the term "Tin Pan Alley" in reference to a location in what city?

A. New York
B. Chicago
C. St. Louis
D. Nashville

2. How long is a lane in a bowling alley, measured from the foul line to the center point of the head pin?

A. 40 feet
B. 50 feet
C. 60 feet
D. 70 feet

3. After 13 years of marriage, what actor endured a messy divorce from *Cheers* and *Veronica's Closet* actress Kirstie Alley?

A. Shaun Cassidy
B. Willie Aames
C. Tim Matheson
D. Parker Stevenson

4. What land that was the prehistoric home of comic strip character Alley Oop?

A. Baa
B. Moo
C. Oink
D. Cluck

5. What performer (yes, all of those names are individual singers, not bands) had a hit with a Grammy-winning piano instrumental titled "Alley Cat"?

A. Eagle-Eye Cherry
B. Falco
C. Bent Fabric
D. Bunker Hill

Answer 1: C—baseball caps.

Answer 2: A—Cenozoic Era.

Answer 3: C—1982.

Answer 4: D—Wisk.

Answer 5: B—3.00 (the number refers to the average number of earned runs allowed per nine innings pitched).

SPORT OF KINGS
Horse racing trivia.

1. How long is one furlong (a standard measurement used in thoroughbred racing)?

A. ⅛ mile
B. ¼ mile
C. ⅓ mile
D. ½ mile

2. In what city is the Kentucky Derby horse race annually held?

A. Frankfort
B. Lexington
C. Louisville
D. Ashland

3. What was the name of the only horse to defeat Man o' War in a race, an event that occurred in 1919?

A. Golden Broom
B. Upset
C. Armistice
D. Seabiscuit

4. Besides Seattle Slew, what other Triple Crown winner has a U.S. city in its name?

A. Omaha
B. Johnstown
C. Belmar
D. Needles

5. In 1978 Affirmed won the Triple Crown. What horse finished second to Affirmed in all three Triple Crown races?

A. Sensitive Prince
B. Track Reward
C. Believe It
D. Alydar

Answer 1: A—New York.

Answer 2: C—60 feet.

Answer 3: D—Parker Stevenson.

Answer 4: B—Moo.

Answer 5: C—Bent Fabric (born in Denmark, his stage name was actually short for his birth name, Bent Fabricius-Bjerre; his composer credit for the song was the more normal-sounding but actually completely made-up pseudonym Frank Bjorn).

SCRATCH THAT ITCH

1. The "scratch test" is usually administered when the doctor suspects the patient has what?

A. hemophilia
B. allergies
C. dyslexia
D. rabies

2. "Old Scratch" is a nickname for whom?

A. Satan
B. Father Time
C. The Sandman
D. Cupid

3. By USGA definition, a male scratch golfer is one who can regularly reach a 470-yard hole in how many shots?

A. two
B. three
C. four
D. five

4. What musician released a 1977 album titled *Cat Scratch Fever?*

A. Ozzy Osbourne
B. Cat Stevens
C. Jeff Beck
D. Ted Nugent

5. What cartoon (based on a video game) featured a bumbling robot named Scratch?

A. *Sonic the Hedgehog*
B. *Pac-Man*
C. *Dragon's Lair*
D. *Mortal Kombat*

Answer 1: A—⅛ mile.

Answer 2: C—Louisville.

Answer 3: B—Upset.

Answer 4: A—Omaha (who won the Triple Crown in 1935).

Answer 5: D—Alydar.

KILLER BB's

1. What name did B.B. King give to his guitar?

A. Louellen
B. Linda
C. Loretta
D. Lucille

2. While scoring a baseball game, the letters "BB" indicate:

A. a broken bat
B. a walk
C. a pitch that hits the batter
D. a bunt

3. The world's largest manufacturer of BB guns shares its name with what flower?

A. carnation
B. daisy
C. rose
D. marigold

4. Ballantine Books (identifiable by their "BB" logo) was bought out in 1973 by what publishing house?

A. Simon & Schuster
B. McGraw-Hill
C. HarperCollins
D. Random House

5. A Web site that ends with a "BB" suffix was registered in what country?

A. Bolivia
B. Belgium
C. Barbados
D. Burkina Faso

Answer 1: B—allergies.

Answer 2: A—Satan.

Answer 3: A—two.

Answer 4: D—Ted Nugent.

Answer 5: A—*Sonic the Hedgehog.*

I CARRY A BADGE

1. *Cops*, the "original reality show," first aired in 1987 on what network?

A. UPN
B. Fox
C. ABC
D. WB

2. The Black Maria, once a staple of law enforcement, was also called a:

A. pie wagon
B. billy club
C. call box
D. drunk tank

3. Who was the lead singer for the band called the Police?

A. Stiv
B. Bono
C. Buzz
D. Sting

4. In the 1984 film *Beverly Hills Cop*, Eddie Murphy portrayed a police officer who worked in what city?

A. Baltimore
B. Chicago
C. Atlanta
D. Detroit

5. What novel by Joseph Wambaugh told of the abduction of two police officers and the execution of one of them?

A. *The Blooding*
B. *The Blue Knight*
C. *The Choirboys*
D. *The Onion Field*

Answer 1: D—Lucille.

Answer 2: B—a walk (the letters stand for "base on balls").

Answer 3: B—daisy.

Answer 4: D—Random House.

Answer 5: C—Barbados.

IN THE "BRIG"

1. Brigham Young was a leader of which religious group?

A. Jehovah's Witnesses
B. Quakers
C. Mormons
D. Christian Scientists

2. Which of these military units is larger than a brigade?

A. regiment
B. company
C. battalion
D. division

3. What is a brigand?

A. an armed bandit
B. a spy
C. a traitor
D. a naval security warden

4. The musical *Brigadoon* takes place in which location?

A. Ireland
B. England
C. Scotland
D. Wales

5. A brigantine is a type of:

A. sailing ship
B. carriage
C. rail car
D. wagon

Answer 1: B—Fox.

Answer 2: A—pie wagon (the same type of vehicle used to deliver pies was also used to hold lawbreakers).

Answer 3: D—Sting (later a successful solo artist, his birth name was Gordon Sumner).

Answer 4: D—Detroit.

Answer 5: D—*The Onion Field*.

HANDS ON

1. Mr. Hands often put what claymation character into dangerous situations?

A. The Noid
B. Mr. Bill
C. Gumby
D. Davey Hansen

2. On May 25, 1986, over five million people formed a human chain in "Hands Across America," which raised money for:

A. farmers
B. sick children
C. the homeless
D. famine relief

3. What baseball Hall of Fame catcher could hold seven baseballs in each of his oversized hands?

A. Yogi Berra
B. Gary Carter
C. Johnny Bench
D. Roy Campanella

4. The four H's of the 4-H club stand for head, heart, hands, and ... what?

A. Health
B. History
C. Happiness
D. Home

5. Members of which monkey variety are used as "Helping Hands," a program that trains primates to assist quadriplegics?

A. Marmoset
B. Spider
C. Squirrel
D. Capuchin

Answer 1: C—Mormons.

Answer 2: D—division.

Answer 3: A—an armed bandit.

Answer 4: C—Scotland.

Answer 5: A—sailing ship.

HOSPITALITY ON PARADE

1. What hotel/motel chain adopted its name based on its original room rate?

A. Four Seasons
B. Super 8
C. Motel 6
D. La Quinta

2. Zsa Zsa Gabor was once married to the founder of what hotel chain?

A. Hilton
B. Westin
C. Marriott
D. Sheraton

3. Who starred in the 1942 film *Holiday Inn*, which inspired the name of the hotel chain?

A. Danny Kaye
B. Bing Crosby
C. Bob Hope
D. Larry Parks

4. The Algonquin Round Table was a group of writers and artists who met regularly at the Algonquin Hotel in what city?

A. New York
B. London
C. Rome
D. Paris

5. What lodging chain's mascot, Sleepy Bear, was introduced back in 1954?

A. Econolodge
B. Clarion
C. Comfort Inn
D. Travelodge

Answer 1: B—Mr. Bill.

Answer 2: C—the homeless.

Answer 3: C—Johnny Bench.

Answer 4: A—Health.

Answer 5: D—Capuchin.

A FUR PIECE

Each clue contains three characters from a TV show; you name the dog that appeared on the program.

1. Joe, Mr. Salt, Mrs. Pepper, and ...

A. Trixie
B. Bear
C. Blue
D. Murray

2. Daphne, Niles, Martin, and ...

A. Eddie
B. Tulip
C. Dreyfuss
D. Rex

3. Steve, Katie, Ernie, and ...

A. Tiger
B. Tramp
C. Barney
D. Winnie

4. Henry, Penelope, Cherie, and ...

A. Brandon
B. Gilbert
C. Mud
D. Parker

5. Doc, the Doozers, the Gorgs, and ...

A. Ralph
B. Scamp
C. Mac
D. Sprocket

Answer 1: C—Motel 6.

Answer 2: A—Hilton.

Answer 3: B—Bing Crosby.

Answer 4: A—New York.

Answer 5: D—Travelodge.

TOO MANY COOKS

1. Julia Child, known as "The French Chef," was born in:

A. the United States
B. Scotland
C. Belgium
D. France

2. What Beverly Hills eatery was launched in 1982 by famed chef Wolfgang Puck?

A. Sonora Café
B. Spago
C. Hamburger Hamlet
D. Delmonico's

3. Who was the "Galloping Gourmet"?

A. Paul Prudhomme
B. Wally Amos
C. Graham Kerr
D. Martin Yan

4. What 1954 film starred Audrey Hepburn as an American studying at the famous Le Cordon Bleu cooking school in Paris?

A. *Funny Face*
B. *Sabrina*
C. *Breakfast at Tiffany's*
D. *Roman Holiday*

5. The traditional chef's hat has 100 pleats, which symbolizes the number of:

A. days in an apprenticeship
B. spices in a properly stocked kitchen
C. kingdoms in the ancient world
D. ways to cook an egg

Answer 1: C—Blue (*Blue's Clues*).

Answer 2: A—Eddie (*Frasier*).

Answer 3: B—Tramp (*My Three Sons*).

Answer 4: A—Brandon (*Punky Brewster*).

Answer 5: D—Sprocket (*Fraggle Rock*).

ARE YOU A HEP CAT?

1. Which of the following is true of the Olympic heptathlon?

A. includes swimming
B. is held over two days
C. is a men-only event
D. never won by the U.S.

2. Hepatitis is the inflammation of which of the body's organs?

A. kidneys
B. gall bladder
C. liver
D. stomach

3. The star of the *The Philadelphia Story* and *The African Queen*, the actress Hepburn spelled her first name in what less-common way?

A. Catherin
B. Katharine
C. Kathryn
D. Catharine

4. A heptagon has how many sides?

A. thirteen
B. eleven
C. nine
D. seven

5. In Greek mythology, Hephaestus was the god of:

A. fire
B. medicine
C. the ocean
D. strength

Answer 1: A—the United States

Answer 2: B—Spago.

Answer 3: C—Graham Kerr.

Answer 4: B—*Sabrina*.

Answer 5: D—ways to cook an egg.

UNUSUAL NAMES

1. Which of the following is NOT the name of a sibling of the late actor River Phoenix?

A. Summer
B. Rain
C. Blossom
D. Liberty

2. Nobel prize–winning author Rudyard Kipling was born in what country?

A. Burma
B. Scotland
C. England
D. India

3. Regis Philbin first gained fame as a sidekick for what TV talk show host?

A. Johnny Carson
B. Joey Bishop
C. Jack Parr
D. Steve Allen

4. Sargent Shriver, father-in-law of Arnold Schwarzenegger, once (unsuccessfully) ran for vice president under what candidate?

A. Barry Goldwater
B. George McGovern
C. Hubert Humphrey
D. Walter Mondale

5. Actress Neve Campbell's first name is based on her mother's maiden name, and is also the Italian word for:

A. Snow
B. Princess
C. Autumn
D. Kitten

Answer 1: B—is held over two days (Jackie Joyner-Kersee was a gold medalist in this series of women-only track & field events).

Answer 2: C—liver.

Answer 3: B—Katharine (the most common spellings are Catherine and Katherine).

Answer 4: D—seven.

Answer 5: A—fire.

BY THE HUNDREDS

1. Britain's Queen Mother lived to be 100. Which of these other politically notable women also reached that age?

A. Indira Nehru Gandhi
B. Bella Abzug
C. Golda Meir
D. Madame Chiang Kai-Shek

2. What musician wrote the music and cowrote the screenplay for the bizarre 1971 motion picture *200 Motels*?

A. Pete Townshend
B. Frank Zappa
C. Lou Reed
D. Iggy Pop

3. The 21st-century reintroduction of what carmaker's "300" model became a hot seller?

A. Chevrolet
B. Nissan
C. Mercury
D. Chrysler

4. The matriarch of what wealthy family began a social register known as "the 400"?

A. Carnegie
B. Rockefeller
C. Astor
D. Vanderbilt

5. Which racecar driver set a record by being on the starting line of the Indianapolis 500 for 35 consecutive years (from 1958 until 1992)?

A. A.J. Foyt
B. Mario Andretti
C. Al Unser
D. Johnny Rutherford

Answer 1: C—Blossom (a fifth sibling, formerly known as Leaf, has since gained fame using his original name, Joaquin).

Answer 2: D—India.

Answer 3: B—Joey Bishop.

Answer 4: B—George McGovern.

Answer 5: A—Snow.

IT'S A LONG, LONG QUIZ

1. A standard U.S. ton weighs 2,000 pounds; how many more pounds are there in a long ton?

A. 16
B. 60
C. 150
D. 240

2. Former Louisiana governor Huey Long was known by what nickname?

A. Sapphire
B. Kingfish
C. Crawdad
D. Shorty

3. Which of the following is a synonym for "long johns"?

A. merry widow
B. boxers
C. union suit
D. maillot

4. Which of the following motion pictures did NOT star Shelley Long?

A. *Hello Again*
B. *The Brady Bunch Movie*
C. *Outrageous Fortune*
D. *Look Who's Talking*

5. Long Island Sound separates Long Island from:

A. New Jersey
B. Manhattan
C. Connecticut
D. the Atlantic Ocean

Answer 1: D—Madame Chiang Kai-Shek (she died in 2003 at the age of 106).

Answer 2: B—Frank Zappa.

Answer 3: D—Chrysler.

Answer 4: C—Astor.

Answer 5: A—A.J. Foyt.

DOOM-DAY

1. What was the name of the youngster who "assisted" the title hero in the motion picture *Indiana Jones and the Temple of Doom*?

A. Toht
B. Short Round
C. Chunk
D. Mola Ram

2. The DC comic book *Doom Patrol* appeared two months before what similar title by rival Marvel (which proved more popular in the long run)?

A. *The Avengers*
B. *X-Men*
C. *The Fantastic Four*
D. *The Defenders*

3. The "chimes of doom" sound might be heard if you experience a problem while operating:

A. an escalator
B. a forklift
C. a garage door
D. a computer

4. What actor from TV's *Taxi* went on to portray Judge Doom in the 1988 film *Who Framed Roger Rabbit*?

A. Christopher Lloyd
B. Tony Danza
C. Judd Hirsch
D. Danny DeVito

5. Michael Wigglesworth's 17th-century book *The Day of Doom* was used to teach Massachusetts schoolchildren about:

A. the seasons
B. war
C. religion
D. marriage

Answer 1: D—240.

Answer 2: B—Kingfish.

Answer 3: C—union suit.

Answer 4: D—*Look Who's Talking* (which starred Long's replacement on TV's *Cheers*, Kirstie Alley).

Answer 5: C—Connecticut.

MOTHER OF OUR COUNTRY

1. Our first First Lady was Martha Washington; what other early president also had a wife named Martha?

A. John Adams
B. Thomas Jefferson
C. James Madison
D. James Monroe

2. How many children did George and Martha Washington have together?

A. none
B. two
C. four
D. six

3. What was Martha Washington's maiden name?

A. Frank
B. Dandridge
C. Custis
D. Mellon

4. Martha Washington's image appeared on late-19th-century U.S. bills—silver certificates, to be exact—in what amount?

A. $1
B. $5
C. $10
D. $20

5. George and Martha Washington are buried just outside what city?

A. Boston
B. New York
C. Philadelphia
D. Washington

Answer 1: B—Short Round.

Answer 2: B—*X-Men*.

Answer 3: D—a computer (specifically, it's the sound a Macintosh makes after experiencing a system error).

Answer 4: A—Christopher Lloyd.

Answer 5: C—religion.

ARE YOU GAME?
Match the term with the related Olympic event:

1. Clean and jerk

A. platform diving
B. weightlifting
C. beach volleyball
D. fencing

2. Dressage

A. canoeing
B. judo
C. modern pentathlon
D. equestrian

3. Cadence action

A. synchronized swimming
B. volleyball
C. badminton
D. racewalking

4. Stalder shoot

A. archery
B. shot put
C. gymnastics
D. small-bore rifle

5. Catch a crab

A. rowing
B. table tennis
C. handball
D. water polo

Answer 1: B—Thomas Jefferson.

Answer 2: A—none (George did adopt Martha's two
children from her previous marriage).

Answer 3: B—Dandridge (Custis was the last name of her
first husband).

Answer 4: A—$1 (she was the first—and to date the
only—real woman to ever appear on U.S.
paper money).

Answer 5: D—Washington (in a mausoleum just outside of
Mount Vernon).

STARRY, STARRY NIGHT

Many classic rock songs are well-known by the words that most often repeat, even if those words aren't in the title. Don McLean's hit "Vincent," for instance, is often called "Starry, Starry Night." Identify these mistakenly titled songs.

1. "Without Love" by the Doobie Brothers

A. "Rockin' Down the Highway"
B. "Long Train Runnin'"
C. "Listen to the Music"
D. "Minute by Minute"

2. "Teenage Wasteland" by the Who

A. "Love Reign O'er Me"
B. "Behind Blue Eyes"
C. "Baba O'Riley"
D. "Long Live Rock"

3. "Hands Across the Water" by Paul McCartney

A. "Another Day"
B. "Uncle Albert/Admiral Halsey"
C. "Mull of Kintyre"
D. "Beware, My Love"

4. "What's That Sound?" by Buffalo Springfield

A. "For What It's Worth"
B. "Mr. Soul"
C. "Bluebird"
D. "Rock & Roll Woman"

5. "I Can Dance" by Leo Sayer

A. "The Show Must Go On"
B. "You Make Me Feel Like Dancing"
C. "More Than I Can Say"
D. "Long Tall Glasses"

Answer 1: B—weightlifting (the clean and jerk is a move in which the barbell is brought to the chest and then lifted overhead).

Answer 2: D—equestrian (dressage is an event during which the horse is guided through a routine by the subtle movements of the rider).

Answer 3: A—synchronized swimming (cadence action is a rapid succession of identical movements a team).

Answer 4: C—gymnastics (a stalder shoot is a high bar or uneven bars maneuver in which the gymnast swings around the bar in a circle with legs straddled).

Answer 5: A—rowing (a rower who "catches a crab" performs a missed stroke, such as when he or she fails to bring his oar out of the water on the return).

POLLY WANNA CRACKER?

1. How many holes are there in a standard Ritz cracker?

A. four
B. five
C. six
D. seven

2. Name the film in which Shirley Temple first sang the song "Animal Crackers in My Soup."

A. *Bright Eyes*
B. *Curly Top*
C. *Dimples*
D. *Captain January*

3. What was the first name of the Presbyterian minister who invented (and provided his last name to) Graham crackers?

A. Samuel
B. Seth
C. Sylvester
D. Sidney

4. What was the first product to bear the National Biscuit Company (later Nabisco) label?

A. Zwieback Toast
B. Honey Grahams
C. Premium Saltines
D. Uneeda Biscuit

5. In what "colorful" motion picture did Charlton Heston try to find out the truth behind a cracker-like product used to feed the starving masses in the year 2022?

A. *Soylent Green*
B. *Color Me Blood Red*
C. *I Am Curious (Yellow)*
D. *Pink Narcissus*

Answer 1: B—"Long Train Runnin'."

Answer 2: C—"Baba O'Riley."

Answer 3: B—"Uncle Albert/Admiral Halsey."

Answer 4: A—"For What It's Worth."

Answer 5: D—"Long Tall Glasses."

TV LODGES

Match the lodge or club with the TV show on which it appeared.

1. Sacred Order of the Stonecutters

A. *Family Guy*
B. *The Simpsons*
C. *King of the Hill*
D. *South Park*

2. Leopard Lodge

A. *Happy Days*
B. *Three's Company*
C. *Night Court*
D. *The Jeffersons*

3. Knights of the Scimitar

A. *Coach*
B. *Major Dad*
C. *Simon & Simon*
D. *Cheers*

4. Loyal Order of Water Buffalo

A. *Futurama*
B. *The Critic*
C. *The PJs*
D. *The Flintstones*

5. Kings of Queens

A. *The Nanny*
B. *All in the Family*
C. *The Odd Couple*
D. *Welcome Back, Kotter*

Answer 1: D—seven.

Answer 2: B—*Curly Top*.

Answer 3: C—Sylvester.

Answer 4: D—Uneeda Biscuit.

Answer 5: A—*Soylent Green*.

MUSIC'S ROYAL FLUSH
Facts that go straight from 10 to ace.

1. 10cc had three Top 40 pop singles in America, and the titles of each of them contained which of the following words?

A. Love
B. Day
C. Things
D. Not

2. Jack Bruce played bass and sang vocals for what "power trio" band?

A. ZZ Top
B. Blue Cheer
C. Cream
D. The James Gang

3. Queen scored the 1981 hit "Under Pressure" with the help of what British singer?

A. Elton John
B. Cliff Richard
C. Roger Daltrey
D. David Bowie

4. Carole King was a college student when she became the subject of the 1959 hit song "Oh, Carol!" by:

A. Frankie Valli
B. Bobby Darin
C. Neil Sedaka
D. Pat Boone

5. Ace Frehley, the original lead guitarist for Kiss, was given what first name upon his birth?

A. Aaron
B. Winfred
C. Edward
D. Paul

Answer 1: B—*The Simpsons.*

Answer 2: A—*Happy Days.*

Answer 3: D—*Cheers.*

Answer 4: D—*The Flintstones.*

Answer 5: B—*All in the Family.*

QZ QUIZ

These questions feature high-scoring word-game words that contain both the letters Q and Z.

1. The quetzal is the national bird and the name of the basic unit of currency in what country?

A. Guatemala
B. Portugal
C. Kenya
D. Laos

2. In its pure form, the mineral known as quartz is:

A. clear
B. yellow
C. pink
D. green

3. Which of these snakes does NOT kill its prey by squeezing it?

A. kingsnake
B. python
C. viper
D. anaconda

4. How many cards are there in the deck used to play the card game bezique?

A. 48
B. 52
C. 64
D. 84

5. Who starred as *The Equalizer* in the 1980s television series of the same name?

A. Edward Fox
B. Edward James Olmos
C. Edward Furlong
D. Edward Woodward

Answer 1: A—Love (the three hits were "The Things We Do for Love," "I'm Not in Love," and "People in Love").

Answer 2: C—Cream.

Answer 3: D—David Bowie.

Answer 4: C—Neil Sedaka.

Answer 5: D—Paul (he used the nickname Ace in Kiss so as to avoid confusion with bandmate Paul Stanley).

SLAMMIN' SPORTS & GAMES

1. What fad involved something known as a slammer?

A. Hula-Hoops
B. Pogs
C. yo-yos
D. Hacky Sack

2. What 1983 college basketball team was known as "Phi Slamma Jamma" due to their high-flying ability to slam-dunk the ball?

A. Duke
B. Richmond
C. Houston
D. UCLA

3. Which of these is NOT part of the professional tennis "grand slam" series?

A. U.S. Open
B. British Open
C. French Open
D. Australian Open

4. In the card game bridge, a "slam" occurs when one team:

A. wins all the tricks
B. forfeits the game
C. has only face cards left
D. passes on a bid

5. Which New York Yankee slugger still holds the Major League Baseball record of hitting 23 career grand slam home runs?

A. Joe DiMaggio
B. Roger Maris
C. Babe Ruth
D. Lou Gehrig

Answer 1: A—Guatemala.

Answer 2: A—clear.

Answer 3: C—viper.

Answer 4: C—64 (7 through ace of the four suits, with two of each card).

Answer 5: D—Edward Woodward.

WHIGGIN' OUT

All about the 19th-century U.S. political party known as the Whigs.

1. The Whig party was founded by key political opponents of what U.S. president?

A. Andrew Jackson
B. Andrew Johnson
C. James Madison
D. James Monroe

2. The Kansas-Nebraska Act that divided the Whig party in 1854 was a federal law that provided for:

A. relocation of Native Americans
B. high incoming trade tariffs
C. free trade with France
D. slavery in western states

3. "Whig" was originally a derogatory term referring to the Presbyterian rebels who fought the establishment in what country?

A. England
B. the U.S.
C. Canada
D. Scotland

4. The Whig party celebrated an 1840 White House victory with the line "Tippecanoe and Tyler, too." Who was this Tippecanoe?

A. Tyler's father, Judge John Tyler
B. a Native American chief
C. Tyler's running mate
D. Tyler's first wife, Letitia

5. Who was the last Whig to be elected U.S. president?

A. James Knox Polk
B. Millard Fillmore
C. William Henry Harrison
D. John Tyler

Answer 1: B—Pogs (the slammer is a plastic disc thrown against a stack of pogs to displace them).

Answer 2: C—Houston.

Answer 3: B—British Open (this is the name of a golf tournament; the British entry in the tennis grand slam is Wimbledon).

Answer 4: A—wins all the tricks.

Answer 5: D—Lou Gehrig.

A BEWITCHING QUIZ

1. According to legend, the "Witch of November" had a hand in the fate of what ship?

A. *Achille Lauro*
B. *Bismarck*
C. *Edmund Fitzgerald*
D. *Titanic*

2. Which of the following actresses was not one of the titular *Witches of Eastwick* in the 1987 film?

A. Susan Sarandon
B. Cher
C. Michelle Pfeiffer
D. Bette Midler

3. What Fleetwood Mac hit single told the story of a Welsh witch?

A. "Gypsy"
B. "Rhiannon"
C. "Sara"
D. "Silver Springs"

4. What company has been selling witch hazel as an astringent since 1866?

A. Dickinson
B. Bayer
C. Johnson & Johnson
D. Carter

5. Billie Hayes portrayed the villainous Witchiepoo on what Krofft Saturday morning TV show of the 1960s–'70s?

A. *Sigmund & the Sea Monsters*
B. *The Bugaloos*
C. *Lidsville*
D. *H.R. Pufnstuf*

Answer 1: A—Andrew Jackson.

Answer 2: D—slavery in western states.

Answer 3: D—Scotland.

Answer 4: C—Tyler's running mate (who happened to be William Henry Harrison, the man Tyler would succeed as president).

Answer 5: B—Millard Fillmore.

GO FOR THE GOLD

1. What brand name recently moved the gold medal (won in Paris in 1900) that had been on the center of its label for over a century?

A. Budweiser Beer
B. Campbell's Soup
C. Ivory Soap
D. Rice-a-Roni

2. In 1775, when James Cook returned to England from the Pacific, the Royal Society awarded him a Copley gold medal for:

A. spy work in the American colonies
B. claiming New Zealand for England
C. finding a scurvy preventative
D. discovering the Hawaiian Islands

3. A 1921 contest by Gold Medal Flour led to the introduction of which fictitious character?

A. Aunt Jemima
B. Duncan Hines
C. Betty Crocker
D. Sara Lee

4. What country was second to the U.S. in gold medals at the 2004 Summer Olympic Games in Athens, Greece?

A. Germany
B. Russia
C. Australia
D. China

5. Which of these famous people has NOT been honored by receiving the Congressional Gold Medal?

A. Stephen King
B. Harry Chapin
C. Tony Blair
D. Billy Graham

Answer 1: C—*Edmund Fitzgerald.*

Answer 2: D—Bette Midler.

Answer 3: B—"Rhiannon."

Answer 4: A—Dickinson.

Answer 5: D—*H.R. Pufnstuf.*

"NANNY NANNY" BOO BOO

1. The female of which of these animals is called a nanny?

A. pig
B. goat
C. sheep
D. llama

2. What was the maiden name of Fran Drescher's character on the sitcom *The Nanny*?

A. Fink
B. Good
C. Best
D. Fine

3. Alexandra Legge-Bourke, who acted as nanny to Prince William and Prince Harry after their royal parents' divorce, was better known by what nickname?

A. Tiggy
B. Lexi
C. Leggy
D. Andy

4. Richard Long, star of TV's *Nanny and the Professor*, also had a starring role on what long-running Western series?

A. *Gunsmoke*
B. *Death Valley Days*
C. *Big Valley*
D. *The Wild, Wild West*

5. After divorcing his wife and marrying his child's nanny (in real life), who starred in a film in which his character divorced his wife and became his children's nanny?

A. Adam Sandler
B. Tom Hanks
C. Robin Williams
D. Mike Myers

Answer 1: B—Campbell's Soup.

Answer 2: C—finding a scurvy preventative (the addition of sauerkraut to the crew's menu protected his crew from the dread disease).

Answer 3: C—Betty Crocker.

Answer 4: D—China (Russia was second in overall medals, while China was second in gold medals).

Answer 5: A—Stephen King.

TEACHER, TEACHER

1. What teacher taught Helen Keller the manual alphabet and Braille?

A. John Macy
B. Anne Sullivan
C. Alexander Graham Bell
D. Polly Thompson

2. What band's "Hot for Teacher" video features a nervous nerd named Waldo?

A. the Rolling Stones
B. Poison
C. Van Halen
D. Aerosmith

3. Vili Fualaau has fathered two children with what controversial schoolteacher?

A. Debra Favre
B. Pamela Smart
C. Mary Kay Letourneau
D. Amy Duane

4. Marcia Wallace, who provides the voice of teacher Mrs. Krabappel on *The Simpsons*, previously portrayed receptionist Carol Kester on what sitcom?

A. *The Bob Newhart Show*
B. *WKRP in Cincinnati*
C. *Bosom Buddies*
D. *Night Court*

5. Which of the following actresses has NOT portrayed famed teacher Anna Leonowens in a feature film?

A. Deborah Kerr
B. Jodie Foster
C. Nicole Kidman
D. Irene Dunne

Answer 1: B—goat.

Answer 2: D—Fine.

Answer 3: A—Tiggy.

Answer 4: C—*Big Valley*.

Answer 5: C—Robin Williams (the film was 1993's *Mrs. Doubtfire*).

Answer 1: B—Anne Sullivan.

Answer 2: C—Van Halen.

Answer 3: C—Mary Kay Letourneau.

Answer 4: A—*The Bob Newhart Show*.

Answer 5: C—Nicole Kidman (Anna Leonowens was the Englishwoman who ventured to Siam in 1862 to teach the king's children, as seen in *The King and I, Anna and the King of Siam,* and *Anna and the King*).